Abraham Lincoln, George M. Van Buren

Abraham Lincoln's Pen and Voice

a complete compilation of his letters, civil, political, and military, also his public addresses, messages to Congress, inaugurals and others, as well as proclamations upon various public concerns

Abraham Lincoln, George M. Van Buren

Abraham Lincoln's Pen and Voice

a complete compilation of his letters, civil, political, and military, also his public addresses, messages to Congress, inaugurals and others, as well as proclamations upon various public concerns

ISBN/EAN: 9783337080358

Printed in Europe, USA, Canada, Australia, Japan

Cover: Foto ©ninafisch / pixelio.de

More available books at **www.hansebooks.com**

ABRAHAM LINCOLN'S
PEN AND VOICE

BEING A COMPLETE COMPILATION OF HIS

LETTERS

CIVIL, POLITICAL, AND MILITARY

ALSO

HIS PUBLIC ADDRESSES, MESSAGES TO CONGRESS

INAUGURALS AND OTHERS

AS WELL AS

PROCLAMATIONS UPON VARIOUS PUBLIC CONCERNS, SHOWING HIM TO HAVE BEEN THE GREATEST CONSTITUTIONAL STUDENT OF THE AGE, AND THE NOBLEST PATTERN FOR FUTURE GENERATIONS AMERICA HAS EVER KNOWN

BY

G. M. VAN BUREN

Late Colonel U. S. Vols.

WITH A FINE STEEL PORTRAIT

CINCINNATI
ROBERT CLARKE & CO
1890

Copyright, 1890,
By G. M. VAN BUREN.

Dedicated to the Memory

OF

ABRAHAM LINCOLN,

GRANDSON OF THE

Martyred President.

By his lamented death the ancestral name becomes extinct.

INTRODUCTION.

The author feels that no one man can say what ought to be said of that great statesman, renowned president, and noble martyr—Abraham Lincoln—and therefore begs leave to present as a preface what has been said of him by the greatest men of our times.

[From Lincoln's Memorial.]

Sprung from the people, with no ancestral renown or services, with none of the auxiliaries which wealth, social position, or academic honors afford the mass of aspirants to great public honors, Abraham Lincoln rose step by step to the highest station in the gift of his fellow-countrymen

And although party virulence, which in our press has no check, persistently coupled his name with odious epithets, there has never been the slightest charge of any thing to detract from a high moral character. He was too great to stoop to vile means to accomplish his ends

> No Cæsar he, whom we lament,
> A man without a precedent,
> Sent, it would seem, to do
> His work, and perish too!

[From a Speech by General B. F. Butler, in New York City.]

Fellow Citizens:—But a day or two since we assembled throughout the nation in joy, gladness, and triumph, at the success of the armies of the republic, which opened to us the promise of a glorious peace and a happy country in the future.

These flags now the token of mourning, were then raised in gladness. To-day, in a short hour, Abraham Lincoln has been struck down by the hand of an assassin, and we assemble to mingle our grief with that of the loved ones at home, who mourn the honest man, the incorruptible patriot, the great statesman, the savior of his country in its crisis.

[From a Speech by Hon. Daniel S. Dickinson.]

It is not merely the death of Abraham Lincoln—great, good, patient, faithful, sincere as he was—but it is the great nation that has been wounded in her Chief Magistrate, that she had, with great and unusual *eclat*, continued in the position, and said, "Well done, good and faithful servant."

[From a Sermon by Rev. Henry W. Bellows.]

Our beloved president, who had enshrined himself not merely in the confidence, the respect, and the gratitude of the people, but in their very hearts, as their true friend, adviser, representative, and brother; whom the nation loved as much as it revered, who had soothed our angry impatience in this fearful struggle with his gentle moderation and passionless calm; who had been the head of the nation, and not the chief of a successful party; and had treated our enemies like rebellious children, and not as foreign foes, providing even in their chastisement for mercy and penitent restoration; our prudent, firm, humble, reverential, God-fearing president is dead.

[Archbishop McClosky, at St. Patrick's Cathedral, in New York.]

We pray that those sentiments of mercy, of clemency, and of conciliation, that filled the heart of the beloved president we have just lost, may animate the heart and guide the actions of him who in this most trying hour is called to fill his place.

[From a Sermon by his Pastor, Rev. D. Gurley.]

I have said that the people confided in the late lamented president with a full and a loving confidence. Probably no man, since the days of Washington, was ever so deeply and firmly imbedded and enshrined in the very hearts of the people as Abraham Lincoln. Nor was it a mistaken confidence and love. He deserved it, deserved it well, deserved it all. He merited it by his character, by his acts, and by the whole tenor, and tone and spirit of his life. He was simple and sincere, plain and honest, truthful and just, benevolent and kind. His perceptions were quick and clear, his judgments were calm and accurate, and his purposes were good and pure beyond a question. Always and every-where he aimed, and endeavored to *be* and to *do* right. His integrity was thorough, all-pervading, all-controlling, and incorruptible.

[Public Address by Ralph Waldo Emerson.]

The president stood before us as a man of the people. He was thoroughly American, had never crossed the sea, had never been spoiled by English insularity or French dissipation; a quiet, native, aboriginal man, as an acorn from the oak; no aping of foreigners, no frivolous accomplishments, Kentuckian born, working on a farm, a flatboatman, a captain in the

Blackhawk war, a country lawyer, a representative in the rural legislature of Illinois—on such modest foundation the broad structure of his fame was laid.

How slowly, and yet by happily prepared steps, he came to his place. . . . There, by his courage, his justice, his even temper, his fertile counsel, his humanity, he stood an heroic figure in the center of an heroic epoch. He is the true history of the American people in his time.

Step by step he walked before them; slow with their slowness, quickening his march by theirs; the true representative of the continent; an entirely public man; father of his country, the pulse of twenty millions throbbing in his heart, the thought of their minds articulated by his tongue.

[General Banks, at New Orleans.]

There is not a man on the continent or globe that will, or can, say that Abraham Lincoln was his enemy; or that he deserved punishment or death for his individual acts. No, Mr. President, it was because he represented *us* that he died, and it is for our good and the glory of our nation that God, in his inscrutable providence, has been pleased to do this, while for the late President it is the great crowning act and security of his career.

[By George Bancroft.]

But after every allowance, it will remain that members of the government which preceded the administration opened the gates to treason, and he closed them; that when he went to Washington the ground on which he trod shook under his feet, and he left the republic on **a solid** foundation; that traitors had seized public forts and arsenals, and he **recovered** them for the United States, to whom they belonged; that the Capital which he found the abode of slaves, is now only the **home of the** free; that the **boundless** public domain **which was** grasped at, **and, in a great** measure, held **for** the diffusion of slavery, is **now irrevocably devoted to** freedom.

[From Bishop Simpson's Funeral Oration.]

But the great cause of the mourning is **to be found in the man** himself. Mr. Lincoln was **no ordinary man, and I** believe the **conviction has been growing on the** nation's mind, as it **certainly has been on my own, especially** in the last years **of his administration.**

By the hand of God he was especially **singled out to guide our** government in these **troublous times, and it seems** to me **that the hand of God** may be **traced in many** events connected with **his** history.

[From a Sermon by Rev. Henry Ward Beecher.]

Who shall recount our martyr's sufferings for **the** people? Since the November of 1860, his horizon has been black with storms. By day and by **night** he trod **a** way of danger and darkness.

On his shoulders rested a government, dearer to him **than his** own life. **At** its life millions were striking at home; upon it foreign eyes were lowered, and it stood like a lone island in a sea full of storms, and every tide and wave seemed eager to devour it.

Upon thousands of hearts great sorrows and anx**ieties have** rested, but upon not one such, and in such were remarkable. He could, upon occasion, rise to the most sublime flight of eloquence.

His little introductory speech at the Gettysburg Cemetery dedication will outlive the elaborate and eloquent oration delivered by Mr. Everett on the same day.

I am indebted to J. C. Power, of Springfield, Ill., author of the "History of the Attempt to Steal the Body of Lincoln," for the use of the plates of the two views of the "*Lincoln Monument.*"

Excavation for the monument commenced September 9, 1869. It is built of granite from quarries at Biddeford, Maine. The rough ashlars were shipped to Quincy, Mass., where they were dressed to perfect ashlars and numbered, thence shipped by railroad to Springfield. It is $72\frac{1}{2}$ feet from east to west, $119\frac{1}{2}$ feet from north to south, and 100 feet high. The total cost is about $230,000, to May 1, 1888. All the statuary is orange-colored bronze. The whole monument was designed by Larkin G. Mead, the statuary was modeled in plaster by him in Florence, Italy, and cast by the Ames Manufacturing Co., of Chicopee, Mass. The statue of Lincoln and coat of arms were first placed on the monument; the statue was unveiled and the monument dedicated October 15, 1874. The infantry and naval groups were put on in September, 1877, the artillery group, April 13, 1882, and the cavalry group, March 13, 1883.

ABRAHAM LINCOLN'S PEN AND VOICE.

MR. LINCOLN'S VERBAL REPLY TO COMMITTEE NOTIFYING HIM OF HIS NOMINATION TO THE PRESIDENCY.

At Springfield, Ill., May 18, 1860.

Mr. Chairman and Gentlemen of the Committee:—
I tender to you, and through you to the Republican National Convention, and all the people represented in it, my profoundest thanks for the high honor done me, which you now formally announce.

Deeply, and even painfully sensible of the great responsibility which is inseparable from the high honor, a responsibility which I could almost wish had fallen upon some one of the far more eminent men and experienced statesmen whose distinguished names were before the convention, I shall, by your leave, consider more fully the resolutions of the convention, denominated the platform, and without any unnecessary or unreasonable delay, report to you, Mr. Chairman, in writing, not doubting that the platform will be found satisfactory, and the nomination gratefully accepted. And now I will no longer defer the pleasure of taking you, and each of you, by the hand.

Springfield, Ill., May 23, 1860.

Sir:—I accept the nomination tendered me by the convention over which you presided, of which I am formally appraised in a letter of yourself and others acting as a committee of the convention for that purpose.

The declaration of principles and sentiments which accompanies your letter meets my approval, and it shall be my care not to violate it, or disregard it, in any part. Imploring the assistance of Divine Providence, and with due regard to the views and feelings of all who were represented in the convention, to the rights of all the states and territories and people of the nation, to the inviolability of the constitution, and the perpetual union, harmony, and prosperity of all; I am most happy to co-operate for the practical success of the principles declared by the convention.

Your obliged friend and fellow-citizen,

ABRAHAM LINCOLN.

HON. GEORGE ASHMUN, *Prest. Republican Convention.*

Springfield, Ill., August 15, 1860.

My Dear Sir:—Yours of the 9th, enclosing the letter of Hon. John Minor Botts, was duly received. The latter is herewith returned according to your request. It contains one of the many assurances I receive from the South, that in no probable event will there be any very formidable effort to break up the Union. The people of the South have too much of good sense and good temper to attempt the ruin of the government rather than see it administered as it was administered by the men who made it. At least, so I hope and believe.

I thank you both for your own letter and a sight of that of Mr. Botts. Yours very truly,
JOHN B. FRY, ESQ. A. LINCOLN.

ABRAHAM LINCOLN TO THURLOW WEED.

Springfield, Ill., August 17, 1860.

My Dear Sir:—Yours of the 13th was received this morning. Douglas is managing the Bell element with great adroitness. He had his men in Kentucky to vote for the Bell candidate, producing a result which has badly alarmed and damaged Breckenridge, and at the same time has induced the Bell men to suppose that Bell will certainly be President, if they can keep a few of the northern states away from us by throwing them to Douglas. But you, better than I, can understand all this.

I think there will be the most extraordinary effort ever made to carry New York for Douglas.

You and all others who write me from your state think the effort can not succeed, and I hope you are right. Still it will require close watching and great efforts on the other side. Herewith I send you a copy of a letter written at New York, which sufficiently explains itself, and which may or may not give you a valuable hint. You have seen that Bell tickets have been put on the track both here and in Indiana. In both cases the object has been, I think, the same as the Hunt movement in New York—to throw states to Douglas.

In our state we know the thing is engineered by

Douglas men, and we do not believe they can make a great deal out of it. Yours very truly,

A. LINCOLN.

THE PRESIDENT ELECT TO THURLOW WEED.

Springfield, Ill., December 17, 1860.

My Dear Sir:—Yours of the eleventh was received two days ago. Should the convention of governors of which you speak seem desirous to know my views on the present aspect of things, tell them you judge from my speeches that I will be inflexible on the territorial question; that I probably think either the Missouri line extended, or Douglas's or Eli Thayer's popular sovereignty would lose us every thing we gain by the election; that filibustering for all the South of us, and making slave states of it would follow, in spite of us in either case; also, that I probably think all opposition, real and apparent, to the fugitive slave clause of the constitution ought to be withdrawn.

I believe you can pretend to find but little, if any thing, in my speeches, about secession. But my opinion is that no state can in any way lawfully get out of the Union without the consent of the others; and that it is the duty of the president and other government functionaries to run the machine as it is.

Truly yours, A. LINCOLN.

INTERVIEW PUBLISHED IN NEW YORK TRIBUNE, JANUARY 30, 1861.

I will suffer death before I will consent or advise my friends to consent to any concession or compromise which looks like buying the privilege of taking possession of the government to which we have a constitutional right; because, whatever I might think of the merit of the various propositions before Congress, I should regard any concession in the face of menace as the destruction of the government itself, and a consent on all hands that our system shall be brought down to a level with the existing disorganized state of affairs in Mexico. But this thing will hereafter be, as it is now, in the hands of the people, and if they desire to call a convention to remove any grievances complained of, or to give new guarantees for the permanence of vested rights, it is not mine to oppose.

THE PRESIDENT ELECT TO THURLOW WEED.

Springfield, Ill., February 4, 1861.

Dear Sir:—I have both your letter to myself, and that to Judge Davis, in relation to a certain gentleman of your state, claiming to dispense patronage in my name, and also to be authorized to use my name to advance the chances of Mr. Greeley for an election to the United States Senate.

It is very strange that such things should be said by any one. The gentleman you mention did speak to me of Mr. Greeley in connection with the senatorial election, and I replied in terms of kindness towards Mr. Greeley, which I really feel, but always with an expressed protest that my name must not be used in the senatorial election in favor of or against any one. Any other representation of me is a misrepresentation.

As to the matter of dispensing patronage, it will perhaps surprise you to learn that I have information that you claim to have my authority to arrange that matter in New York. I do not believe you have so claimed, but still so some men say. On that subject you know all I have said to you is "justice to all," and I have said nothing more particular to any one. I say this to reassure you that I have not changed my position.

In the hope, however, that you will not use my name in the matter, I am, yours truly,

A. LINCOLN.

MR. LINCOLN'S SPEECH AT SPRINGFIELD, FEBRUARY 11, 1861, ON LEAVING FOR WASHINGTON, TO BE INAUGURATED AS PRESIDENT.

Friends:—No one who has never been placed in a like position can understand my feeling at this hour, nor the oppressive sadness I feel at this parting.

For more than a quarter of a century I have lived among you, and during all that time I have received nothing but kindness at your hands. Here I have lived from my youth, until now I am an old man. Here the most sacred ties of earth were assumed. Here all my children were born; and here one of them lies buried. To you, dear friends, I owe all that I have, all that I am. *All the strange, checkered past seems to crowd now upon my mind.* To-day I leave you. I go to assume a task more difficult than that which devolved upon Washington. Unless the great God, who assisted him, shall be with and aid me, I must fail; but if the same omniscient mind and almighty arm that directed and protected him shall guide and support me. I shall not fail—I shall succeed. Let us all pray that the God of our fathers may not forsake us now. To Him I commend you all. Permit me to ask, that, with equal security and faith, you will invoke His wisdom and guidance for me. With these few words I must leave you, for how long I know not. Friends, one and all, I must now bid you an affectionate farewell.

Mr. Lincoln's Speech at Indianapolis, February 11, 1861.

Governor Morton and Fellow-citizens of the State of Indiana:—Most heartily do I thank you for this magnificent reception, and while I can not take to myself any share of the compliment thus paid, more than that which pertains to a mere instrument, an accidental instrument, perhaps I should say, of a great cause, I yet must look upon it as a most magnificent reception, and as such, most heartily do thank you for it. You have been pleased to address yourself to me chiefly in behalf of this glorious Union in which we live, in all of which you have my hearty sympathy, and, as far as may be within my power, will have, one and inseparably, my hearty consideration. While I do not expect, upon this occasion, or until I get to Washington, to attempt any lengthy speech, I will only say to the salvation of the Union, there needs but one single thing, the hearts of a people like yours.

The people, when they rise in mass in behalf of the Union, and the liberties of their country, truly may it be said, "The gates of hell can not prevail against them." In all trying positions in which I shall be placed, and, doubtless, I shall be placed in many such, my reliance will be placed upon you and the people of the United States; and I wish you to remember, now and forever, that it is your business, and not mine; that if the union of these states, and the liberties of this people shall be lost, it is but little to any one man of fifty-two years of age, but a great deal to the thirty millions of people who inhabit these United States, and to their posterity in all coming time.

It is your business to rise up and preserve the Union and liberty for yourselves, and not for me.

I desire they should be constitutionally performed. I, as already intimated, am but an accidental instrument, temporary, and to serve but for a limited time, and I appeal to you again to constantly bear in mind that with you, and not with politicians, not with presidents, not with office-seekers, but with you, is the question, Shall the Union, and shall the liberties of this country be preserved to the latest generation?

Continued at Indianapolis in the Evening, Before the Legislature, February 11, 1861.

Fellow-citizens of the State of Indiana:—I am here to thank you much for this magnificent welcome, and still more for the generous support given by your state to that political cause which I think is the true and great cause of the whole country and the whole world.

Solomon says there is "a time to keep silence," and

when men wrangle by the mouth with no certainty that they *mean* the same *thing*, while using the same *word*, it perhaps were as well if they would keep silence.

The words "coercion" and "invasion" are much used in these days, and often with some temper and hot blood. Let us make sure, if we can, that we do not misunderstand the meaning of those who use them. Let us get the exact definition of these words, not from dictionaries, but from the men themselves, who certainly deprecate the *things* they would represent by the use of the words. What, then, is "coercion?" What is "invasion?" Would the marching of an army into South Carolina, without the consent of her people, and with hostile intent toward them, be "invasion?" I certainly think it would; and it would be "coercion" also if the South Carolinians were forced to submit.

But if the United States should merely hold and retake its own forts and other property, and collect the duties on foreign importations, and even withhold the mails from places where they were habitually violated, would any or all these things be "invasion" or "coercion?" Do our professed lovers of the Union, but who spitefully resolve that they will resist coercion and invasion, understand that such things as these on the part of the United States, would be coercion or invasion of a state? If so, their idea of means to preserve the object of their affection would seem exceedingly thin and airy. If sick, the little pills of the homeopathists would be much too large for it to swallow. In their view, the Union, as a family relation, would seem to be no regular marriage, but a sort of "free love" arrangement, to be maintained only on "passional attraction."

By the way, in what consists the special sacredness of a state? I speak not of the position assigned to a state in the Union, by the constitution; but that, by the bond we all recognize.

That position, however, a state can not carry out of the Union with it. I speak of that assumed primary right of a state to rule all which is *less* than itself, and ruin all which is larger than itself.

If a state and a county in a given case, should be equal in extent of territory, and equal in number of inhabitants, in what, as a matter of principle, is the state better than the county? Would an exchange of names be an exchange of *rights* upon principle? On what rightful principle may a state, being not more than one-fiftieth part of the nation, in soil and population, break up the nation, and then coerce a proportionally larger subdivision of itself, in the most arbitrary way? What mysterious right to play tyrant is conferred on a district of country, with its people, by merely calling it a state?

Fellow-citizens, I am not asserting any thing; I am merely asking questions for you to consider. And now allow me to bid you farewell.

Speech at Cincinnati, February 12, 1861.

Mr. Mayor, Ladies and Gentlemen:—Twenty-four hours ago, at the capital of Indiana, I said to myself, "I have never seen so many people assembled together in winter weather." I am no longer able to say that. But it is what might reasonably have been expected—that this great city of Cincinnati would thus acquit herself on such an occasion. My friends, I am entirely overwhelmed by the magnificence of the reception which has been given, I will not say to me, but to the President-elect of the United States of America. Most heartily do I thank you, one and all, for it. I am reminded by the address of your worthy Mayor, that this reception is given not by one political party; and even if I had not been so reminded by His Honor, I could not have failed to know the fact by the extent of the multitude I see before me now. I could not look upon this vast assemblage without being made aware that all parties were united in this reception. This is as it should be. It is as it should have been if Senator Douglas had been elected; it is as it should have been if Mr. Bell had been elected; as it should have been if Mr. Breckinridge had been elected; as it should ever be when any citizen of the United States is constitutionally elected President of the United States. Allow me to say that I think what has occurred here to-day could not have occurred in any other country on the face of the globe, without the influence of the free institutions which we have unceasingly enjoyed for three-quarters of a century.

There is no country where the people can turn out and enjoy this day precisely as they please, save under the benign influence of the free institutions of our land.

I hope that, although we have some threatening national difficulties now, while these free institutions shall continue to be in the enjoyment of millions of free people of the United States, we will see repeated every four years what we now witness.

In a few short years I and every other individual man who is now living will pass away. I hope that our national difficulties will also pass away, and I hope we shall see in the streets of Cincinnati—good old Cincinnati—for centuries to come, once every four years, the people give such a reception as this to the constitutionally elected President of the whole United States. I hope you will all join in that reception, and that you shall also welcome your brethren across the river to participate in it. We will welcome them in every state in the Union, no matter where they are from. From away South, we shall extend to them a cordial good will, when our present differences shall have been forgotten and blown to the winds forever.

I have spoken but once before this in Cincinnati. That was a year previous to the late presidential election. On that occasion, in a playful manner, but with sincere words, I addressed much of what I said to the Kentuckians. I gave as my opinion that we, as Republicans, would ultimately beat them as Democrats, but that they could postpone that result longer by nominating Senator Douglas for the presidency than they could in any other way. They did not, in the true sense of the word nominate Douglas, and the result has come certainly as soon as I expected. I also told them how I expected they would be treated after they should have been beaten; and I now wish to call or recall their attention to what I then said upon that subject. I then said: "When we do, as we say, beat you, you perhaps will want to know what we will do with you. We mean to treat you as near as we possibly can as Washington, Jefferson and Madison treated you. We mean to leave you alone, and in no way to interfere with your institutions, to abide by all and every compromise of the Constitution; and, in a word, coming back to the original proposition to treat you as far as degenerated men, if we have degenerated, may, according to the examples of those noble fathers, Washington, Jefferson and Madison. We mean to remember that you are as good as we—that there is no difference between us—other than the difference of circumstances. We mean to recognize and bear in mind always that you have as good hearts in your bosoms as other people, or as good as we claim to have, and treat you accordingly."

Fellow-citizens of Kentucky, friends, brethren: may I call you such? In my new position I see no occasion, and feel no inclination to retract a word of this. If it shall not be made good, be assured that the fault shall not be mine.

Speech at Columbus, February 13, 1861.

Mr. President and Mr. Speaker, and Gentlemen of the General Assembly:—It is true, as has been said by the president of the Senate, that very great responsibility rests upon me in the position to which the votes of the American people have called me. I am deeply sensible of that weighty responsibility. I can not but know what you all know, that without a name per-

3

haps without a reason why I should have a name, there has fallen upon me a task such as did not rest even upon the Father of his country, and so feeling I can not but turn and look for the support without which it will be impossible for me to perform that great task. I turn, then, and look to the great American people, and to that God who has never forsaken them.

Allusion has been made to the interest felt in relation to the policy of the new administration. In this I have received from some a degree of credit for having kept silence, and from others some depreciation. I still think that I was right. In the varying and repeatedly shifting scenes of the present, and without a precedent which could enable me to judge by the past, it has seemed fitting that before speaking upon the difficulties of the country, I should have gained a view of the whole field so as to be sure after all—at liberty to modify and change the course of policy as future events may make a change necessary. I have not maintained silence from any want of real anxiety. It is a good thing that there is no more than anxiety, for there is nothing going wrong.

It is a consoling circumstance that when we look out, there is nothing that really hurts anybody. We entertain different views upon political questions, but nobody is suffering any thing. This is a most consoling circumstance, and from it we may conclude that all we want is time, patience, and a reliance on God, who has never forsaken this people. Fellow-citizens, what I have said I have said altogether extemporaneously, and will now come to a close.

Speech at Pittsburg, before the Mayor and Common Council, February 15, 1861.

I most cordially thank his Honor Mayor Wilson and the citizens of Pittsburg generally, for their flattering reception. I am the more grateful because I know that it is not given to me alone, but to the cause I represent, which clearly proves to me their good will, and that sincere feeling is at the bottom of it. And here I may remark, that in every short address I have made to the people, in every crowd through which I have passed, of late, some allusion has been made to the distracted condition of the country. It is natural to expect that I should say something on this subject; but to touch upon it at all would involve an elaborate discussion of a great many questions and circumstances, requiring more time than I can at present command, and would, perhaps, commit me upon matters that have not yet fully developed themselves. The condition of the country is an extraordinary one, and fills the mind of every patriot with anxiety. It is my intention to give this subject all the consideration I possibly can, before specially deciding in regard to it, so that when I do speak it may be as nearly right as possible. When I do speak, I hope I may say nothing in opposition to the spirit of the Constitution, contrary to the integrity of the Union, or which will prove inimical to the liberties of the people or to the peace of the whole country. And, furthermore, when the time arrives for me to speak on this great subject, I hope I may say nothing to disappoint the people generally throughout the country, especially if the expectation has been based upon any thing which I may have heretofore said. Notwithstanding the troubles across the river [the speaker pointing southwardly across the Monongahela, and smiling], there is no crisis but an artifical one. What is there now to warrant the condition of affairs presented by our friends over the river? Take even their own view of the questions involved, and there is nothing to justify the course they are pursuing. I repeat, then, there is no crisis, excepting such a one as may be gotten up at any time by turbulent men, aided by designing politicians. My advice to them, under such circumstances, is to keep cool. If the great American people only keep their temper on both sides of the line, the troubles will come to an end, and the question which now distracts the country will be settled, just as surely as all other difficulties of a like character which have originated in this government have been adjusted. Let the people on both sides keep their self-possession, and just as other clouds have cleared away in due time, so will this great nation continue to prosper as heretofore. But, fellow-citizens, I have spoken longer on this subject than I intended at the outset.

It is often said that the tariff is the specialty of Pennsylvania. Assuming that direct taxation is not to be adopted, the tariff question must be as durable as the government itself. It is a question of national housekeeping. It is to the government what replenishing the meal-tub is to the family.

Every varying circumstance will require frequent

modifications as to the amount needed, and the sources of supply. So far there is little difference of opinion among the people. It is only whether, and how far, the duties on imports shall be adjusted to favor home productions. In the home market that controversy begins. One party insists that too much protection oppresses one class for the advantage of another, while the other party argues that with all its incidents, in the long run, all classes are benefited. In the Chicago platform there is a plank upon this subject, which should be a general law to the incoming administration. We should do neither more nor less than we gave people reason to believe we would when they gave us their votes. . . .

In regard to the plank from Chicago platform, Mr. Lincoln resumed: As with all general propositions, doubtless there will be shades of difference in construing this. I have by no means a thoroughly matured judgment upon this subject, especially as to details; some general ideas are about all. I have long thought to produce any necessary article at home which can be made of as good quality and with as little labor at home as abroad, would be better policy, at least by the difference of the carrying from abroad. In such a case the carrying is demonstrably a dead loss of labor. For instance, labor being the true standard of value, is it not plain that if equal labor gets a bar of railroad iron out of a mine in England, and another out of a mine in Pennsylvania, each can be laid down in a track at home cheaper than they could exchange countries, at least by the cost of carriage. If there be a present cause why one can be both made and carried cheaper in money price than the other can be made without carrying, that cause is an unnatural and injurious one, and ought naturally, if not rapidly, to be removed. The condition of the treasury at this time would seem to render an early revision of the tariff indispensable. The Morrill Tariff bill, now pending before Congress, may or may not become a law. I am not posted as to its particular provisions, but if they are generally satisfactory and the bill shall now pass, there will be an end of the matter for the present. If, however, it shall not pass, I suppose the whole subject will be one of the most pressing and important for the next Congress. By the Constitution, the executive may recommend measures which he may think proper, and he may veto those he thinks improper, and it is supposed that he may add to these, certain indirect influences to affect the action of Congress. My political education strongly inclines me against a very free use of any of these means by the executive to control the legislation of the country. As a rule, I think it better that Congress should originate as well as perfect its measures without external bias. I, therefore, would rather recommend to every gentleman who knows he is to be a member of the next Congress, to take an enlarged view and inform himself thoroughly, so as to contribute his part to such an adjustment of the tariff as shall prove sufficient revenue, and in its other bearings, so far as possible, be just and equal to all sections of the country and all classes of the people.

At Albany, N. Y., February 18, 1861, from the Steps of the Capitol.

Mr. Governor:—I was pleased to receive an invitation to visit the capital of the great Empire State of the nation, on my way to the Federal Capital, and I now thank you, Mr. Governor, and the people of this Capital, and the people of the State of New York, for this most hearty and magnificent welcome.

If I am not at fault, the great Empire State at this time contains a greater population than did the United States of America, at the time she achieved her national independence. I am proud to be invited to pass through your Capital and meet them, as I now have the honor to do.

I am notified by your Governor that the reception is given without distinction of party. I accept it the more gladly because it is so. Almost all men in the country, and in any country where freedom of thought is tolerated, attach themselves to political parties. It is but ordinary charity to attribute this to the fact that in so attaching himself to the party which his judgment prefers, the citizen believes he thereby promotes the best interests of the whole country; and when an election is passed, it is altogether befitting a free people that, until the next election, they should be as one people. The reception you have extended to me to-day is not given to me personally.

It should not be so, but as the representative for the time being of the majority of the nation.

If the election had resulted in the selection of either of the other candidates, the same cordiality should have been extended to him as is extended to me this day, in testimony of the devotion of the whole people to the Constitution and the whole Union, and of their desire to perpetuate our institutions, and to hand them down in their perfection to succeeding generations.

I have neither the voice nor the strength to address you at any greater length. I beg you will accept my most grateful thanks for the devotion, not to me, but to this great and glorious free country.

AFTERWARD IN THE ASSEMBLY HALL AS FOLLOWS, FEBRUARY 18, 1861.

Mr. President and Gentlemen of the Legislature of the State of New York:—It is with feelings of great diffidence, and, I may say, with feelings of awe, perhaps greater than I have recently experienced, that I meet you here in this place.

The history of this great state, the renown of those great men who have stood here, and spoke here, and been heard here, all crowd around my fancy, and incline me to shrink from any attempt to address you. Yet I have some confidence given me by the generous manner in which you have invited me, and by the still more generous manner in which you have received me, to speak further.

You have invited and received me without distinction of party. I can not for a moment suppose that this has been done in any considerable degree with reference to my personal services, but that it is done in so far as I am regarded at this time, as the representative of the majesty of the great nation. I doubt not this is the truth, and the whole truth, of the case, and this is as it should be.

It is much more gratifying to me that this reception has been given to me as the representative of a free people, than it could possibly be if tendered as an evidence of devotion to me, or to any one man personally.

And now I think it were more fitting that I should close these hasty remarks.

It is true that, while I hold myself, without mock modesty, the humblest of all individuals that have ever been elevated to the Presidency, I have a more difficult task to perform than any one of them.

You have generously tendered me the united support of the great Empire State. For this, in behalf of the nation—in behalf of the present and future of the nation—in behalf of civil and religious liberty for all time to come, most gratefully do I thank you. I do not propose to enter into an explanation of any particular line of policy, as to our present difficulties, to be adopted by the incoming administration.

I deem it just to you, to myself, and to all, that I should see every thing, that I should hear every thing, that I should have every light that can be brought within my reach, in order that when I do so speak, I shall have enjoyed every opportunity to take correct and true grounds; and for this reason I don't propose to speak, at this time, of the policy of the government. But when the time comes I shall speak, as well as I am able, for the good of the present and future of the country—for the good both of the North and the South of this country—for the good of the one and the other, and of all sections of the country. [Rounds of applause.] In the meantime, if we have patience, if we restrain ourselves, if we allow ourselves not to run off in a passion, I still have confidence that the Almighty, the maker of the universe, will, through the instrumentality of this great and intelligent people, bring us through this as He has through all the other difficulties of our country. Relying on this, I again thank you for this generous reception.

The President elect en route from Albany to New York. Speech at Troy, February 18, 1861.

Mr. Mayor and Ladies and Gentlemen of the city of Troy:—I can not fail to remark to you here that, since I entered upon this journey from my home to the Federal Capital, I have never seen a meeting so compact and yet so good-natured as the one before which I now stand. I thank you for this reception. I thank you, because it is a demonstration made without distinction of party. I appear before you that I may see you and you see me; but with the large attendance of the fair who face this vast assemblage, I must say I have the best of the bargain. Having said this much in response to your cordial greeting, I will now bid you farewell.

Speech at Hudson, N. Y., February 19, 1861.

Fellow-citizens:—I see that you are providing a platform for me. I shall have to decline standing upon it, because the President of the company [Mr. Sloane] tells me that I shall not have time to wait until it is brought to me. As I said yesterday under similar circumstances to another gathering, you must not draw any inference that I have any intention of deserting any platform of which I have any legitimate connection because I do not stand on yours. Allow me to thank you for this splendid reception, and I now bid you farewell.

SPEECH AT POUGHKEEPSIE, N. Y., FEBRUARY 19, 1861.

It is altogether impossible that I make myself heard by any considerable proportion of this vast assemblage. I am grateful for this cordial welcome, and I am gratified that this immense multitude has come together, not to meet the individual man, but the man who, for the time being, will humbly but earnestly represent the majesty of the nation. These receptions have been given me at other places, and as here, by men of different parties, and not by one party alone. It shows an earnest effort on the part of all to save, not the country, for the country can save itself, but to save the institutions of the country —those institutions under which, for at least three-quarters of a century, we have become the greatest, the most intelligent, and the happiest people in the world. These manifestations show that we all make common cause for these objects; that if some of them are successful in an election and others are beaten, those who are beaten are not in favor of sinking the ship in consequence of defeat, but are earnest in their purpose to sail it safely through the voyage in hand, and, in so far as they may think there has been any mistake in the election, satisfying themselves to take their chance at setting the matter right the next time. That course is entirely right. I am not sure— I do not pretend to be sure—that in the selection of the individual who has been elected this term, the wisest choice has been made. I fear it has not. In the purposes and in the principles that have been sustained, I have been the instrument selected to carry forward the affairs of this government. I can rely upon you, and upon the people of the country; and with their sustaining hand I think that even I shall not fail in carrying the ship of state through the storm. I have only time, in conclusion, to bid you an affectionate farewell.

SPEECH AT FISHKILL LANDING, N. Y., FEB. 19, 1861.

I appear before you not to make a speech. I have no sufficient time, if I had the strength, to repeat speeches at every station where the people kindly gather to welcome me as we go along. If I had the strength and should take the time, I should not get to Washington until after inauguration, which you must be aware would not fit exactly. That such an untoward event might not transpire, I know you will readily forego any further remarks.

SPEECH AT PEEKSKILL, N. Y., FEBRUARY 19, 1861.

I have but a moment to stand before you and thank you for this cordial reception tendered by your authorities. In regard to the difficulties that lie before me, and to which your president has alluded, let me say that if I shall only be as generously and unanimously sustained as this meeting would seem to indicate I shall be, in my management of public affairs, I shall probably not fail; but without that sustaining arm I am quite sure that the difficulties that lie before me will not only be too great for my humble self, but too great for any individual man. I thank you, then, as I have thanked the assembled thousands upon various occasions as I have passed along my route, for such demonstrations, which, if they mean any thing, mean that I shall be supported, not only by the party who gave me the election, but by the free, intelligent and earnest support of all the parties in the country.

SPEECH AT NEW YORK CITY, FEBRUARY 20, 1861.

I am rather an old man to avail myself of such excuses as I am now about to do; yet the truth is so distinct and presses so distinctly upon me, that I can not well avoid it—that is, that I did not understand, when I was brought into this room, that I was to make a speech. It was not intimated to me that I was brought into a room where Daniel Webster and Henry Clay had made speeches, and where I, in my position, am expected to do something like those men, or at least say something worthy of myself. I, therefore, beg you to make allowance for the circumstances under which I have been by surprise brought before you. I have been very much in the habit of thinking and sometimes speaking on the questions that have agitated the people. If I were disposed to do so, and we were to take up some of the issues, and I was called upon to make an argument, I could do it without much deliberation. But that is not what you desire to have done here tonight. I have been occupying the position since election, of silence—of avoiding public speaking. I have been doing so because I thought, upon due consideration, that was the proper course for me to take. I am brought before you now to make a speech, while you all approve, more than any thing else, that I have been keeping silence.

It seems to me the response you give to that remark ought to justify me in closing right here.

I have not kept silence since the presidential election from any party craftiness or from any indifference to anxieties that pervade the minds of men in this country. I have kept silence for the reason that it was peculiarly proper for me to wait until the time should come when, according to the custom of the country, I would speak officially. I hear some one say, "according to the custom of the country." I allude to the custom, on the president's taking the oath of office, of his declairing what course he thinks should be pursued. That is what I mean. The political drama acting before the country at this time is rapidly shifting its scenes. It was eminently fitting that I should wait till the last minute; so that I could chose a position from which I should not be obliged to deviate.

I have said several times on this journey, and now repeat to you, I shall then take the ground that I think is right—the ground that I shall then think right for the North, the South, the East, the West, and the whole country. And in doing so, I hope to feel no necessity pressing upon me to say any thing in conflict with the Constitution, in conflict with the continued union of these United States, in conflict with the liberty of the people, nor any thing in conflict with any thing whatever I have given you reason to expect from me. Now, my friends, have I not said enough? Now, my friends, there is a difference of opinion between you and me, and I insist on deciding the question.

SPEECH AT TRENTON, N. J., FEBRUARY 21, 1861, BEFORE THE SENATE.

Mr. President, and Gentlemen of the Senate of the State of New Jersey:—I am very grateful to you for the honorable reception of which I have been the object. I can not but remember the place that New Jersey holds in our early history. In the early revolutionary struggle, few of the states among the old thirteen had more of the battle field of the country within their limits than old New Jersey. May I be pardoned if, upon this occasion, I mention that away back in my childhood, the earliest days of my being able to read, I got hold of a small book, such a one as few of the younger members have ever seen, "*Weems's Life of Washington.*" I remember all the accounts then given of the battle fields and struggles for the liberties of the country, and none fixed themselves upon my imagination so deeply as the struggle here at Trenton, New Jersey.

The crossing of the river; the contest with the Hessians; the great hardships endured at that time, all fixed themselves in my memory, more than any single revolutionary event; and you all know, for you have all been boys, how these early impressions last longer than any others. I recollect thinking then, boy even though I was, that there must have been something more than common that these men struggled for. I am exceedingly anxious that that thing which they struggled for; that something even more than national independence; that something that held out a great promise to all the people of the world in all time to come—I am exceedingly anxious that the Union, the Constitution, and the liberties of the people shall be perpetuated in accordance with the original idea for which that struggle was made, and I shall be most happy indeed if I shall be an humble instrument in the hands of the Almighty, and of these, his most chosen people, as the chosen instrument—also in the hands of the Almighty—for perpetuating the object of that great struggle. You give me this reception, as I understand, without distinction of party. I learn that this body is composed of a majority of gentlemen who, in the exercise of their best judgment in the choice of a chief magistrate, did not think I was the man. I understand, nevertheless, that they came forward here to greet me as the constitutional President of the United States —as citizens of the United States, to meet the man who, for the time being, is the representative man of the nation—united by a purpose to perpetuate the Union and liberties of the people.

As such, I accept the reception more gratefully than I could do did I believe it was tendered to me as an individual.

Speech at Philadelphia, Pa., February 22, 1861.

I am filled with deep emotion at finding myself standing here, in this place, where were collected the wisdom, the patriotism, the devotion to principle, from which sprang the institution under which we live. You have kindly suggested to me that in my hands is the task of restoring peace to the present distracted condition of the country. I can say in return, sir, that all the political sentiments I entertain have been drawn, so far as I have been able to draw them, from the sentiments which originated and were given to the world from this hall. I have never had a feeling, politically, that did not spring from the sentiments embodied in the Declaration of Independence. I have pondered over the toils that were endured by the officers and soldiers of the army who achieved that independence. I have often inquired of myself what great principle or idea it was that kept this confederacy so long together. It was not the mere matter of the separation of the colonies from the mother-land, but that sentiment in the Declaration of Independence which gave liberty not alone to the people of this country, but, I hope, to the world for all future time. It was that which gave promise that in due time the weight would be lifted from the shoulders of all men. This is a sentiment embodied in the Declaration of Independence. Now, my friends, can the country be saved upon this basis? If it can, I will consider myself one of the happiest men in the world if I can help to save it. If it can not be saved upon that principle, it will be truly awful.

4

But if this country can not be saved without giving up that principle, I was about to say I would rather be assassinated on this spot than surrender it. Now, in my view of the present aspect of affairs, there need be no bloodshed or war. There is no necessity for it. I am not in favor of such a course; and I may say, in advance, that there will be no bloodshed unless it will be forced upon the government, and then it will be compelled to act in self-defense.

Speech before the Legislature of Pennsylvania at Harrisburg, Pa., February 22, 1861.

I appear before you only for a very few, brief remarks, in response to what has been said to me. I thank you most sincerely for this reception and the generous words in which support has been promised me upon this occasion. I thank your great commonwealth for the overwhelming support it recently gave, not me personally, but the cause which I think a great one, in the late election. Allusion has been made to the fact—the interesting fact, perhaps, we should say—that I for the first time appear at the capital of the great Commonwealth of Pennsylvania upon the birthday of the Father of this country, in connection with that beloved anniversary connected with the history of this country.

I have already gone through one exceedingly interesting scene this morning in the ceremonies at Philadelphia.

Under the high conduct of gentlemen, thus I was for the first time allowed the privilege of standing in old Independence Hall [enthusiastic cheering] to have a few words addressed to me there, and opening up to me an opportunity of expressing, with much regret, that I had not more time to express something of my own feelings, excited by the occasion, somewhat to harmonize and give shape to the feelings that had been really the feelings of my whole life. Besides this, my friends there had provided a magnificent flag of the country. They had arranged it so that I was given the honor of raising it to the head of its staff. And when it went up I was pleased that it went to its place by the strength of my own feeble arm, when according to the arrangement, the cord was pulled, and it floated gloriously to the wind, without an accident, in the light, glowing sunshine of the morning, I could not help hoping that there was, in the entire success of that beautiful ceremony, at least something of an omen of what is to come. [Loud applause.] How could I help feeling then as I often have felt? In the whole of that proceeding I was a very humble instrument. I had not provided the flag; I had not made the arrangement for elevating it to its place; I had applied but a very small portion of my feeble strength in raising it. In the whole transaction I was in the hands of the people who had arranged it, and if I can have the same generous co-operation of the people of the nation, I think the flag of our country may still be kept flaunting gloriously. [Loud enthusiastic and continued cheering.] I recur for a moment but to repeat some words uttered at the hotel, in regard to what has been said about the military support which the general government may expect from the Commonwealth of Pennsylvania in a proper emergency.

To guard against any possible mistake do I recur to this. It is not with any pleasure that I contemplate the possibility that a necessity may arise in this country for the use of the military arm. [Applause.] While I am exceedingly gratified to see the manifestations upon your streets of your military force here, and exceedingly gratified at your promises here to use that force upon a proper emergency—while I make these acknowledgments, I desire to repeat, in order to preclude any possible misconstruction, that I do most sincerely hope that we shall have no use for them. [Applause.] That it will never become their duty to shed blood, and most especially never to shed fraternal blood, I promise that, so far as I may have wisdom to direct, if so painful a result shall any wise be brought about, it shall be through no fault of mine. [Cheers.]

Allusion has also been made by one of your honored speakers to some remarks made by myself at Pittsburg, in regard to what is supposed to be the especial interest of this great Commonwealth of Pennsylvania.

I now wish only to say, in regard to that matter, that the few remarks which I uttered on that occasion were rather carefully worded. I took pains that they should be so. I have seen no occasion since to add to them, or subtract from them. I leave them precisely as they stand [applause] adding only now that I am pleased to have an expression from you, gentlemen of Pennsylvania, significant that they are satisfactory to you. And now, gentlemen of the General Assembly of the Commonwealth of Pennsylvania, allow me to return you again my most sincere thanks.

Lincoln's Own Statement of How He Entered Washington, D. C., February 23, 1861.

I arrived at Philadelphia on the 21st. I agreed to stop over night, and on the following morning to hoist the flag over Independence Hall. In the evening there was a great crowd where I received my friends, at the Continental Hotel. Mr. Judd, a warm personal friend from Chicago, sent for me to come to his room. I went, and found there Mr. Pinkerton, a skillful police detective, also from Chicago, who had been employed for some days in Baltimore, watching and searching for suspicious persons there. Pinkerton informed me that a plan had been laid for my assassination, the exact time when I expected to go through Baltimore being publicly known. He was well informed as to the plan, but did not know that the conspirators would have pluck enough to execute it. He urged me to go right through with him to Washington that night. I didn't like that. I had made engagements to visit Harrisburg, and go from there to Baltimore, and I resolved to do so. I could not believe that there was a plot to murder me. I made arrangements, however, with Mr. Judd for my return to Philadelphia the next night, if I should be convinced that there was danger in going through Baltimore. I told him if I should meet at Harrisburg, as I had at other places, a delegation to go with me to the next place (then Baltimore), I should feel safe and go on. When I was making my way back to my room, through crowds of people, I met Frederick Seward. We went together to my room, when he told me that he had been sent, at the instance of his father and General Scott, to inform me that their detectives in Baltimore had discovered a plot to assassinate me. They knew nothing of Pinkerton's movements. I now believed such a plot to be in existence. The next morning I raised the flag over Independence Hall, and then went on to Harrisburg with Mr. Sumner, Major (now General) Hunter, Mr. Judd, Mr. Lamon, and others. There I met the Legislature and people, dined, and waited until the time appointed for me to leave. In the meantime, Mr. Judd had so secured the telegraph that no communication could pass to Baltimore and give the conspirators knowledge of a change in my plans. In New York some friend had given me a new beaver hat in a box, and in it had placed a soft wool hat. I had never worn one of the latter in my life. I had this box in my room. Having informed a very few friends of the secret of my new movements, and the cause, I put on an old overcoat I had with me, and putting the soft hat in my pocket, I walked out of the house at a back door, bareheaded, and without exciting any special curiosity. Then I put on the soft hat and joined my friends without being recognized by strangers, for I was not the same man. Sumner and Hunter wished to accompany me. I said no; you are known, and your presence might betray me. I will only take Lamon (now marshal of this district), whom nobody knew, and Mr. Judd. Sumner and Hunter felt hurt. We went back to Philadelphia, and found a message there from Pinkerton (who had returned to Baltimore), that the conspirators had held their final meeting that evening, and it was doubtful whether they had the nerve to attempt the execution of their purpose. I went on, however, as the arrangement had been made, in a special train. We were not long in the station at Baltimore. I heard people talking around, but no one particularly observed me. At an early hour on Saturday morning, at about the time I was expected to leave Harrisburg, I arrived in Washington.

Speech at Washington, February 28, 1861, in Response to a Serenade by Republican Associations.

My friends:—I suppose that I may take this as a compliment paid to me, and as such please accept my thanks for it. I have reached this city of Washington under circumstances considerably differing from those under which any other man ever reached it. I am here for the purpose of taking an official position amongst the people, almost all of whom were politically opposed to me, and are yet opposed to me, as I suppose.

I propose no lengthy address to you. I only propose to say, as I did yesterday, when your worthy Mayor and Board of Aldermen called upon me, that I thought much of the ill-feeling that has existed between you and the people of your surroundings, and that people from among whom I came, has depended, and now depends, upon a misunderstanding.

I hope that if things shall go along as prosperously as I believe we all desire they may, I may have it in my power to remove something of the misunderstanding; that I may be enabled to convince you, and the people of your section of the country, that we regard you as in all things our equals, and in all things entitled to the same respect and the same treatment that we claim for ourselves; that we are in nowise disposed, if it were in our power to oppress you, to deprive you of any of your rights under the Constitution of the United States, or over-narrowly to split hairs with you in regard to these rights, but are determined to give you, as far as lies in our hands, all your rights under the Constitution—not grudgingly, but fully and fairly. (Applause). I hope that, by thus dealing with you, we will become better acquainted, and be better friends.

And now, with these few remarks, and again returning my thanks for this compliment, and expressing my desire to hear a little more of your good music, I bid you good-night.

Inaugural Address at Washington, D. C., March 4, 1861.

Fellow Citizens of the United States:—In compliance with a custom as old as the government itself, I appear before you to address you briefly, and to take, in your presence, the oath prescribed by the Constitution of the United States, to be taken by the president before he enters on the execution of his office.

I do not consider it necessary, at present, for me to discuss those matters of administration about which there is no special anxiety or excitement. Apprehension seems to exist among the people of the Southern

States, that by the accession of a Republican administration, their property and their peace and personal security are to be endangered. There has never been any reasonable cause for such apprehension. Indeed, the most ample evidence to the contrary has all the while existed, and been open to their inspection. It is found in nearly all the published speeches of him who now addresses you. I do but quote from one of those speeches, when I declare that "I have no purposes directly or indirectly, to interfere with the institution of slavery, in the states where it exists." I believe I have no lawful right to do so, and I have no inclination to do so. Those who nominated and elected me did so with the full knowledge that I had made this and many similar declarations, and had never recanted them. And, more than this, they placed in the platform for my acceptance, and as a law to themselves and to me, the clear and emphatic resolution which I now read:—

"*Resolved*, that the maintainance inviolate of the rights of the states, and especially the right of each state to order and control its own domestic institutions according to its own judgment exclusively, is essential to that balance of power on which the perfection and endurance of our political fabric depend; and we denounce the lawless invasion by armed force of the soil of any state or territory, no matter under what pretext, as among the gravest of crimes."

I now reiterate these sentiments, and, in doing so, I only press upon the public attention the most conclusive evidence of which the case is susceptible, that the property, peace and security of no section are to be in any wise endangered by the now incoming administration.

I add, too, that all the protection which, consistently with the Constitution and the laws, can be given, will be cheerfully given to all the states, when lawfully demanded, for whatever cause, as cheerfully to one section as to another. There is much controversy about the delivering up of fugitives from service or labor. The clause I now read is as plainly written in the Constitution as any other of its provisions:

"No person held to service or labor in one state under the laws thereof, escaping into another, shall, in consequence of any law or regulation therein, be discharged from such service or labor, but shall be delivered up on claim of the party to whom such service or labor may be due."

It is scarcely questioned that this provision was intended by those who made it for the reclaiming of what we call fugitive slaves; and the intention of the law-giver is the law.

All members of Congress swear their support to the whole Constitution,—to this provision as well as any other. To the proposition then that slaves whose cases come within the terms of this clause, "shall be delivered up," their oaths are unanimous. Now, if they would make the effort in good temper, could they not, with nearly equal unanimity, frame and pass a law by means of which to keep good that unanimous oath?

There is some difference of opinion whether this clause should be enforced by national or by state authority; but surely that difference is not a very material one. If the slave is to be surrendered, it can be of but little consequence to him or to others by which authority it is done, and should any one in any case be content that this oath shall go unkept on a merely unsubstantial controversy, as to how it shall be kept?

Again, in any law upon this subject, ought not all the safe-guards of liberty known in civilized and humane jurisprudence to be introduced, so that a free man be not, in any case, surrendered as a slave? And might it not be well at the same time to provide by law for the enforcement of that clause in the Constitution which guarantees that "the citizens of each state shall be entitled to all the privileges and immunities of citizens in the several states?"

I take the official oath to-day with no mental reservations, and with no purpose to construe the Constitution or laws by any hypercritical rules; and, while I do not chose now to specify particular acts of Congress as proper to be enforced, I do suggest that it will be much safer for all, both in official and private stations, to conform to and abide by all those acts which stand unrepealed, than to violate any of them, trusting to find impunity in having them held to be unconstitutional.

It is seventy-two years since the first inauguration of a president under our national Constitution. During that period, fifteen different and very distinguished citizens have in succession administered the executive branch of the government. They have conducted it through many perils, and generally with great success. Yet, with all this scope for precedent, I now enter upon the same task, for the brief constitutional term of four years, under great and peculiar difficulties.

A disruption of the Federal Union, heretofore only menaced, is now formidably attempted. I hold, that, in the contemplation of universal law and the Constitution, the union of these states is perpetual. Perpetuity is implied, if not expressed, in the fundamental law of all national governments. It is safe to assert that no government proper ever had a provision in its organic law for its own termination. Continue to execute all the express provisions of our national Constitution, and the Union will endure forever; it being impossible to destroy it, except by some action not provided for in the instrument itself. Again, if the United States be not a government proper, but an association of states in the nature of a contract merely, can it, as a contract, be peaceably unmade by less than all the parties who made it? One party to a contract may violate it—break it, so to speak; but does it not require all to lawfully rescind it? Descending from these general principles, we find the proposition that in legal contemplation the Union is perpetual, confirmed by the history of the Union in itself.

The Union is much older than the Constitution. It was formed, in fact, by the Articles of Association in 1774. It was matured and continued in the Declaration of Independence in 1776. It was further matured, and the faith of all the then thirteen states expressly plighted and engaged that it should be perpetual, by the Articles of Confederation, in 1778;

and, finally, in 1787, one of the declared objects for ordaining and establishing the Constitution was to form a more perfect Union. But, if the destruction of the Union by one or by a part only of the states be lawfully possible, the Union is less than before, the Constitution having lost the vital element of perpetuity.

It follows from these views that no state, upon its own mere motion, can lawfully get out of the Union; that resolves and ordinances to that effect are legally void; and that acts of violence within any state or states against the authority of the United States, are insurrectionary or revolutionary according to circumstances. I therefore consider, that, in view of the Constitution and the laws, the Union is unbroken; and, to the extent of my ability I shall take care, as the Constitution itself expressly enjoins upon me, that the laws of the Union shall be faithfully executed in all the states. Doing this, which I deem to be only a simple duty on my part, I shall perfectly perform it so far as is practicable, unless my rightful masters, the American people, shall withhold the requisite power, or in some authoritative manner direct the contrary. I trust this will not be regarded as a menace, but only as the declared purpose of the Union that it will constitutionally defend and maintain itself. In doing this, there need be no bloodshed nor violence; and there shall be none unless it is forced upon the national authority. The power confided to me *will be used to hold, occupy, and possess the property and places belonging to the Government,* and collect the duties and imposts; but, beyond what may be necessary for these objects, there will be no invasion, no using of force against or among the people anywhere.

Where hostility to the United States shall be so great and so universal as to prevent competent resident citizens from holding the Federal offices, there will be no attempt to force obnoxious strangers among the people for that object. While the strict legal right may exist of the Government to enforce the exercise of these offices, the attempt to do so would be so irritating, and so nearly impracticable withal, that I deem it better to forego for the time the uses of such offices.

The mails, unless repelled, will continue to be furnished in all parts of the Union.

So far as possible, the people every-where shall have that sense of perfect security which is most favorable to calm thought and reflection.

The course here indicated will be followed, unless current events and experience shall show a modification or change to be proper; and in every case and exigency my best discretion will be exercised according to the circumstances actually existing, and with a view and hope of a peaceful solution of the national troubles, and the restoration of fraternal sympathies and affections. That there are persons in one section or another, who seek to destroy the Union at all events, and are glad of any pretext to do it, I will neither affirm nor deny. But, if there be such, I need address no word to them.

To those, however, who really love the Union, may I not speak? Before entering upon so grave a matter as the destruction of our national fabric, with all its benefits, its memories, and its hopes, would it not be well to ascertain why we do it? Will you hazard so desperate a step, while any portion of the ills you fly from have no real existence? Will you, while the certain ills you fly to are greater than all the real ones you fly from? Will you risk the commission of so fearful a mistake? All profess to be content in the Union if all constitutional rights can be maintained. Is it true, then, that any right, plainly written in the Constitution, has been denied? I think not. Happily the human mind is so constituted, that no party can reach to the audacity of doing this.

Think, if you can, of a single instance in which a plainly written provision of the Constitution has ever been denied. If, by the mere force of numbers, a majority should deprive a minority of any clearly written constitutional right, it might, in a moral point of view, justify revolution; it certainly would, if such right were a vital one. But such is not our case.

All the vital rights of minorities and of individuals are so plainly assured to them by affirmations and negations, guarantees and prohibitions, in the Constitution, that controversies never arise concerning them. But no organic law can ever be framed with a provision specifically applicable to every question which may occur in practical administration. No foresight can anticipate, nor any document of reasonable length contain, express provision for all possible questions. Shall fugitives from labor be surrendered by National or by state authority? The Constitution does not expressly say. Must Congress protect slavery in the territories? The Constitution does not expressly say. From questions of this class spring all our constitutional controversies, and we divide upon them into majorities and minorities. If the minority will not acquiesce, the majority must, or the government must cease. There is no alternative for continuing the government but acquiescence on the one side or the other.

If a minority, in such a case, will secede rather than acquiesce, they make a precedent which in turn will ruin and divide them; for a minority of their own will secede from them, whenever a majority refuses to be controlled by such a minority. For instance, why not any portion of a new confederacy, a year or two hence, arbitrarily secede again, precisely as portions of the present Union now claim to secede from it? All who cherish disunion sentiments are now being educated to the exact temper of doing this. Is there such perfect identity of interests among the states to compose a new Union as to produce harmony only, and prevent renewed secession? Plainly, the central idea of secession is the essence of anarchy.

A majority held in restraint by constitutional check and limitation and always changing easily with deliberate changes of popular opinions and sentiments, is the only true sovereign of a free people. Whoever rejects it does, of necessity, fly to anarchy or to despotism. Unanimity is impossible: the rule of a minority as a permanent arrangement, is wholly inadmissible; so that, rejecting the majority principle, anarchy or despotism in some form is all that is left.

I do not forget the position assumed by some, that

Constitutional questions are to be decided by the Supreme Court, nor do I deny that such decisions must be binding in any case upon the parties to a suit, as to the object to that suit; while they are also entitled to very high respect and consideration in all parallel cases by other departments of the government; and, while it is obviously possible that such decision may be erroneous in any given case, still, the evil effect following it, being limited to that particular case, with the chance that it may be overruled and never become a precedent for other cases, can better be borne than could the evils of a different practice.

At the same time, the candid citizen must confess that, if the policy of the government upon the vital questions affecting the whole people is to be irrevocably fixed by the decisions of the Supreme Court the instant they are made, as in ordinary litigation between parties in personal actions, the people will have ceased to be their own masters, having to that extent practically resigned their government into the hands of that eminent tribunal.

Nor is there in this view any assault upon the court or the judges. It is a duty from which they may not shrink, to decide cases properly brought before them; and it is no fault of theirs if others seek to turn their decisions to political purposes. One section of our country believes that slavery is right and ought to be extended, while the other believes it is wrong, and ought not to be extended; and this is the only substantial dispute. And the fugitive-slave clause of the Constitution, and the law for the suppression of the foreign slave trade, are each as well enforced, perhaps, as any law can ever be in a community where the moral sense of the people imperfectly supports the law itself. The great body of the people abide by the dry, legal obligation in both cases, and a few break over in each.

This, I think, can not be perfectly cured; and it would be worse in both cases after the separation of the sections than before. The foreign slave trade, now imperfectly suppressed, would be ultimately revived, without restriction, in one section; while fugitive slaves, now only partially surrendered, would not be surrendered at all by the other.

Physically speaking, we can not separate; we cannot move our respective sections from each other, nor build an impassable wall between them. A husband and wife may be divorced, and go out of the presence and beyond the reach of each other; but the different parts of our country can not do this. They can not but remain face to face; and intercourse, either amicable or hostile, must continue between them. Is it possible, then, to make that intercourse more advantageous or more satisfactory after separation than before? Can aliens make treaties easier than friends can make laws? Can treaties be more faithfully enforced between aliens than laws can among friends? Suppose you go to war, you can not fight always; and when, after much loss on both sides, and no gain on either, you cease fighting, the identical questions as to terms of intercourse are again upon you.

This country, with its institutions, belongs to the people who inhabit it. Whenever they shall grow weary of the existing government, they can exercise their constitutional right of amending, or their revolutionary right to dismember or overthrow it. I can not be ignorant of the fact, that many worthy and patriotic citizens are desirous of having the national Constitution amended. While I make no recommendation of amendment, I fully recognize the full authority of the people over the whole subject, to be exercised in either of the modes prescribed in the instrument itself; and I should, under existing circumstances, favor rather than oppose a fair opportunity being afforded the people to act upon it.

I will venture to add, that to me the convention mode seems preferable, in that it allows amendments to originate with the people themselves, instead of only permitting them to take or reject propositions originated by others not especially chosen for the purpose, and which might not be precisely such as they would wish either to accept or refuse. I understand that a proposed amendment to the Constitution [which amendment, however, I have not seen] has passed Congress, to the effect that the Federal government shall never interfere with the domestic institutions of states, including that of persons held to service. To avoid misconstruction of what I have said, I depart from my purpose not to speak of particular amendments so far as to say, that, holding such a provision to now be implied constitutional law, I have no objection to its being made express and irrevocable. The chief magistrate derives all his authority from the people, and they have conferred none upon him to fix the terms for the separation of the states. The people, themselves, also can do this if they choose; but the Executive, as such, has nothing to do with it. His duty is to administer the present government as it came to his hands, and to transmit it unimpaired by him to his successor.

Why should there not be a patient confidence in the ultimate justice of the people? Is there any better or equal hope in the world? In our present differences, is either party without faith of being in the right? If the Almighty Ruler of Nations, with his eternal truth and justice, be on your side of the North, or on yours of the South, that truth and that justice will surely prevail by the judgment of this great tribunal—the American people. By the frame of the government under which we live, this same people have wisely given their public servants but little power for mischief, and have with equal wisdom provided for the return of that little to their own hands at very short intervals. While the people retain their virtue and vigilance, no administration, by any extreme wickedness or folly, can very seriously injure the government in the short space of four years.

My countrymen, one and all, think calmly and well upon this whole subject. Nothing valuable can be lost by taking time.

If there be an object to hurry any of you, in hot haste, to a step which you would never take deliberately, that object will be frustrated by taking time; but no good object can be frustrated by it Such of you as are now dissatisfied still have the old Constitution unimpaired, and, on the sensitive point, the laws of your own framing under it; while the new administration will have no immediate power, if it would, to change either.

If it were admitted that you who are dissatisfied hold the right side in the dispute, there is still no single reason for precipitate action. Intelligence, patriotism, Christianity, and a firm reliance on Him who has never yet forsaken this favored land, are still competent to adjust, in the best way, all our present difficulties.

In your hands, my dissatisfied fellow-countrymen, and not in mine, is the momentous issue of civil war. The government will not assail you.

You can have no conflict without being yourselves the aggressors. You can have no oath registered in Heaven to destroy the government; while I shall have the most solemn one to "preserve, protect and defend" it.

I am loath to close. We are not enemies, but friends. We must not be enemies. Though passion may have strained, it must not break our bonds of affection. The mystic cords of memory, stretching from every battle-field and patriot grave to every living heart and hearthstone all over this broad land, will yet swell the chorus of the Union, when again touched, as surely they will be, by the better angels of our nature.

OH! WHY SHOULD THE SPIRIT OF MORTAL BE PROUD.

[The following poem, written by William Knox, a Scottish poet of considerable talent, has been widely

published. It was a great favorite with President
Lincoln, by whom it was often recited.]

Oh, why should the spirit of mortal be proud?
Like a swift, fleeting meteor, a fast-flying cloud,
A flash of the lightning, a break of the wave,
He passeth from life to his rest in the grave.

The leaves of the oak and the willow shall fade,
Be scattered around and together be laid;
And the young and the old, and the low and the high
Shall molder to dust, and together shall lie.

The infant a mother attended and loved;
The mother that infant's affection who proved;
The husband that mother and infant who blessed,
Each, all, are away to their dwellings of rest.

The hand of the king that the scepter hath born;
The brow of the priest that the miter hath worn;
The eye of the sage and the heart of the brave,
Are hidden and lost in the depths of the grave.

The peasant, whose lot was to sow and to reap;
The herdsman, who climbed with his goats up the steep;
The beggar, who wandered in search of his bread,
Have faded away like the grass that we tread.

The maid on whose cheek, on whose brow, in whose eye
Shone beauty and pleasure—her triumphs are by;
And the memory of those who loved her and praised,
Are alike from the minds of the living erased.

The saint who enjoyed the communion of heaven,
The sinner who dared to remain unforgiven,
The wise and the foolish, the guilty and just,
Have quietly mingled their bones in the dust.

So the multitude goes, like the flower or the weed
That withers away to let others succeed;
So the multitude comes, even those we behold,
To repeat every tale that has often been told.

For we are the same our fathers have been;
We see the same sights our fathers have seen
We drink the same stream and view the same sun —
And run the same course our fathers have run.

The thoughts we are thinking our fathers would think;
From the death we are shrinking our fathers would shrink;
To the life we are clinging they also would cling;
But it speeds for us all, like a bird on the wing.

They loved, but the story we can not unfold;
They scorned, but the heart of the haughty is cold;
They grieved, but no wail from their slumber will come;
They joyed, but the tongue of their gladness is dumb.

They died, aye! they died; we things that are now,
That walk on the turf that lies over their brow,
And make in their dwellings a transient abode,
Meet the things that they met on their pilgrimage road.

Yea! hope and despondency, pleasure and pain,
We mingle together in sunshine and rain;
And the smile and the tear, the song and the dirge,
Still follow each other, like surge upon surge.

'Tis the wink of an eye, 'tis the draught of a breath;
From the blossom of health to the paleness of death,
From the gilded saloon to the bier and the shroud —
Oh, why should the spirit of mortal be proud?

Lincoln's Letter to Senor Molina, March 17, 1861.

I am happy to receive the letters you present, and to recognize you, sir, as Envoy Extraordinary and Minister Plenipotentiary of Nicaragua, near the U. S. In conferring a higher rank upon you, as a token of regard on the part of the Government and people of Nicaragua toward this country, they have done our Government and people an honor, for which we are duly grateful; while they have also manifested an increased confidence in you, which we can attest is deserved, and thereby have done you a distinguished honor, upon which we congratulate you. On behalf of the United States I fully reciprocate toward your government and people the kind wishes and friendly purposes you so generously express toward ours. Please communicate to his Excellency, the President of Nicaragua, my high esteem and consideration, and my earnest wish for his health, happiness and long life. Be assured, sir, I do not allow myself to doubt that your public duties and social intercourse here will be so conducted as to be entirely acceptable to the government and people of the United States.

A. LINCOLN.

LINCOLN'S REPLY TO THE DELEGATES FROM VIRGINIA, APRIL 13, 1861.

Hon. Messrs. Preston, Stuart, and Randolph, Gentlemen:—As a committee of the Virginia Convention, now in session, you present me a preamble and resolution in these words:

"Whereas, in the opinion of this Convention, the uncertainty which prevails in the public mind as to the policy which the Federal executive intends to pursue towards the seceded states is extremely injurious to the industrial and commercial interests of the country, tends to keep up an excitement which is unfavorable to an adjustment of pending difficulties, and threatens a disturbance of the public peace: therefore,

"*Resolved*, That a committee of three delegates be

appointed to wait on the President of the United States, present to him this preamble and resolution, and respectfully ask him to communicate to this Convention the policy which the Federal executive intends to pursue in regard to the Confederate States."

In answer, I have to say that, having at the beginning of my official term expressed my intended policy as plainly as I was able, it is with deep regret and some mortification that I now learn that there is great and injurious uncertainty in the public mind as to what that policy is, and what course I intend to pursue. Not having as yet seen occasion to change, it is now my purpose to pursue the course marked out in the inaugural address. I commend a careful consideration of the whole document as the best expression I can give of my purposes. As I then and therein said, I now repeat :

"The power confided to me will be used to hold, occupy, and possess the property and places belonging to the government, and to collect the duties and imports; but beyond what is necessary for these objects, there will be no invasion, no using of force against or among the people anywhere."

By the words "property and places belonging to the government," I chiefly allude to the military posts and property which were in the possession of the government when it came to my hands. But if, as now appears to be true, in pursuit of a purpose to drive the United States authority from these places, an unprovoked assault has been made upon Fort Sumter, I shall hold myself at liberty to repossess, if I can, like places which had been seized before the government was devolved upon me. And, in any event, I shall, to the best of my ability, repel force by force. In case it proves true that Fort Sumter has been assaulted, as is reported, I shall, perhaps, cause the United States mails to be withdrawn from all the states which claim to have seceded, believing that the commencement of actual war against the government justifies and possibly demands it.

I scarcely need to say that I consider the military posts and property situated within the states which claim to have seceded as yet belonging to the government of the United States as much as they did before the supposed secession.

Whatever else I may do for the purpose, I shall not attempt to collect the duties and imposts by any armed invasion of any part of the country—not meaning by this, however, that I may not land a force deemed necessary to relieve a fort upon the border of the country.

From the fact that I have quoted a part of the inaugural address, it must not be inferred that I repudiate any other part, the whole of which I reaffirm, except so far as what I now say of the mails may be regarded as a modification.

PROCLAMATION, APRIL 15, 1861.

Whereas, the laws of the United States have been for some time past and now are opposed, and the execution thereof obstructed, in the States of South Carolina, Georgia, Alabama, Florida, Mississippi, Louisiana, and Texas, by combination too powerful to be surpassed by the ordinary course of judicial proceedings, or by the powers vested in the marshals by law; now, therefore, I, Abraham Lincoln, President of the United States, in virtue of the power in me vested by the Constitution and the laws, have thought fit to call forth and hereby do call forth, the militia of the several states of the Union, to the aggregate number of seventy-five thousand, in order to suppress said combination, and to cause the laws to be duly executed.

The details for the object will be immediately communicated to the state authorities through the War Department. I appeal to all local citizens to favor, facilitate, and aid this effort to maintain the honor, the integrity and existence of our National Union, and the perpetuity of popular government, and to redress laws already long enough endured. I deem it proper to say, that the first service assigned to the forces hereby called forth, will probably be to repossess the forts, property, and places which have been seized from the Union; and in every event, the utmost care will be observed, consistently with the objects aforesaid, to avoid any devastation, any destruction of, or interference with, property, or any disturbance of peaceful citizens of any part of the country; and I hereby command the persons composing the combinations aforesaid to disperse and retire peaceably to their respective abodes, within twenty days from this date.

Deeming that the present condition of public affairs presents an extraordinary occasion, I do hereby, in virtue of the power in me vested by the Constitution, convene both houses of Congress. The senators and representatives are, therefore, summoned to assemble at their respective chambers at twelve o'clock noon, on Thursday, the fourth day of July next, then and there to consider and determine such measures as, in their wisdom, the public safety and interest may seem to demand.

In witness whereof, I have hereunto set my hand, and caused the seal of the United States to be affixed.

Done at the city of Washington, this fifteenth day of April, in the year of our Lord one thousand eight hundred and sixty-one, and of the independence of the United States the eighty-fifth.

ABRAHAM LINCOLN.

PRESIDENT LINCOLN TO GOVERNOR HICKS AND MAYOR BROWN.

Washington, April 20, 1861.

Gentlemen:—Your letter by Messrs. Bond, Dobbin and Brune is received. I tender you both my sincere thanks for your efforts to keep the peace in the trying situation in which you are placed. For the future, troops *must* be brought here, but I make no point of bringing them *through* Baltimore.

Without any military knowledge myself, of course I must leave details to General Scott. He hastily said this morning, in the presence of these gentlemen, "March them *around* Baltimore, and not through it."

I sincerely hope the General, on fuller reflection, will consider this practical and proper, and that you will not object to it. By this a collision of the people of Baltimore with the troops will be avoided, unless they go out of their way to seek it. I hope you will exert your influence to prevent this. Now and ever I shall do all in my power for peace, consistently with the maintenance of the government. Your obedient servant, ABRAHAM LINCOLN.

PRESIDENT LINCOLN'S REPLY TO FRONTIER GUARDS, APRIL 28, 1861.

I have desired as sincerely as any man—I sometimes think more than any other man—that our present difficulties might be settled without the shedding of blood. I will not say that all hope is yet gone. But if the alternative is presented, whether the Union is to be broken in fragments, and the liberties of the people lost, or blood be shed, you will probably make the choice, with which I shall not be dissatisfied.

PRESIDENT LINCOLN'S REPLY TO A BALTIMORE COMMITTEE, APRIL 28, 1861.

You, gentlemen, come here to me and ask for peace on any terms, and yet have no word of condemnation for those who are making war on us. You express great horror of bloodshed, and yet would not lay a straw in the way of those who are organizing in Virginia and elsewhere to capture this city. The rebels attack Fort Sumter, and your citizens attack troops sent to the defense of the government, and the lives and property in Washington, and yet you would have me break my oath and surrender the government without a blow. There is no Washington in that—no Jackson in that—there is no manhood or honor in that. I have no desire to invade the

South; but I must have troops to defend this Capital. Geographically it lies surrounded by the soil of Maryland; and mathematically the necessity exists that they should come over her territory. Our men are not moles, and can't dig under the earth; they are not birds, and can't fly through the air. There is no way but to march across, and that they must do. But in doing this, there is no need of collision. Keep your rowdies in Baltimore, and there will be no bloodshed. Go home and tell your people that if they will not attack us, we will not attack them; but if they do attack us, we will return it, and that severely.

Proclamation.

Washington, Friday, May 3, 1861.

Whereas, existing exigencies demand immediate and adequate measures for the protection of the National Constitution and the preservation of the National Union by the suppression of the insurrectionary combination now existing in several states for opposing the laws of the Union, and obstructing the execution thereof, to which end a military force, in addition to that called forth by my proclamation of the fifteenth day of April in the the present year, appears to be indispensably necessary: now, therefore, I, Abraham Lincoln, President of the United States, and Commander-in-chief of the Army and Navy thereof, and of the militia of the several states when called into actual service, do hereby call into the service of the United States forty-two thousand and thirty-four volunteers, to serve for a period of three years, unless sooner discharged, and to be mustered into service as infantry and cavalry. The proportions of each arm, and the details of enrollment, and organization, will be made known through the Department of War; and I also direct that the regular army of the United States be increased by the addition of eight regiments of infantry, one regiment of cavalry, and one regiment of artillery, making altogether a maximum aggregate increase of 22,714 officers and enlisted men, the details of which increase will also be made known through the War Department; and I farther direct the enlistment, for not less than one, nor more than three years, of 18,000 seamen, in addition to the present force, for the naval service of the United States. The details of the enlistment and organization will be made known through the Department of the Navy. The call for volunteers hereby made, and the direction of the increase of the regular army, and for the enlistment of seamen hereby given, together with the plan of organization adopted for the volunteers and for the regular forces hereby authorized, will be submitted to Congress as soon as assembled.

In the meantime I earnestly invoke the co-operation of all good citizens in the measures hereby adopted for the effectual suppression of unlawful violence, for the impartial enforcement of constitutional laws, and for the speediest possible restoration of peace and order, and with those of happiness and prosperity throughout our country.

In testimony whereof, I have hereunto set my hand, and caused the seal of the United States to be affixed.

Done at the city of Washington, this third day of

May, in the year of our Lord, one thousand eight hundred and sixty-one, and of the Independence of the United States the eighty-fifth. A. LINCOLN.

TO THE SECRETARY OF THE NAVY.

Executive Mansion, May 11, 1861.

Sir:—Lieutenant D. D. Porter was placed in command of the steamer Powhatan, and Captain Samuel Mercer was detached therefrom by my special order, and neither of them is responsible for any apparent or real irregularity on their part in connection with that vessel.

Hereafter Captain Porter is relieved from that special service and placed under the direction of the Navy Department, from which he will receive instructions and to which he will report.

Very respectfully, A. LINCOLN.

PRESIDENT LINCOLN'S FIRST MESSAGE TO CONGRESS, JULY 4, 1861.

Having been convened on an extraordinary occasion, as authorized by the Constitution, your attention is not called to any ordinary subject of legislation.

At the beginning of the present presidential term, four months ago, the functions of the Federal government were found to be generally suspended within the several states of South Carolina, Georgia, Alabama, Mississippi, Louisiana, and Florida, excepting only those of the Post-office Department.

Within these states, all the forts, arsenals, dockyards, custom-houses, and the like, including the movable and stationary property in and about them, had been seized, and were held in open hostility to this government, excepting only Forts Pickens, Taylor, and Jefferson, on and near the Florida coast, and Fort Sumter in the Charleston Harbor, South Carolina. The forts thus seized had been put in improved condition; new ones had been built, and armed forces had been organized, and were organizing, all avowedly with the same hostile purpose.

The forts remaining in the possession of the Federal government in and near these states were either besieged or menaced by war-like preparations, and especially Fort Sumter was nearly surrounded by well-protected hostile batteries, with guns equal in quality to the best of its own, and outnumbering the latter as perhaps ten to one. A disproportionate share of the Federal muskets and rifles had somehow found their way into these states, and been seized to be used against the government. Accumulations of the public revenue, lying within them, had been seized for the same object. The navy was scattered in distant seas, leaving but a very small part of it within the immediate reach of the government. Officers of the Federal army and navy had resigned in great numbers; and of those resigning a large proportion had taken up arms against the government. Simultaneously, and in connection with all this, the purpose to sever the Federal Union was openly avowed. In accordance with this purpose an ordinance had been adopted in each of these states, declaring the states, respectively, to be separated from the national Union.

A formula for instituting a combined government

of these states had been promulgated; and this illegal organization, in the character of Confederate States, was already invoking recognition, aid and intervention from foreign powers.

Finding this condition of things, and believing it to be an imperative duty upon the incoming Executive to prevent, if possible, the consummation of such attempt to destroy the Federal Union, a choice of means to that end became indispensable. This choice was made, and was declared in the inaugural address. The policy chosen looked to the exhaustion of all peaceful measures, before a resort to any stronger ones. It sought only to hold the public places and property not already wrested from the government, and to collect the revenue; relying for the rest on time, discussion, and the ballot-box. It promised a continuance of the mails, at government expense, to the very people who were resisting the government; and it gave repeated pledges against any disturbance to any of the people, or any of their rig'ts. Of all that which a President might constitutionally and justifiably do in such a case, every thing was forborne, without which it was believed possible to keep the government on foot.

On the 5th of March [the present incumbent's first full day in office] a letter of Major Anderson, commanding at Fort Sumter, written on the 28th of February, and received at the War Department on the 4th of March, was, by that Department, placed in his hands. This letter expressed the professional opinion of the writer that reinforcements could not be thrown into the fort within the time for his relief, rendered necessary by the limited supply of provisions, and with a view of holding possession of the same, with a force of less than twenty thousand good and well-disciplined men. This opinion was concurred in by all the officers of his command, and their *memoranda* on the subject were made inclosures of Major Anderson's letter. The whole was immediately laid before Lieut.-General Scott, who at once concurred with Major Anderson in opinion. On reflection, however, he took full time, consulting with other officers, both of the army and the navy, and, at the end of four days, came reluctantly, but decidedly to the same conclusion as before. He also stated at the same time that no such sufficient force was then at the control of the government, or could be raised and brought to the ground within the time when the provisions in the fort would be exhausted. In a purely military point of view this reduced the duty of the administration in the case to mere matter of getting the garrison safely out of the fort.

It was believed, however, that to so abandon that position, under the circumstances, would be utterly ruinous; that the necessity under which it was to be done would not be fully understood; that by many it would be construed as a part of a *voluntary* policy; that at home it would discourage the friends of the Union, embolden its adversaries, and go far to insure to the latter a recognition abroad; that in fact it would be our national destruction consummated. This would not be allowed. Starvation was not yet upon the garrison, and ere it would be reached *Fort Pickens* might be re-inforced.

This last would be a clear indication *of policy*, and would better enable the country to accept the evacuation of Fort Sumter as a military *necessity*. An order was at once directed to be sent for the landing of the troops from the steamship Brooklyn into Fort Pickens. This order could not go by land, but must take the longer and slower route by sea. The first return news from the order was received just one week before the fall of Fort Sumter. The news itself was that the officer commanding the Sabine, to which vessel the troops had been transferred from the Brooklyn, acting upon some *quasi* armistice of the late administration (and of the existence of which the present administration, up to the time the order was dispatched, had only too vague and uncertain rumors to fix attention), had refused to land the troops. To now reinforce Fort Pickens, before a crisis would be reached at Fort Sumter, was impossible, rendered so by the near exhaustion of provisions in the latter named fort. In precaution against such a conjuncture the government had, a few days before, commenced preparing an expedition, as well adapted as might be, to relieve Fort Sumter, which expedition was intended to be ultimately used, or not, according to circumstances. The strongest anticipated case for using it was now presented; and it was resolved to send it forward. As had been intended in this contingency, it was resolved to notify the governor of South Carolina that he might expect an attempt would be made to provision the fort; and that if the attempt should not be resisted there would be no effort to throw in men, arms, or ammunition, without further notice, or in case of an attack upon the fort. This notice was accordingly given; whereupon the fort was attacked and bombarded to its fall, without even awaiting the arrival of the provisioning expedition.

It is thus seen that the assault upon and reduction of Fort Sumter was, in no sense, a matter of self-defense on the part of the assailants.

They knew well that the garrison in the fort could, by no possibility, commit aggression upon them. They knew—they were expressly notified—that the giving of bread to the few brave and hungry men of the garrison was all which would on that occasion be attempted, unless themselves, by resisting so much, should provoke more. They knew that this government desired to keep the garrison in the fort, not to assail them, but merely to maintain in visible possession, and thus to preserve the Union from actual and immediate dissolution, trusting, as hereinbefore stated, to time, discussion, and the ballot-box for final adjustment; and they assailed and reduced the fort for precisely the reverse object, to drive out the visible authority of the Federal Union, and thus force it to immediate dissolution. That this was their object the Executive well understood; and having said to them, in the inaugural address, "You can have no conflict without being yourselves the aggressors," he took pains not only to keep this declaration good, but also to keep the case so free from the power of ingenious sophistry, as that the world should not be able to misunderstand it. By the affair at Fort Sumter, with its surrounding circumstances, that point was reached. Then and there, by the assailants of the government, began the conflict of arms, without a gun in sight or in expectancy to return their fire, save only the few in the fort sent to that harbor years before for their own protection, and still ready to give that protection in whatever was lawful. In this act, discarding all else, they have forced upon the country, the distinct issue, "Immediate dissolution or blood."

And this issue embraces more that the fate of these United States. It presents to the whole family of man the question whether a constitutional republic or democracy—a government of the people, by the same people—can or can not maintain its territorial integrity against its own domestic foes. It presents the question whether discontented individuals, too few in numbers to control administration according to organic law in any case, can always, upon the pretenses made in this case, or on any other pretenses, or arbitrarily without any pretense, break up their government, and thus practically put an end to free government upon the earth. It forces us to ask, "Is there, in all republics, this inherent and fatal weakness?" "Must a government of necessity be too *strong* for the liberties of its own people, or too *weak* to maintain its own existence?"

So viewing the issue, no choice was left but to call out the war power of the government; and so to resist force, employed for its destruction, by force for its preservation.

Ths call was made, and the response of the country was most gratifying, surpassing in unanimity and spirit the most sanguine expectations. Yet none of the states commonly called slave states, except Delaware, gave a regiment through regular state organization. A few regiments have been organized within some others of those states by individual enterprise, and received into the government service. Of course, the seceded states, so called (and to which Texas had been joined about the time of the inauguration), gave no troops to the cause of the Union. The Border States, so called, were not uniform in their action; some of them being almost for the Union, while in others—as Virginia, North Carolina, Tennessee and Arkansas—the Union sentiment was nearly repressed and silenced. The course taken in Virginia was the most remarkable, perhaps the most important. A convention, elected by the people of that state to consider this very question of disrupting the Federal Union, was in session at the Capital of Virginia when Fort Sumter fell. To this body the people had chosen a large majority of *professed* Union men.

Almost immediately after the fall of Sumter, many members of that majority went over to the original disunion minority, and, with them, adopted an ordinance for withdrawing the state from the Union. Whether this change was wrought by their great approval of the assault upon Sumter, or their great resentment at the government's resistance to that assault, is not definitely known. Although they submitted the ordinance, for ratification, to a vote of the people, to be taken on a day then somewhat more than a month distant, the convention, and the legislature (which was also in session at the same time and place), with leading men of the state, not members of either, immediately commenced acting as if the state were already out of the Union. They pushed military preparations vigorously forward all over the state. They seized the United States armory at Harper's Ferry, and the navy-yard at Gosport, near Norfolk. They received, perhaps invited, into their state large bodies of troops, with their warlike appointments, from the so-called seceded states. They formally entered into a treaty of temporary alliance and co-operation with the so-called "Confederate states," and sent members to their congress at Montgomery. And, finally, they permitted the insurrectionary government to be transferred to their capital at Richmond.

The people of Virginia have thus allowed this giant insurrection to make its nest within her borders; and this government has no choice left but to deal with it *where* it finds it. And it has the less regret, as the loyal citizens have, in due form, claimed its protection. Those loyal citizens this government is bound to recognize and protect, as being Virginia.

In the Border States, so called—in fact, the Middle States—there are those who favor a policy which they call "armed neutrality;" that is, an arming of those states to prevent the Union forces passing one way, or the disunion the other, over their soil. This would be disunion completed. Figuratively speaking, it would be the building of an impassable wall along the line of separation; and yet not quite an impassable one, for under the guise of neutrality, it would tie the hands of the Union men, and freely pass supplies from among them to the insurrectionists, which it could not do as an open enemy. At a stroke, it would take all the trouble off the hands of secession, except only what proceeds from the external blockade. It would do for the disunionists that which, of all things, they most desire—feed them well, and give them disunion without a struggle of their own. It recognizes no fidelity to the Constitution, no obligation to maintain the Union; and while very many who have favored it are doubtless loyal citizens, it is, nevertheless, very injurious in effect.

Recurring to the action of the government, it may be stated that, at first, a call was made for seventy-five thousand militia; and rapidly following this, a proclamation was issued for closing the ports of the insurrectionary districts by proceedings in the nature of blockade. So far, all was believed to be strictly legal. At this point, the insurrectionists announced their purpose to enter upon the practice of privateering.

Other calls were made for volunteers to serve three years, unless sooner discharged, and also for large additions to the regular army and navy. These measures, whether strictly legal or not, were ventured upon under what appeared to be a popular demand and a public necessity; trusting then, as now, that Congress would readily ratify them. It is believed that nothing has been done beyond the constitutional competency of Congress.

Soon after the first call for militia, it was considered a duty to authorize the commanding general, in proper cases, according to his discretion, to suspend the privilege of the writ of habeas corpus, or, in other words, to arrest and detain, without resort to the ordinary processes and forms of law, such individuals as he might deem dangerous to the public safety. This authority has purposely been exercised but very sparingly. Nevertheless, the legality and propriety of what has been done under it are questioned, and the attention of the country has been called to the proposition that one who is sworn to "take care" that the laws be faithfully executed should not himself violate them. Of course, some consideration was given to the questions of power and propriety before this matter was acted upon. The whole of the laws which were required to be faithfully executed were being resisted and failing of execution in nearly one-third of the states. Must they be allowed to finally fail of execution, even had it been perfectly clear, that, by the use of the means necessary to their execution, some single law, made in such extreme tenderness of the citizens' liberty, that practically it relieves more of the guilty than of the innocent, should to a very limited extent be violated?

To state the question more directly, are all the laws *but one* to go unexecuted, and the government itself go to pieces, lest that one be violated? Even in such a case, would not the official oath be broken, if the government should be overthrown, when it was believed that disregarding the single law would tend to preserve it? But it was not believed that this question was presented. It was not believed that any law was violated. The provision of the Constitution that "the privilege of the writ of habeas corpus shall not be suspended unless when, in cases of rebellion or invasion, the public safety may require it," is equivalent to a provision, is a provision, that such privilege may be suspended when, in cases of rebellion or invasion, the public safety *does* require it. It was decided that we have a case of rebellion, and that the public safety does require the qualified suspension of the privilege of the writ which was authorized to be made. Now it is insisted that Congress, and not the executive, is vested with this power.

But the Constitution itself is silent as to which or who is to exercise the power; and as the provision was plainly made for a dangerous emergency, it can not be believed that the framers of the instrument intended that in every case the danger should run its course until Congress could be called together, the very assembling of which might be prevented, as was intended in this case, by the rebellion.

No more extended argument is now offered, as an opinion at some length will probably be presented by the Attorney-General. Whether there shall be any legislation upon the subject, and if any, what, is submitted entirely to the better judgment of Congress.

The forbearance of this government has been so extraordinary and so long continued as to lead some foreign nations to shape their action as if they supposed the early destruction of our National Union was probable. While this, on discovery, gave the executive some concern, he is now happy to say that the sovereignty and rights of the United States are now every-where practically respected by foreign powers, and a general sympathy with the country is manifested throughout the world.

The reports of the Secretaries of the Treasury, War and the Navy, will give the information in detail deemed necessary and convenient for your deliberation and action; while the Executive, and all the departments, will stand ready to supply omissions, or to communicate new facts considered important for you to know.

It is now recommended that you give the legal means for making this contest a short and a decisive one; that you place at the control of the government, for the work, at least four hundred thousand men and four hundred millions of dollars. That number of men is about one-tenth of those of proper ages within the regions where, apparently, *all* are willing to engage; and the sum is less than a twenty-third part of the money value owned by the men who seem ready to devote the whole. A debt of six hundred millions of dollars now, is a less sum per head than was the debt of our Revolution when we came out of that struggle: and the money value in the country now bears even a greater proportion to what it was *then*, than does the population. Surely, each man has as strong a motive now to preserve our liberties as each had *then* to *establish* them. A right result, at this time, will be worth more to the world than ten times the men and ten times the money. The evidence reaching us from the country leaves no doubt that the material for the work is abundant; and that it needs only the hand of legislation to give it legal sanction, and the hand of the Executive to give it practical shape and efficiency.

One of the greatest perplexities of the government is to avoid receiving troops faster than it can provide for them. In a word, the people will save their government if the government itself will do its part only indifferently well.

It might seem, at first thought, to be of little difference whether the present movement at the South be called "secession" or "rebellion." The movers, however, well understand the difference. At the beginning, they knew they could never raise their treason to any respectable magnitude by any name which implies violation of law. They knew their people possessed as much of moral sense, as much of devotion to law and order, and as much pride in, and reverence for the history and government of their common country, as any other civilized and patriotic people. They knew they could make no advancement directly in the teeth of these strong and noble sentiments. Accordingly, they commenced by an insidious debauching of the public mind. They invented an ingenious sophism, which, if conceded, was followed by perfectly logical steps, through all the incidents, to the complete destruction of the Union. The sophism itself is, that any state of the Union may, consistently with the National Constitution, and therefore lawfully and peacefully withdraw from the Union without the consent of the Union, or of any other state. The little disguise that the supposed right is to be exercised only for just cause, themselves to be the sole judges of its justice, is too thin to merit any notice.

With rebellion thus sugar-coated, they have been drugging the public mind of their section for more than thirty years, and until at length they have brought many good men to a willingness to take up arms against the government the day after some assemblage of men have enacted the farcical pretense of taking their state out of the Union, who could have been brought to no such thing the day before.

This sophism derives much, perhaps the whole, of its current from the assumption that there is some omnipotent and sacred supremacy pertaining to a state—to each state of our Federal Union. Our states have neither more nor less power than that reserved to them in the Union by the Constitution—no one of them ever having been a state out of the Union. The original ones passed into the Union even before they cast off their British colonial dependence; and the new ones each came into the Union directly from a condition of dependence, excepting Texas. And even Texas, in its temporary independence, was never designated a state. The new ones only took the designation of states on coming into the Union, while that name was first adopted by the old ones in and by the Declaration of Independence. Therein the "United Colonies" were declared to be "free and independent states;" but, even then, their object plainly was not to declare their independence of one another, or of the Union, but directly the contrary, as their mutual pledge and their mutual action before, at the time, and afterward, abundantly shows.

The express plighting of faith by each and all of the original thirteen in the Articles of Confederation, two years later, that the Union shall be perpetual, is most conclusive.

Having never been states, either in substance or in name, outside of the Union, whence this magical omnipotence of "state rights," asserting a claim of power to lawfully destroy the Union itself? Much is said about the "sovereignty" of the states; but the word even is not in the National Constitution; nor, as is believed, in any of the state constitutions. What is a "sovereignty" in the political sense of the term? Would it be far wrong to define it "a political community without a political superior?"

Tested by this, no one of our states, except Texas, ever was a sovereignty. And even Texas gave up the character on coming into the Union; by which act she acknowledged the Constitution of the United States and the laws and treaties of the United States made in pursuance of the Constitution, to be for her the supreme law of the land. The states have their *status* in the Union, and they have no other legal *status*. If they break from this, they can only do so against law and by revolution. The Union, and not themselves, separately, procured their independence and their liberty. By conquest or purchase the Union gave each of them whatever of independence or liberty it has. The Union is older than any of the states, and, in fact, it created them as states. Originally, some dependent colonies made the Union, and, in turn, the Union threw off their old dependence for them, and made them states, such as they are.

Not one of them ever had a state constitution independent of the Union. Of course, it is not forgotten that all the new states framed their constitutions before they entered the Union—nevertheless dependent upon and preparatory to coming into the Union. Unquestionably the states have the powers and rights reserved to them in and by the National Constitution; but among them, surely, are not included all conceivable powers, however mischievous or destructive; but, at most, such only as were known in the world, at the time, as governmental powers: and, certainly, a power to destroy the government itself had never been known as a governmental—as a merely administrative power. This relative matter of national power and state rights, as a principle, is no other than the principle of generality and locality. Whatever concerns the whole should be confided to the whole—to the general government; while whatever concerns only the state should be left exclusively to the state. This is all there is of original principle about it. Whether the National Constitution in defining boundaries between the two has applied the principle with exact accuracy, is not to be questioned. We are all bound by that defining, without question.

What is now combated, is the position that secession is consistent with the Constitution—is lawful and peaceful. It is not contended that there is any express law for it, and nothing should ever be implied as law which leads to unjust or absurd consequences. The nation purchased with money the countries out of which several of these states were formed: is it just that they shall go off without leave and without refunding? The nation paid very large sums (in the aggregate, I believe, nearly a hundred millions) to relieve Florida of the aboriginal tribes; is it just that she shall now be off without consent, or without making any return? The nation is now in debt for money applied to the benefit of these so-called seceding states in common with the rest; is it just either that creditors shall go unpaid, or the remaining states pay the whole? A part of the present national debt was contracted to pay the old debts of Texas, is it just that she shall leave and pay no part of this herself?

Again, if one state may secede, so may another; and when all shall have seceded, none is left to pay the debts. Is this quite just to creditors? Did we notify them of this sage view of ours when we borrowed their money? If we now recognize this doctrine by allowing the seceders to go in peace, it is difficult to see what we can do if others choose to go, or to extort terms upon which they will promise to remain.

The seceders insist that our Constitution admits of secession. They have assumed to make a national constitution of their own, in which, of necessity, they have either discarded or retained the right of secession, as they insist it exists in ours. If they have discarded it, they thereby admit that on principle it ought not to exist in ours; if they have retained it, by their own construction of ours they show that, to be consistent, they must secede from one another whenever they shall find it the easiest way of settling their debts, or effecting any other selfish or unjust object. The principle itself is one of disintegration, and upon which no government can possibly endure.

If all the states save one should assert the power to

drive that one out of the Union, it is presumed the whole class of seceder politicians would at once deny the power, and denounce the act as the greatest outrage upon state rights. But suppose that precisely the same act, instead of being called " driving the one out," should be called " the seceding of the others from that one," it would be exactly what the seceders claim to do, unless, indeed, they make the point that the one, because it is a minority, may rightfully do what the others, because they are a majority, may not rightfully do. These politician are subtle, and profound on the rights of minorities. They are not partial to that power which made the Constitution, and speaks from the preamble, calling itself " We, the people."

It may well be questioned whether there is to-day a majority of the legally qualified voters of any state, except perhaps South Carolina, in favor of disunion. There is much reason to believe that the Union men are the majority in many, if not in every other one, of the so-called seceded states. The contrary has not been demonstrated in any one of them. It is ventured to affirm this, even of Virginia and Tennessee: for the results of an election, held in military camps, where the bayonets are all on one side of the question voted upon, can scarcely be considered as demonstrating popular sentiment. At such an election, all the large class who are, at once, *for* the Union, and *against* coercion, would be coerced to vote against the Union.

It may be affirmed, without extravagance, that the free institutions we enjoy have developed the powers and improved the condition of our whole people beyond any example in the world. Of this we now have a striking and an impressive illustration. So large an army as the government has now on foot was never before known, without a soldier in it but who had taken his place there of his own free choice. But more than this; there are many single regiments whose members, one and another, possess full practical knowledge of all the arts, sciences, professions, and whatever else, whether useful or elegant, is known in the world; and there is scarcely one from which there could not be selected a president, a cabinet, a congress, and perhaps a court, abundantly competent to administer the government itself. Nor do I say that this is not true also in the army of our late friends, now adversaries, in this contest; but if it is so, so much better the reason why the government, which has conferred such benefits on both them and us, should not be broken up. Whoever, in any section, proposes to abandon such a government would do well to consider in deference to what principle it is that he does it, what better he is likely to get in its stead, whether the substitute will give or be intended to give so much of good to the people. There are some fore-shadowings on this subject.

Our adversaries have adopted some declaration of independence, in which, unlike the good old one penned by Jefferson, they omit the words "all men are created equal." Why? They have adopted a temporary national constitution, in the preamble of which, unlike our good old one signed by Washington, they omit "We, the people," and substitute "We, the deputies of the sovereign and independent states."

Why? Why this deliberate pressing out of view the rights of men and the authority of the people? This is essentially a people's contest. On the side of the Union it is a struggle for maintaining in the world that form and substance of government whose leading object is to elevate the condition of men, to lift artificial weights from all shoulders, to clear the paths of laudable pursuit for all, to afford all an unfettered start and a fair chance in the race of life.

Yielding to partial and temporary departures from necessity, this is the leading object of the government for whose existence we contend.

I am most happy to believe that the plain people understand and appreciate this. It is worthy of note that, while in this, the government's hour of trial, large numbers of those in the army and navy who have been favored with the offices have resigned, and proved false to the hand which had pampered them, not one common soldier or common sailor is known to have deserted his flag.

Great honor is due to those officers who remained true, despite the example of their treacherous associates; but the greatest honor and most important fact of all is the unanimous firmness of the common soldiers and common sailors. To the last man, so far as known, they have successfully resisted the traitorous efforts of those whose commands but an hour before they obeyed as absolute law. This is the patriotic instinct of plain people. They understand, without an argument, that the destroying the government which was made by Washington means no good to them. Our popular government has often been called an experiment. Two points in it our people have already settled—the successful *establishing*, and the successful *administering* of it. One still remains—its successful *maintenance* against a formidable internal attempt to overthrow it. It is now for them to demonstrate to the world that those who can fairly carry an election can also suppress a rebellion; that ballots are the rightful and peaceful successors of bullets; and that when ballots have fairly and constitutionally decided, there can be no successful appeal back to bullets; that there can be no successful appeal except to ballots themselves at succeeding elections. Such will be a great lesson of peace, teaching men that what they can not take by an election, neither can they take it by a war; teaching all the folly of being beginners of a war.

Lest there be some uneasiness in the minds of candid men as to what is to be the course of the government toward the Southern states *after* the rebellion shall have been suppressed, the Executive deems it proper to say, it will be his purpose then, as ever, to be guided by the constitution and the laws; and that he will probably have no different understanding of the powers and duties of the Federal government relatively to the rights of the states and the people, under the Constitution, than that expressed in the inaugural address.

He desires to preserve the government, that it may be administered for all, as it was administered by the men who made it.

Loyal citizens every-where have the right to claim this of their government, and the government has no right to withhold or neglect it. It is not perceived that, in giving it, there is any coercion, any conquest, or any subjugation, in any just sense of those terms.

The constitution provides, and all the states have accepted the provision, that "the United States shall guarantee to every state in this Union a republican form of government." But, if a state may lawfully go out of the Union, having done so, it may also discard the republican form of government; so that to prevent its going out is an indispensable *means* to *the end* of maintaining the guarantee mentioned; and when an end is lawful and obligatory, the indispensable means to it are also lawful and obligatory. It was with the deepest regret that the Executive found the duty of employing the war power in defense of the government forced upon him. He could but perform this duty or surrender the existence of the government.

No compromise by public servants could in this case be a cure: not that compromises are not often proper, but that no popular government can long survive a marked precedent, that those who carry an election can only save the government from immediate destruction by giving up the main point upon which the people gave the election. The people themselves, and not their servants, can safely reverse their own deliberate decisions.

As a private citizen, the Executive could not have consented that these institutions shall perish; much less could he in betrayal of so vast and so sacred a trust as these free people had confided to him. He felt that he had no moral right to shrink, nor even to count the chances of his own life, in what might follow. In full view of his great responsibility he has so far, done what he has deemed his duty. You will now, according to your own judgment, perform yours. He sincerely hopes that your views, and your action, may so accord with his as to assure all faithful citizens who have been disturbed in their rights, of a certain and speedy restoration to them under the Constitution and the laws. And having thus chosen our course, without guile and with pure purpose, let us renew our trust in God, and go forward without fear and with manly hearts.   ABRAHAM LINCOLN.

July 4, 1861.

MR. LINCOLN'S MEMORANDUM OF MILITARY PROGRAMME.

July 23, 1861.

1. Let the plan for making the blockade effective be pushed forward with all possible dispatch.

2. Let the volunteer forces at Fort Monroe and vicinity, under General Butler, be constantly drilled, disciplined, and instructed without more for the present.

3. Let Baltimore be held as now, with a gentle but firm and certain hand.

4. Let the force now under Patterson or Banks be strengthened and made secure in its position.

5. Let the forces in western Virginia act till further orders according to instructions or orders from General McClellan.

6. General Fremont push forward his organization and operations in the West as rapidly as possible, giving rather special attention to Missouri.

7. Let the forces late before Manassas, except the three months' men, be organized as rapidly as possible in their camps, here and about Arlington.

8. Let the three months' forces who decline to enter the longer service be discharged as rapidly as circumstances will permit.

9. Let the new volunteer forces be brought forward as fast as possible; and especially into the camps on the two sides of the river here.

July 27, 1861.

When the foregoing shall have been substantially attended to—

1. Let Manassas Junction (or some point on one or the other of the railroads nearest it) and Strasburg be seized, and permanently held, with an open line from Washington to Manassas, and an open line from Harper's Ferry to Strasburg, the military men to find the way of doing these.

2. This done, a joint movement from Cairo on Memphis, and from Cincinnati on east Tennessee.

War Department, Washington, Aug. 15, 1861.

Major-General Fremont, St. Louis:—Been answering your messages ever since day before yesterday. Do you receive the answers? The War Department has notified all the governors you designated to forward all available force, and so telegraphed you. Have you received these messages? Answer immediately.

A. LINCOLN.

Honorable Secretary of War.

Executive Mansion, August 17, 1861.

My Dear Sir:—Unless there be reason to the contrary, not known to me, make out a commission for Simon (B.) Buckner, of Kentucky, as a brigadier-general of volunteers. It is to be put into the hands of General Anderson, and delivered to General Buckner or not, at the discretion of General Anderson. Of course it is to remain a secret unless and until the commission is delivered. Yours truly, A. Lincoln.

To His Excellency, B. Magoffin, Governor of Kentucky.

Washington, D. C., August 24, 1861.

Sir:—Your letter of the 19th inst., in which you urge the removal from the limits of Kentucky of the military force now organized and in camp within that state, is received. I may not possess full and precisely accurate knowledge upon the subject, but I believe it is true that there is a military force in camp within Kentucky, acting by authority of the United States, which force is not very large, and is not now being augmented.

I also believe that some arms have been furnished to this force by the United States.

I also believe this force consists exclusively of Kentuckians, having their camp in the immediate vicinity of their homes, and not assailing or menacing any of the good people of Kentucky. In all I have done in the premises, I have acted upon the urgent solicitation of many Kentuckians, and in accordance with all the Union-loving people of Kentucky.

While I have conversed on this subject with many of the eminent men of Kentucky, including a large majority of her members of Congress, I do not remember that any one of them, or any other person except your excellency and the bearers of your excellency's letter, has urged me to move the military force from Kentucky, or to disband it. One very worthy citizen of Kentucky did solicit me to have the augmenting of the force suspended for a time.

Taking all the means within my reach to form a judgment. I do not believe it is the popular wish of Kentucky that this force shall be removed beyond her limits; and, with this impression I must respectfully decline to remove it.

I most cordially sympathize with your Excellency in the wish to preserve the peace of my own native State of Kentucky. It is with regret I search for, and can not find, in your not very short letter, any declaration or intimation that you entertain any desire for the preservation of the Federal Union.

Your obedient servant,— A. LINCOLN.

PRIVATE LETTER TO MAJ.-GEN. FREMONT. SEPT. 2. 1861.

Two points in your proclamation of August 30th, give me some anxiety. *First.*—Should you shoot a man, according to the proclamation, the Confederates would very certainly shoot our best men in their hands, in retaliation; and so, man for man, indefinitely. It is, therefore, my order that you allow no man to be shot, under the proclamation, without first having my approbation and consent.

Second.—I think there is a great danger that the

closing paragraph in relation to the confiscation of property, and the liberating slaves of traitorous owners, will alarm our Southern Union friends, and turn them against us—perhaps ruin our rather fair prospect for Kentucky. Allow me, therefore, to ask that you will, as of your own motion, modify that paragraph so as to conform to the *first* and *fourth* sections of the Act of Congress entitled, "An Act to Confiscate Property used for Insurrectionary Purposes," approved August 6, 1861, and a copy of which act I herewith send you. This letter is written in a spirit of caution, and not of censure. I send it by special messenger in order that it may certainly and speedily reach you. Yours very truly,

A. LINCOLN.

To MRS. GENERAL FREMONT.

Washington, D. C., Sept. 12, 1861.

My Dear Madam:—Your two notes of to-day are before me. I answered the letter you bore me from General Fremont, on yesterday, and not hearing from you during the day, I sent the answer to him by mail. It is not exactly correct, as you say you were told by the elder Mr. Blair, to say that I had sent Postmaster-General Blair to St. Louis to examine into the department and report. Postmaster-General Blair did go with my approbation, to see and converse with General Fremont as a friend. I do not feel authorized to furnish you with copies of letters in my possession without the consent of the writers. No impression has been made upon my mind against the honor or integrity of General Fremont, and I now enter my protest against being understood as acting in any hostility toward him.

Your obedient servant.   A. LINCOLN.

HON. SECRETARY OF WAR.

Executive Mansion, September 18, 1861.

My Dear Sir:—To guard against misunderstanding, I think fit to say that the joint expedition of the army and navy, agreed upon some time since, and in which General W. T. Sherman was and is to bear a conspicuous part, is in nowise to be abandoned, but must be ready to move by the first of, or very early in October. Let all preparations go forward accordingly.   Yours truly,   A. LINCOLN.

MAJOR-GENERAL FREMONT.

Washington, September 22, 1861.

Governor Morton telegraphs as follows: Colonel Lane, just arrived by special train, represents Owensborough, forty miles above Evansville, in possession of secessionists. Green river is navigable. Owensborough must be seized. We want a gun-boat sent up from Paducah for that purpose. Send up the gun-boat if, in your discretion, you think it right. Perhaps you had better order those in charge of the Ohio river, to guard it vigilantly at all points.

A. LINCOLN.

HON. O. H. BROWNING.

Executive Mansion, Washington, Sept. 22, 1861.

My Dear Sir:—Yours of the seventeenth is just received; and coming from you, I confess it astonishes me. That you should object to my adhering to a law, which you had assisted in making, and presenting to me, less than a month before, is odd enough. But this is a very small part. General Fremont's proclamation, as to confiscation of property, and the liberation of slaves, is *purely political*, and not within the range of *military* law or necessity. If a commanding general finds a necessity to seize the farm of a private owner, for a pasture, an encampment, or a fortification, he has the right to do so, and to so hold it, as long as the necessity lasts; and this is within military law, because within military necessity. But to say the farm shall no longer belong to the owner, or his heirs forever, and this, as well when the farm is *not* needed for military purposes as when it is, is purely political, without the savor of military law about it. And the same is true of slaves. If the general needs them, he can seize them and use them, but when the need is past, it is not for him to fix their permanent future condition. That must be settled according to laws made by law-makers, and not by military proclamations. The proclamation in the point in question is simply "dictatorship." It assumes that the general may do *any thing* he pleases—confiscate the lands and free the slaves of *loyal* people, as well as disloyal ones.

And going the whole figure, I have no doubt, would be more popular, with some thoughtless people, than that which has been done. But I can not assume this reckless position, nor allow others to assume it on my responsibility.

You speak of it as being the only means of saving the government. On the contrary, it is itself the surrender of the government. Can it be pretended that it is any longer the government of the United States—any government of Constitution and laws—wherein a general or a president may make permanent rules of property by proclamation.

I do not say Congress might not, with propriety, pass a law on the point, just such as General Fremont proclaimed. I do not say I might not, as a member of Congress, vote for it. What I object to is, that I, as President, shall expressly and impliedly seize and exercise the permanent legislative functions of the government.

So much as to principle. Now as to policy. No doubt the thing was popular in some quarters, and would have been more so if it had been a general declaration of emancipation. The Kentucky legislature would not budge till that proclamation was modified; and General Anderson telegraphed me that on the news of General Fremont having actually issued deeds of manumission, a whole company of our volunteers threw down their arms and disbanded. I was so assured as to think it probable that the very arms we had furnished Kentucky would be turned against us.

I think to lose Kentucky is nearly the same as to lose the whole game. Kentucky gone, we can not hold Missouri, nor, as I think, Maryland. These all against us, and the job on our hands is too large for us. We would as well consent to separation at once, including the surrender of this capital. On the contrary, if you will give up your restlessness for new positions, and back me manfully on the grounds upon which you and other kind friends gave me the election, and have approved in my public documents, we shall go through triumphantly.

You must not understand I took my course on the proclamation *because* of Kentucky. I took the same ground in a private letter to General Fremont before I heard from Kentucky.

You think I am inconsistent because I did not also forbid General Fremont to shoot men under the proclamation. I understand that part to be within military law, but I also think, and so privately wrote General Fremont, that it is impolitic in this, that our adversaries have the power, and will certainly exercise it, to shoot as many of our men as we shoot of theirs. I did not say this in the public letter, because it is a subject I prefer not to discuss in the hearing of our enemies.

There has been no thought of removing General Fremont on any ground connected with his proclamation; and if there has been any wish for his removal on any ground, our mutual friend, Sam Glover, can probably tell you what it was. I hope no real necessity for it exists on any ground. Your friend, as ever, A. LINCOLN.

TO THE COMMANDER OF THE DEPARTMENT OF THE WEST.

Washington, D. C., October 24, 1861.

Sir:—The command of the Department of the West having devolved upon you, I propose to offer you a few suggestions. Knowing how hazardous it is to bind down a distant commander in the field to specific lines and operations, as so much always depends upon a knowledge of localities and passing events, it is intended, therefore, to leave a considerable margin for the exercise of your judgment and discretion.

The main rebel army (Price's) west of the Mississippi is believed to have passed Dade county in full retreat upon North-western Arkansas, leaving Missouri almost freed from the enemy, excepting in the south-east of the state. Assuming this basis of fact, it seems desirable, as you are not likely to overtake Price, and are in danger of making too long a line from your base of supplies and re-inforcements, that you should give up the pursuit, halt your main army, divide it into two corps of observation, one occupying Sedalia and the other Rolla, the present termini of railroad; then recruit the condition of both corps by re-establishing and improving their discipline and instructions, perfecting their clothing and equipments, and providing less uncomfortable quarters.

Of course, both railroads must be guarded and kept open, judiciously employing just so much force as is necessary for this. From these two points, Sedalia and Rolla, and especially in judicious co-operation with Lane on the Kansas border, it would be so easy to concentrate and repel any army of the enemy returning on Missouri, from the south-west, that it is not probable any such attempt to return will be made before or during the approaching cold weather. Before spring the people of Missouri will probably be in no favorable mood to renew for the next year the troubles which have so much afflicted and impoverished them during this.

If you adopt this line of policy, and if, as I anticipate, you will see no enemy in great force approaching, you will have a surplus of force, which you can withdraw from these points and direct to others, as may be needed, the railroads furnishing ready means of re-inforcing their main points if necessity requires. Doubtless local uprisings will for a time continue to occur, but these can be met by detachments and local forces of our own, and will ere long tire out of themselves.

While, as stated in the beginning of the letter, a large discretion must be and is left to yourself, I feel sure that an indefinite pursuit of Price, or any attempt by this long and circuitous route to reach Memphis, will be exhaustive beyond endurance, and will end in the loss of the whole force engaged in it.

Your obedient servant, A. LINCOLN.

LETTER OF THE PRESIDENT ON THE OCCASION OF THE RESIGNATION OF GEN. SCOTT.

On the first day of November, A. D. 1861, upon his own application to the President of the United States, Brevet Lieutenant-Gen. Winfield Scott is ordered to be placed, and hereby is placed, upon the list of retired officers of the army of the United States, without reduction in his current pay, subsistence or allowances. The American people will hear with sadness and deep emotion that Gen. Scott has withdrawn from the active control of the army, while the President and the unanimous cabinet express their own and the nation's sympathy in his personal affliction, and their profound sense of the important public services rendered by him to his country during his long and brilliant career, among which will ever be gratefully distinguished his faithful devotion to the Constitution, the Union, and the flag, when assailed by parricidal rebellion. A. LINCOLN.

Upon presenting the foregoing letter the President added:—

General:—You will naturally feel solicitude about the gentlemen of your staff, who have rendered you and their country such faithful service. I have taken that subject into consideration. I understand that they go with you to New York. I shall desire them at their earliest convenience, after their return, to make their wishes known to me. I desire you now, however, to be satisfied that, except the unavoidable privation of your counsel, and society, which they have so long enjoyed, the provision which will be made for them will be such as to render their situation hereafter as agreeable as it has been heretofore.

LETTER ON MISSOURI MATTERS.

Executive Mansion, Washington, Nov. 5, 1861.

The governor of the State of Missouri, acting under the direction of the convention of that state, proposes to the government of the United States, that he will raise a military force, to serve within the state as state militia during the war there, to co-operate with the troops in the service of the United States in repelling the invasion of the state and suppressing rebellion therein; the said state militia to be embodied and to be held in the camp and in the field, drilled, disciplined and governed according to the army regulations and subject to the Articles of War; the said state militia not to be ordered out of the state except for the immediate defense of the State of Missouri, but to co-operate with the troops in the service of the United State in military operations within the state or necessary to its defense, and when officers of the state militia act with officers in the service of the United States of the same grade, the officers of the United States shall command the combined force; the state militia to be armed, equipped, clothed, subsisted, transported, and paid by the United States during such time as they shall be actually engaged as an embodied military force in the service in accordance with regulations of the United States army or general orders as issued from time to time.

In order that the Treasury of the United States may not be burdened with the pay of unnecessary officers, the governor proposes that, although the state law requires him to appoint upon the general staff an adjutatant-general, a commissary-general, an inspector-general, a quartermaster-general, a paymaster-general, and a surgeon-general, each with the rank of colonel of cavalry, yet he proposes that the government of the United States pay only the adjutant-general, the quartermaster-general, and the inspector-general, their services being necessary in the relations which would exist between the state militia and the United States.

The governor further proposes that, while he is allowed by the state law to appoint aides-de-camp to the governor at his discretion, with the rank of colonel, three only shall be reported to the United States for payment. He also proposes that the state militia shall be commanded by a single major-general, and by such number of brigadier-generals as shall allow one for a brigade of not less than four regiments, and that no greater number of staff officers shall be appointed for regimental, brigade and division duties than is provided for in the act of Congress of the 22d of July, 1861, and that whatever be the rank of such officers as fixed by the law of the state, the compensation that they shall receive from the United States shall only be that which belongs to the rank given by said act of Congress to officers in the United States service performing the same duties.

The field officers of a regiment in the state militia are one colonel, one lieutenant-colonel, and one major, and the company officers are a captain, a first lieutenant, and a second lieutenant.

The governor proposes that, as the money to be disbursed is the money of the United States, such staff officers in the service of the United States as may be necessary to act as disbursing officers for the state militia shall be assigned by the War Department for that duty; or, if such can not be spared from their present duty, he will appoint such persons disbursing officers for the state militia as the President of the United States may designate. Such regulations as may be required, in the judgment of the president, to insure regularity of returns and to protect the United States from any fraudulent practices, shall be observed and obeyed by all in office in the state militia.

The above propositions are accepted on the part of United States, and the Secretary of War is directed to make the necessary orders upon the ordnance, commissary, pay and medical department to carry this agreement into effect. He will cause the necessary staff officers in the United States service to be detailed for duty in connection with the Missouri state militia, and will order them to make the necessary provision in their respective offices for fulfilling this agreement. All requisitions upon the different officers of the United States, under this agreement, to be made in substance in the same mode for the Missouri state militia, as similar requisitions are made for troops in the service of the United States, and the Secretary of War will cause any additional regulations that may be necessary to insure regularity and economy in carrying this agreement into effect to be adopted and communicated to the governor of Missouri, for the government of the Missouri state militia.

November 6, 1861.

This plan approved, with the modification that the governor stipulates that when he commissions a major-general of militia, it shall be the same person at the time in command of the United States Department of the West; and in case the United States shall change such commander of the department, he, the Governor, will revoke the state commission given to person relieved, and give one to the person substituted to the United States command of said department. A. LINCOLN.

TO MAJOR-GENERAL H. W. HALLECK, COMMANDING IN THE DEPARTMENT OF MISSOURI.

December 2, 1861.

General:—As an insurrection exists in the United States and is in arms in the State of Missouri, you are hereby authorized and empowered to suspend the writ of *habeas corpus* within the limits of the military division under your command, and to exercise martial law as you find it necessary in your discretion, to secure the public safety and the authority of the United States.

In witness whereof I have hereunto set my hand and cause the seal of the United States to be affixed, at Washington, this second day of December, A. D. 1861. A. LINCOLN.

PRESIDENT LINCOLN'S FIRST ANNUAL MESSAGE, DECEMBER 3, 1861.

Fellow-citizens of the Senate and House of Representatives:—In the midst of unprecedented political troubles, we have cause of great gratitude to God for unusual good health and most abundant harvests.

You will not be surprised to learn that in the peculiar exigencies of the times, our intercourse with foreign nations has been attended with profound solicitude, chiefly turning upon our own domestic affairs.

A disloyal portion of the American people have, during the whole year, been engaged in an attempt to divide and destroy the Union. A nation which endures factious domestic divisions, is exposed to disrespect abroad; and one party, if not both, is sure, sooner or later, to invoke foreign intervention.

Nations thus tempted to interfere are not always able to resist the counsels of seeming expediency and ungenerous ambition, although measures adopted under such influences seldom fail to be unfortunate and injurious to those adopting them.

The disloyal citizens of the United States, who have offered the ruin of our country in return for the aid and comfort which they have invoked abroad, have received less patronage and encouragement than they probably expected. If it were just to suppose, as the insurgents have seemed to assume, that foreign nations in this case, discarding all moral, social, and treaty obligations, would act solely and selfishly for the speedy restoration of commerce, including especially, the acquisition of cotton, those nations appear, as yet, not to have seen their way to their object more directly or clearly through the destruction than through the preservation of the Union. If we could dare to believe that foreign nations are actuated by no higher principle than this, I am quite sure a sound argument could be made to show them that they can reach their aim more readily and easily by aiding to crush this rebellion than by giving encouragement to it.

The principal lever relied on by these insurgents for exciting foreign nations to hostility against us, as already intimated, is the embarrassment of commerce. Those nations, however, not improbably, saw from

the first that it was the Union which made as well
our foreign as our domestic commerce. They can
scarcely have failed to perceive that the effort for disunion produces the existing difficulty; and that one
strong nation promises more durable peace, and a
more extensive, valuable, and reliable commerce, than
can the same nation broken into hostile fragments.
It is not my purpose to review our discussions with
foreign states, because whatever might be their wishes
or dispositions, the integrity of our country, and the
stability of our government, mainly depend not upon
them, but upon the loyalty, virtue, patriotism, and
intelligence of the American people. The correspondence itself, with the usual reservations, is herewith submitted. I venture to hope it will appear
that we have practiced prudence and liberality toward foreign powers, averting causes of irritation,
and, with firmness, maintaining our own rights and
honor.

Since, however, it is apparent that here, as in every
other state, foreign dangers necessarily attend domestic difficulties, I recommend that adequate and ample
measures be adopted for maintaining the public defenses on every side. While, under this general recommendation, provision for defending our sea-coast line
readily occurs to the mind, I also, in the same connection, ask the attention of Congress to our great
lakes and rivers. It is believed that some fortifications and depots of arms and munitions, with harbor
and navigation improvements, all at well selected
points upon these, would be of great importance to
the national defense and preservation. I ask atten-

tion to the views of the Secretary of War, expressed in his report, upon the same general subject. . . .

By the act of the 5th of August last, Congress authorized the president to instruct the commanders of suitable vessels to defend themselves against, and to capture pirates. This authority has been exercised in single instances only. For the more effectual protection of our extensive and valuable commerce, in the eastern seas especially, it seems to me that it would also be advisable to authorize the commanders of sailing vessels to recapture any prizes which pirates may make of United States vessels and their cargoes, and the consular courts, now established by law in eastern countries, to adjudicate the case, in the event that this should not be objected to by the local authorities.

If any good reason exists why we should persevere longer in withholding our recognition of the independence and sovereignty of Hayti and Liberia, I am unable to discern it. Unwilling, however, to inaugurate a novel policy in regard to them without the approbation of Congress, I submit for your consideration the expediency of an appropriation for maintaining a *charge d'affaires* near each of those new states. It does not admit of doubt that important commercial advantages might be secured by favorable treaties with them. . . .

The execution of the laws for the suppression of the African slave-trade has been confided to the Department of the Interior. It is a subject of gratulation that the efforts which have been made for the suppression of this inhuman traffic have been recently attended with unusual success. Five vessels being fitted out for the slave-trade have been seized and condemned.

Two mates of vessels engaged in the trade, and one person in equipping a vessel as a slaver, have been convicted and subjected to the penalty of fine and imprisonment; and one captain, taken with a cargo of Africans on board his vessel, has been convicted of the highest grade of offense under our laws, the punishment of which is death.

The territories of Colorado, Dakota, and Nevada, created by the last Congress, have been organized, and civil administration has been inaugurated therein under auspices especially gratifying, when it is considered that the leaven of treason was found existing in some of these new countries when the Federal officers arrived there. The abundant natural resources of these territories, with the security and protection afforded by organized government, will doubtless invite to them a large immigration when peace shall restore the business of the country to its accustomed channels. I submit the resolutions of the legislature of Colorado, which evidence the patriotic spirit of the people of the territory. So far the authority of the United States has been upheld in all the territories, as it is hoped it will be in the future. I commend their interests and defense to the enlightened and generous care of Congress.

I recommend to the favorable consideration of Congress the interests of the District of Columbia. The insurrection has been the cause of much suffering and sacrifice to its inhabitants, and as they have no representative in Congress, that body should not overlook their just claims upon the Government. . . .

The war continues. In considering the policy to be adopted for suppressing the insurrection, I have been anxious and careful that the inevitable conflict for this purpose shall not degenerate into a violent and remorseless revolutionary struggle. I have, therefore, in every case, thought it proper to keep the integrity of the Union prominent as the primary object of the contest on our part, leaving all questions which are not of vital importance to the more deliberate action of the legislature.

In the exercise of my best discretion, I have adhered to the blockade of the ports held by the insurgents, instead of putting in force, by proclamation, the law of Congress enacted at the late session, for closing those ports.

So, also, obeying the dictates of prudence, as well as the obligations of law, instead of transcending, I have adhered to the act of Congress to confiscate property used for insurrectionary purposes. If a new law upon the same subject shall be proposed, its propriety will be duly considered. The Union must be preserved; and hence all indispensable means must be employed. We should not be in haste to determine that radical and extreme measures, which may reach the loyal as well as the disloyal, are indispensable.

The inaugural address at the beginning of the administration, and the message to Congress at the late special session, were both mainly devoted to the domestic controversy out of which the insurrection and consequent war have sprung.

Nothing now occurs to add or substract, to or from, the principles or general purposes, stated and expressed in those documents. . . .

The last ray of hope for preserving the Union peaceably, expired at the assault upon Fort Sumter; and a general review of what has occured since may not be unprofitable. What was painfully uncertain then, is much better defined and more distinct now; and the progress of events is plainly in the right direction. The insurgents confidently claimed a strong support from north of Mason and Dixon's line; and the friends of the Union were not free from apprehension on the point. This, however, was soon settled definitely, and on the right side. South of the line, noble little Delaware led off right from the first. Maryland was made to seem against the Union. Our soldiers were assaulted, bridges were burned, and railroads were torn up within her limits; and we were many days, at one time, without the ability to bring a single regiment over her soil to the capital. Now her bridges and railroads are repaired and open to the Government; she already gives seven regiments to the cause of the Union, and none to the enemy; and her people, at a regular election, have sustained the Union by a larger majority and a larger aggregate vote than they ever before gave to any candidate or any question. Kentucky, too, for some time in doubt, is now decidedly, and I think, unchangeably ranged on the side of the Union. Missouri is comparatively quiet, and, I believe, can not again be overrun by the insurrectionists. These three states of Maryland, Kentucky and Missouri, neither of which would promise a single soldier at first, have now an aggregate of not less than forty thousand in the field for the Union; while of their citizens, certainly not more than a third of that number, and they of doubtful whereabouts and doubtful existence, are in arms against it. After a somewhat bloody struggle of months, winter closes on the Union people of western Virginia, leaving them masters of their own country.

An insurgent force of about fifteen hundred, for months dominating the narrow peninsular region constituting the counties of Accomac and Northampton, and known as the eastern shore of Virginia, together with some contiguous parts of Maryland, have laid down their arms; and the people there have renewed their allegiance to, and accepted the protection of the old flag. This leaves no armed insurrectionist north of the Potomac, or east of the Chesapeake.

Also, we have obtained a footing at each of the isolated points on the southern coast—of Hatteras, Port Royal, Tybee Island near Savannah, and Ship Island; and we likewise have some general accounts of popular movements in behalf of the Union in North Carolina and Tennessee.

These things demonstrate that the cause of the Union is advancing steadily and certainly southward.

. . . .

It is not needed, nor fitting here, that a general argument should be made in favor of popular institutions; but there is one point, with its connections, not so hackneyed as most others, to which I ask a brief attention. It is the effort to place *capital* on an equal footing with, if not above, *labor*, in the structure of the Government. It is assumed that labor is available only in connection with capital; that nobody labors unless somebody else, owning capital, somehow by the use of it induces him to labor.

This assumed, it is next considered whether it is best that capital shall hire laborers, and thus induce them to work by their own consent, or buy them, and drive them to it without their consent. Having proceeded so far, it is naturally concluded that all laborers are either hired laborers or what we call slaves. And further, it is assumed that whoever is once a hired laborer, is fixed in that condition for life.

Now, there is no such relation between capital and labor as assumed; nor is there any such thing as a free man being fixed for life in the condition of a hired laborer. Both these assumptions are false, and all inferences from them are groundless. Labor is prior to and independent of capital—capital is only the fruit of labor, and could never have existed if labor had not first existed. Labor is the superior of capital, and deserves much the higher consideration. Capital has its rights, which are as worthy of protection as any other rights. Nor is it denied that there is, and probably always will be, a relation between labor and capital, producing mutual benefits. The error is in assuming that the whole labor of the community exists within that relation. A few men own capital, and those few avoid labor themselves, and with their capital, hire or buy another few to labor for them. A large majority belong to neither class—neither work for others, nor have others working for them. In most of the southern states, a majority of the whole people of all colors are neither slaves nor masters; while in the northern, a large majority are neither hirers nor hired. Men, with their families, wives, sons and daughters—work for themselves, on their farms, in their houses, and in their shops, taking the whole product to themselves, and asking no favors of capital on the one hand, nor of hired laborers or slaves on the other.

It is not forgotten that a considerable number of persons mingle their own labor with capital—that is, they labor with their own hands, and also buy or hire others to labor for them; but this is only a mixed, and not a distinct class. No principle stated is disturbed by the existence of this mixed class. Again: as has already been said, there is not of necessity any such thing as the free hired laborer being fixed to that condition for life. Many independent men every-where in these states, a few years back in their lives, were hired laborers. The prudent, penniless beginner in the world, labors for wages awhile, saves a surplus with which to buy tools or land for himself, then labors on his own account another while, and at length hires another new beginner to help him. This is the just and generous and prosperous system, which opens the way to all, gives hope to all, and consequent energy and progress, and improvement of condition to all.

No men living are more worthy to be trusted, than those who toil up from poverty—none less inclined to take or touch aught which they have not honestly earned. Let them beware of surrendering a political power which they already possess, and which, if surrendered, will surely be used to close the door of advancement against such as they, and to fix new disabilities and burdens upon them, till all of liberty shall be lost.

. . . .

It continues to develop that the insurrection is largely, if not exclusively, a war upon the first principle of popular government—the rights of the people. Conclusive evidence of this is found in the most grave and maturely considered public documents, as well as in the general tone of the insurgents. In those documents we find the abridgment of the existing right of suffrage, and the denial to the people of all right to participate in the selection of public officers, except the legislative, boldly advocated, with labored arguments to prove that large control of the people in government is the source of all political evil. Monarchy itself is sometimes hinted at as a possible refuge from the power of the people.

In my present position, I could scarcely be justified were I to omit raising a warning voice against this approach of returning despotism.

. . . .

From the first taking of our national census to the last are seventy years: and we find our population at the end of the period eight times as great as it was in the beginning. The increase of those other things which men deem desirable has been even greater. We thus have, at one view, what the popular principle applied to government, through the machinery of the states and the Union, has produced in a given time, and also what, if firmly maintained, it promises for the future. There are already among us those who, if the Union be preserved, will live to see it contain two hundred and fifty millions. The struggle of to-day is not altogether *for* to-day—it is for a vast future also. With a reliance on Providence, all the more firm and earnest, let us proceed in the great task which events have devolved upon us.

Washington, December 3, 1861. A. LINCOLN.

Executive Mansion, Washington, January 1, 1862.
My Dear General Halleck:—General McClellan is not dangerously ill, as I hope, but would better not be disturbed with business. I am very anxious that, in case of General Buell's moving toward Nashville, the enemy shall not be greatly re-inforced, and I think there is danger he will be from Columbus. It seems to me that a real or feigned attack upon Columbus from up river at the same time, would either prevent this or compensate for it, by throwing Columbus into our hands. I wrote General Buell a letter similar to this, meaning that he and you shall communicate and act in concert, unless it be your judgment and his that there is no necessity for it. You and he will understand much better than I how to do it. Please do not lose time in this matter. Yours, very truly, A. LINCOLN.

TO BRIGADIER-GENERAL BUELL.

Executive Mansion, Washington, Jan. 6, 1862.
My Dear Sir:—Your dispatch of yesterday has been received, and it disappoints and distresses me. I have shown it to General McClellan, who says he will

write you to-day. I am not competent to criticise your news, and therefore what I offer is merely in justification of myself. Of the two, I would rather have a point on the railroad south of Cumberland Gap than Nashville—first, because it cuts a great artery of the enemy's communication, which Nashville does not; and, secondly, because it is in the midst of loyal people, who would rally around it, while Nashville is not. Again, I can not see why the movement on East Tennessee would not be a diversion in your favor rather than a disadvantage, assuming that a movement toward Nashville is the main object. But my distress is that our friends in East Tennessee are being hanged and driven to despair, and even now I fear are thinking of taking rebel arms for the sake of personal protection. In this we lose the most valuable stake we have in the South. My dispatch, to which yours is an answer, was sent with the knowledge of Senator Johnson and Representative Maynard, of East Tennessee, and they will be upon me to know the answer, which I can not safely show them. They would despair, possibly resign, to go and save their families somehow or die with them. I do not intend this to be an order in any sense, but merely as intimated before, to show you the grounds of my anxiety.

Yours very truly, A. LINCOLN.

To BRIGADIER-GENERAL D. C. BUELL, LOUISVILLE.

Washington, January 7, 1862.

Please name as early a day as you safely can, on or before which you can be ready to move northward in concert with Major-General Halleck. Delay is ruining us, and it is indispensable for me to have something definite. I send a like dispatch to Major-General Halleck. A. LINCOLN.

To Brigadier-General Buell.

Executive Mansion, Washington, Jan. 13, 1862.

My Dear Sir:—Your dispatch of yesterday is received, in which you say, " I received your letter and General McClellan's, and will at once devote my efforts to your views and his." In the midst of my many cares I have not seen, nor asked to see, General McClellan's letter to you. For my own views, I have not offered, and do not now offer them as orders; and while I am glad to have them respectfully considered, I would blame you to follow them contrary to your own clear judgment, unless I should put them in the form of orders. As to General McClellan's views, you understand your duty in regard to them better than I do. With this preliminary I state my general idea of this war to be, that we have the greater numbers and the enemy has the greater facility of concentrating forces upon points of collision; that we must fail unless we can find some way of making our advantage an overmatch for his; and that this can only be done by menacing him with superior forces at different points at the same time, so that we can safely attack one or both if he makes no change; and if he weakens one to strengthen the other, forbear to attack the strengthened one, but seize and hold the weakened one, gaining so much.

To illustrate: Suppose last summer when Winchester ran away to enforce Manassas, we had forborne to attack Manassas, but had seized and held Winchester. I mention this to illustrate and not to criticise. I did not lose confidence in McDowell, and I think less harshly of Patterson than some others seem to. Application of the general rule I am suggesting, every particular case will have its modifying circumstances, among which the most constantly present and most difficult to meet will be the want of perfect knowledge of the enemy's movements. This had its part in the Bull Run case; but worse in that case was the expiration of the terms of the three months' men.

Applying the principle to your case, my idea is that Halleck shall menace Columbus and "down-river" generally, while you menace Bowling Green and East Tennessee. If the enemy shall concentrate at Bowling Green do not retire from his front, yet do not fight him there either, but seize Columbus and East Tennessee, one or both, left exposed by the concentration at Bowling Green.

It is a matter of no small anxiety to me, and one which I am sure you will not overlook, that the East Tennessee is so long and over so bad a road.

Yours very truly,   A. LINCOLN.

To Major-General Halleck.

Executive Mansion, Washington, Jan. 15, 1862.

My Dear Sir:—The Germans are true and patriotic, and so far as they have got cross in Missouri it is upon mistake and misunderstanding.

Without a knowledge of its contents Governor Koerner, of Illinois, will hand you this letter. He is an educated and talented German gentleman, as true a man as lives.

With his assistance you can set every thing right with the Germans. I write this without his knowledge, asking him at the same time, by letter, to deliver it. My clear judgment is that, with reference to the German element in your command, you should have Governor Koerner with you; and if agreeable to you and him, I will make him a brigadier-general, so that he can afford to so give his time.

He does not wish to command in the field, though he has more military knowledge than many who do. If he goes into the place he will simply be an efficient, zealous, and unselfish assistant to you. I say all this upon intimate personal acquaintance with Governor Koerner. Yours very truly, A. LINCOLN.

TO THE SECRETARY OF WAR.

Executive Mansion, Washington, January 31, 1862.

My Dear Sir:—It is my wish that the expedition commonly called the "Lane Expedition," shall be as much as has been promised at the adjutant-general's office under the supervision of General McClellan, *and not any more*. I have not intended, and do not now intend that it shall be a *great, exhausting affair*, but a snug, sober column of 10,000 or 15,000. General Lane has been told by me many times that he is under the command of General Hunter, and assented to it as often as told. It was the distinct agreement between him and me when I appointed him, that he was to be under Hunter. Yours truly,

A. LINCOLN.

Special War Order No. 1, January 31, 1862.

Ordered: That all the disposable forces of the Army of the Potomac, after providing safely for the defense of Washington, be formed into an expedition for the immediate object of seizing and occupying a point upon the railroad southwestward of what is known as Manassas Junction; all details to be in the direction of the general-in-chief, and the expedition to move before or on the 22d day of February next.

A. Lincoln.

Letter to General McClellan, February 3, 1862.

My Dear Sir:—You and I have distinct and different plans for a movement of the Army of the Potomac. Yours to be done by the Chesapeake, up the Rappahannock to Urbanna, and across to the terminus of the railroad on the York river; mine to move directly to a point on the railroad south-west of Manassas.

If you will give me satisfactory answers to the following questions, I shall gladly yield my plan to yours:

1. Does not your plan involve a greatly larger expenditure of *time* and *money* than mine?
2. Wherein is a victory *more certain* by your plan than mine?
3. Wherein is a victory *more valuable* by your plan than mine?
4. In fact, would it not be *less* valuable in this: that it would break no great line of the enemy's communications, while mine would?

5. In case of disaster, would not a retreat be more difficult by your plan than mine. Yours truly,
A. LINCOLN.

TO MAJOR-GENERAL HUNTER AND BRIGADIER-GENERAL LANE, LEAVENWORTH, KANSAS.

Executive Mansion, Washington, February 10, 1862.

My wish has been and is to avail the Government of the services of both General Hunter and General Lane, and, so far as possible, to personally oblige both.

General Hunter is the senior officer, and must command when they serve together; though in so far as he can, consistently with the public service and his own honor, oblige General Lane, he will also oblige me.

If they can not come to an amiable understanding, General Lane must report to General Hunter for duty, according to rules, or decline the service.
A. LINCOLN.

TO MAJOR-GENERAL HALLECK, ST. LOUIS MO.

Executive Mansion, Washington, February 16, 1862.

You have Fort Donelson safe, unless Grant shall be overwhelmed from outside; to prevent which latter will, I think, require all the vigilance, energy and skill of yourself and Buell, acting in full co-operation. Columbus will not get at Grant, but the full force from Bowling Green will. They hold the railroad from Bowling Green to within a few miles of Fort Donelson, with the bridge at Clarksville undisturbed. It is unsafe to rely that they will not dare to expose Nashville to Buell. A small part of their force can retire slowly toward Nashville, breaking up the railroad as they go, and keep Buell out of that city twenty days. Meanwhile, Nashville will be abundantly defended by forces from all south, and perhaps from here at Manassas. Could not a cavalry force from General Thomas on the upper Cumberland dash across, almost unresisted, and cut the railroad at or near Knoxville, Tenn.? In the midst of a bombardment at Fort Donelson, why could not a gun-boat run up and destroy the bridge at Clarksville? Our success or failure at Fort Donelson is vastly important, and I beg you to put your soul in the effort. I send a copy of this to Buell. A. LINCOLN.

RECOMMENDATION TO CONGRESS, MARCH 6, 1862.

I recommend the adoption of a joint resolution by your honorable bodies, which shall be substantially as follows:

Resolved, That the United States ought to co-operate with any state which may adopt gradual abolishment of slavery, giving to such state pecuniary aid, to be used by such state in its discretion, to compensate for the inconvenience, both public and private, produced by such change of system.

If the proposition contained in the resolution does not meet the approval of Congress and the country, there is the end; but if it does command such approval, I deem it of importance that the states and people immediately interested should be at once distinctly notified of the fact, so that they may begin to consider whether to accept or reject it. The Federal government would find its highest interest in such a measure, as one of the most efficient means of self-preservation. The leaders of the existing insurrection entertain the hope that this government will ultimately be forced to acknowledge the independence of some part of the disaffected region, and that all the slave states north of such part will then say, "the Union for which we have struggled being already gone, we now choose to go with the southern section." To deprive them of this hope, substantially ends the rebellion; and the initiation of emancipation completely deprives them of it as to all the states initiating it. The point is not that *all* the states tolerating slavery, would very soon, if at all, initiate emancipation; but that, while the offer is equally made to all, the more northern shall, by such initiation, make it certain to the more southern that in no event will the former ever join the latter in their proposed confederacy. I say "initiation," because, in my judgment gradual, and not sudden emancipation, is better for all. In the mere financial or pecuniary view, any member of Congress, with the census tables and treasury reports before him, can readily see for himself how very soon the current expenditures of this war would purchase, at fair valuation, all the slaves in any named state. Such a proposition on the part of the general government sets up no claim of a right by Federal authority to interfere with slavery within state limits, referring, as it does, the absolute control of the subject in each case to the state and its people immediately interested. It is proposed as a matter of perfectly free choice with them.

In the annual message last December, I thought fit

to say, "the Union must preserved; and hence all indispensable means must be employed." I said this not hastily, but deliberately. War has been made, and continues to be an indispensable means to this end. A practical re-acknowledgement of the national authority would render the war unnecessary, and it would at once cease. If, however, resistance continues, the war must also continue; and it is impossible to foresee all the incidents which may attend, and all the ruin which may follow it. Such as may seem indispensable, or may obviously promise great efficiency toward ending the struggle, must and will come. The proposition now made, though an offer only, I hope it may be esteemed no offense to ask whether the pecuniary consideration tendered would not be of more value to the states and private persons concerned, than are the institution and property in it, in the present aspect of affairs.

While it is true that the adoption of the proposed resolution would be merely initiatory, and not within itself a practical measure, it is recommended in the hope that it would soon lead to important practical results. In full view of my great responsibility to my God and to my country, I earnestly beg the attention of Congress and the people to the subject.

ABRAHAM LINCOLN.

GENERAL WAR ORDER No. 3, MARCH 8, 1862.

Ordered: That no change of the base of operations of the Army of the Potomac shall be made without leaving in and about Washington such a force as, in the opinion of the general-in-chief and the commanders of all the army corps, shall leave the said city entirely secure.

That no more than two army corps (about 50,000 troops), of said Army of the Potomac shall be moved en route for a new base of operations until the navigation of the Potomac from Washington to the Chesapeake bay shall be freed from the enemy's batteries and obstructions, or until the president shall hereafter give express permission.

That any movement aforesaid en route for a new base of operations, which may be ordered by the general-in-chief, and which may be intended to move upon the Chesapeake bay, shall begin to move upon the bay as early as the 18th March inst., and the general-in-chief shall be responsible that it so move as early as that day.

Ordered: That the army and navy co-operate in an immediate effort to capture the enemy's batteries upon the Potomac between Washington and the Chesapeake bay. A. LINCOLN.

To GENERAL D. C. BUELL.

Washington, March 10, 1862.

The evidence is very strong that the enemy in front of us here is breaking up and moving off. General McClellan is after him. Some part of the force may be destined to meet you. Look out and be prepared. I telegraphed Halleck, asking him to assist you, if needed. A. LINCOLN.

GENERAL WAR ORDERS, MARCH 13, 1862.

First. Leave such force at Manassas Junction as

shall make it entirely certain that the enemy shall not repossess himself of that position and line of communication.

Second. Leave Washington secure.

Third. Move the remainder of the force down the Potomac, choosing a new base at Fort Monroe, or anywhere between here and there, or, at all events, move such remainder of the army, at once, in pursuit of the enemy, by some route.   A. LINCOLN.

NOMINATION.

March 22, 1862.

The President of the United States of America to all who shall see these presents, greeting: Know ye that, reposing special trust and confidence in the patriotism, valor, fidelity, and abilities of John Pope, I have nominated, and by and with the advice and consent of the senate, do appoint him major-general of volunteers in the service of the United States, to rank as such from the 21st day of March, 1862. He is, therefore, carefully and diligently to discharge the duty of major-general, by doing and performing all manner of things thereunto belonging. And I do strictly charge and require all officers and soldiers under his command to be obedient to his orders as major-general. And he is to observe and follow such orders and directions, from time to time, as he shall receive from me, or the future President of the United States of America, or the general or other superior officers set over him, according to the rules and discipline of war. This commission to continue in force during the pleasure of the President of the United States for the time being.

Given under my hand, at the city of Washington, this 22d day of March, in the year of our Lord one thousand eight hundred and sixty-two, and in the eighty-sixth year of the independence of the United States. ABRAHAM LINCOLN.

LETTER TO GEN. MCCLELLAN, APRIL 9, 1862.

My Dear Sir.—Your dispatches, complaining that you are not properly sustained, while they do not offend me, do pain me very much.

Blenker's division was withdrawn from you before you left here, and you know the pressure under which I did it, and, as I thought, acquiesced in it, certainly not without reluctance.

After you left I ascertained that less than twenty thousand unorganized men, without a single field battery, were all you designed to be left for the defense of Washington and Manassas Junction; and part of this even was to go to General Hooker's old position. General Banks's corps, once designed for Manassas Junction, was diverted and tied upon the line of Winchester and Strasburg, and could not leave it without again exposing the upper Potomac, and the Baltimore and Ohio Railroad. This presented (or would present, when McDowell and Sumner should be gone) a great temptation to the enemy to turn back from the Rappahannock and sack Washington. My explicit order that Washington should, by the judgment of *all* the commanders of army corps, be left entirely secure, had been neglected. It was precisely this that drove me to detain McDowell.

I do not forget that I was satisfied with your arrangement to leave Banks at Manassas Junction; but when that arrangement was broken up, and *nothing* was substituted for it, of course, I was constrained to substitute something for it myself. And allow me to ask, do you really think I should permit the line from Richmond via Manassas Junction to this city to be entirely open, except what resistance could be presented by twenty thousand unorganized troops? This is a question which the country will not allow me to evade.

There is a curious mystery about the number of the troops now with you. When I telegraphed you on the 6th, saying you had over a hundred thousand with you, I had just obtained from the secretary of war a statement, taken, as he said, from your own returns, making one hundred and eight thousand then with you and *en route* to you. You now say you will have but eighty-five thousand when all *en route* to you shall have reached you.

How can the discrepancy of twenty-three thousand be accounted for?

As to General Wool's command, I understand it is doing for you precisely what a like number of your own would have to do if that command was away.

I suppose the whole force which has gone forward for you is with you by this time, and if so, I think it is the precise time to strike a blow. By delay the enemy will relatively gain upon you—that is, he will gain faster, by *fortifications* and *re-inforcements*, than you can by re-inforcements alone.

And once more let me tell you it is indispensable to *you* that you strike a blow. *I* am powerless to help this. You will do me the justice to remember I always insisted that going down the bay in search of a field, instead of fighting at or near Manassas, was only shifting, and not surmounting, a difficulty; that we would find the same enemy, and the same or equal intrenchments, at either place. The country will not fail to note—is now noting—that the present hesitation to move upon an intrenched enemy is but the story of Manassas repeated.

I beg to assure you that I have never written you, or spoken to you, in greater kindness of feeling than now, nor with a fuller purpose to sustain you, so far as in my most anxious judgment, I consistently can. But you must act. Yours, very truly,

A. LINCOLN.

Proclamation, April 10, 1862.

It has pleased Almighty God to vouchsafe signal victories to the land and naval forces engaged in suppressing an internal rebellion, and at the same time to avert from our country the dangers of foreign intervention and invasion.

It is therefore recommended to the people of the United States, that at their next weekly assemblages in their accustomed places of public worship, which shall occur after the notice of this proclamation shall have been received, they especially acknowledge and render thanks to our Heavenly Father for these inestimable blessings; that they then and there implore spiritual consolation in behalf of all those who have been brought into affliction by the casualties and calamities of sedition and civil war; and that they reverently invoke the divine guidance for our national councils, to the end that they may speedily result in the restoration of peace, harmony, and unity throughout our borders, and hasten the establishment of fraternal relations among all the countries of the earth.

In witness whereof I have hereunto set my hand and caused the seal of the United States to be affixed.

Done at the city of Washington, the tenth day of April, in the year of Our Lord one thousand eight hundred and sixty-two, and of the independence of the United States the eighty-sixth.

ABRAHAM LINCOLN.

MESSAGE TO CONGRESS, APRIL 16, 1862.

The act entitled "An act for the release of certain persons held to service or labor in the District of Columbia," has this day been approved and signed.

I have never doubted the constitutional authority of Congress to abolish slavery in this district; and I have ever desired to see the national capital freed from the institution in some satisfactory way. Hence, there has never been in my mind any question upon the subject except the one of expediency, arising in view of all the circumstances. If there be matters within and about this act which might have taken a course or shape more satisfactory to my judgment, I do not attempt to specify them. I am gratified that the two principles of compensation and colonization, are both recognized and practically applied in the act. In the matter of compensation, it is provided that claims may be presented within ninety days from the passage of the act, "but not thereafter;" and there is no saving for minors, *femmes covert*, insane, or absent persons. I presume this is an omission by mere oversight, and I recommend that it be supplied by an amendatory or supplemental act. ABRAHAM LINCOLN.

To GOVERNOR ANDREW JOHNSON, NASHVILLE, TENN.

War Department, April 27, 1862.

Your dispatch of yesterday just received, as also, in due course, was your former one. The former one was sent to General Halleck, and we have his answer, by which I have no doubt he (General Halleck) is in communication with you before this. General Halleck understands better than we can here, and he must be allowed to control in that quarter.

If you are not in communication with Halleck, telegraph him at once, freely and frankly.

A. LINCOLN.

To FLAG OFFICER GOLDSBOROUGH.

Fort Monroe, Virginia, May 7, 1862.

Sir:—Major-General McClellan telegraphs that he has ascertained, by a reconnaissance, that the battery at Jamestown has been abandoned, and he again requests that gun-boats may be sent up the James river. If you have tolerable confidence that you can successfully contend with the Merrimac without the help of the Galena and two accompanying gun-boats, send the Galena and two gun-boats up the James river at once. Please report your action on this to me at once. I shall be found either at General Wool's headquarters or on board the Miami.

Your obedient servant,   A. LINCOLN.

LETTER TO GENERAL McCLELLAN, MAY 9, 1862.

My Dear Sir:—I have just assisted the Secretary of War in forming the part of a dispatch to you relating to army corps, which dispatch, of course, will have reached you long before this will. I wish to say a few words to you privately on this subject. *I ordered the army corps organization not only on the unanimous opinion of the twelve generals of division, but also on the unanimous opinion of every military man I could get an opinion from, and every modern military book, yourself only excepted.* Of course I did not, on my own judgment, pretend to understand the subject. *I now think it indispensable for you to know how your struggle against it is received in quarters which we can not entirely disregard. It is looked upon as merely an effort to pamper one or two pets, and to persecute and degrade their supposed rivals. I have had no word from Sumner, Heintzelman, or Keyes.* The commanders of these corps are, of course, the three highest officials with you, but I am constantly told that you have no consultation or communication with them, that you consult and communicate with nobody but Fitz John Porter, and perhaps General Franklin. I do not say these complaints are true or just, but, at all events, it is proper that you should know of their existence.

Do the commanders of corps disobey your orders in any thing?

When you relieved General Hamilton of his command the other day you thereby lost the confidence of at least one of your best friends in the senate. And here let me say, not as applicable to you personally, that senators and representatives speak of me in their places as they please without question; and that officers of the army must cease addressing insulting letters to them for taking no greater liberty with them. But to return, *are you strong enough, even with my help, to set your foot upon the neck of Sumner, Heintzelman, and Keyes, all at once? This is a practical and very serious question for you.* Yours truly, A. LINCOLN.

To Flag Officer Goldsborough.

Fort Monroe, Va., May 10, 1862.

My Dear Sir:—I send you this copy of your report of yesterday for the purpose of saying to you in writing, that you are quite right in supposing the movement made by you and therein reported was made in accordance with my wishes, verbally expressed to you in advance. I avail myself of the occasion to thank you for your courtesy and all your conduct, so far as known to me, during my brief visit here.

Yours very truly, A. LINCOLN.

Proclamation Declaring Major-General Hunter's Emancipation Orders Null and Void.

May 19, 1862.

I, Abraham Lincoln, President of the United States, proclaim and declare that the government of the

United States had no knowledge or belief of an intention on the part of General Hunter to issue such a proclamation, nor has it yet any authentic information that the document is genuine, and further, that neither General Hunter, nor any other commander, or person, has been authorized by the government of the United States to make a proclamation declaring the slaves of any state free, and that the supposed proclamation now in question is altogether void, so far as respects such declaration.

I further make known that whether it be competent for me, as commander-in-chief of the army and navy, to declare the slaves of any state or states free, and whether at any time or in any case, it shall have become a necessity, indispensable to the maintenance of the government, to exercise such supposed power, are questions which, under my responsibility, I reserve to myself, and which I can not feel justified in leaving to the decision of commanders in the field. These are totally different questions from those of police regulations in armies and corps.

On the 6th day of March last, by a special message, I recommended to Congress the adoption of a joint resolution, to be substantially as follows:

Resolved, That the United States ought to co-operate with any state which may adopt a gradual abolishment of slavery, giving aid to such state, in its discretion, to compensate for the inconveniences, public and private, produced by such change of system.

The resolution, in the language above quoted, was adopted by large majorities in both branches of Congress; and now stands an authentic, definite and solemn proposal of the nation to the states and people most immediately interested in the subject-matter. To the people of these states I now earnestly appeal. I do not argue, I beseech you to make the arguments for yourselves. You can not, if you would, be blind to the signs of the times. I beg of you a calm and enlarged consideration of them, ranging, if it may be, far above personal and partisan politics.

This proposal makes common cause for a common object, casting no reproaches upon any It acts not the Pharisee. The change it contemplates would come gently as the dews of heaven, not rending or wrecking any thing. Will you not embrace it? So much good has not been done by one effort in all past time, as in the providence of God it is now your high privilege to do. May the vast future not have to lament that you have neglected it.

In witness whereof I have hereunto set my hand and caused the seal of the United States to be affixed.

Done at the city of Washington this 19th day of May, in the year of our Lord one thousand eight hundred and sixty-two, and of the Independence of the United States the eighty-sixth. A. LINCOLN.

To MAJOR-GENERAL McCLELLAN.

Washington City, May 21, 1862.

Your long dispatch of yesterday (to-day) just received. You will have just such control of General McDowell and his force as you therein indicate. McDowell can reach you by land sooner than he could get aboard of boats, if the boats were ready at Fredericksburg, unless his march shall be resisted, in which case the force resisting him will certainly not be confronting you at Richmond. By land he can reach you in five days after starting, whereas by water he would not reach you in two weeks, judging by past experience. Franklin's single division did not reach you in ten days after I ordered it.

A. LINCOLN.

To GENERAL SAXTON.

War Department, May 24, 1862, 1 *P. M.*

Geary reports Jackson with 20,000 moving from Ashby's Gap, by the Little River Turnpike, through Aldie, toward Centreville. This he says is reliable. He is also informed of large forces south of him. We know of a force of some 15,000 broke up Saturday night from in front of Fredericksburg, and went we know not where. Please inform us, if possible, what has become of the force which pursued Banks yesterday; also any other information you have.

A. LINCOLN.

To MAJOR-GENERAL FREMONT, FRANKLIN.

War Department, May 24, 1862, 4 *P. M.*

You are authorized to purchase 400 horses or take them whenever and however you can get them. The exposed condition of General Banks makes his immediate relief a point of paramount importance. You are therefore directed by the president to move against Jackson at Harrisonburg, and operate against the enemy in such way as to relieve Banks. The movement must be made immediately.

You will acknowledge the receipt of this order and specify the hour it was received by you.

A. LINCOLN.

To Major-General McDowell.

Washington, May 24, 1862.

General Fremont has been ordered by telegraph to move to Franklin and Harrisonburg to relieve General Banks, and capture or destroy Jackson's and Ewell's forces.

You are instructed, laying aside for the present the movement on Richmond, to put twenty thousand men in motion at once for the Shenandoah, moving on the line, or in advance of the line, of the Manassas Gap Railroad. Your object will be to capture the forces of Jackson and Ewell, either in co-operation with General Fremont, or, in case want of supplies or transportation has interfered with his movement, it is believed that the force which you move will be sufficient to accomplish the object alone. The information thus far received here makes it probable that, if the enemy operates actively against General Banks, you will not be able to count upon much assistance from him, but may have even to re-relieve him.

Reports received this morning are that Banks is fighting with Ewell eight miles from Harper's Ferry.

A. Lincoln.

To Major-General Fremont, Franklin, Va.

War Department, May 24, 1862, 7:15 *P. M.*

Many thanks for the promptness with which you have answered that you will execute the order. Much—perhaps all—depends upon the celerity with which you can execute it. Put the utmost speed into it. Do not lose a moment. A. Lincoln.

To Major-General Halleck, near Corinth, Miss.

War Department, May 24, 1862.

Several dispatches from Assistant Secretary Scott, and one from Governor Martin, asking reinforcements for you, have been received. I beg you to be assured we do the best we can. I mean to cast no blame when I tell you each of our commanders along our line from Richmond to Corinth supposes himself to be confronted by numbers superior to his own.

Under this pressure, we thinned the line on the Upper Potomac, until yesterday it was broken at heavy loss to us, and General Banks put in great peril, out of which he is not yet extricated, and may be actually captured. We need men to repair this breach, and have them not at hand.

My dear general, I feel justified to rely very much on you. I believe you, and the brave officers and men with you, can and will get the victory at Corinth. A. LINCOLN.

To General Saxton, Harper's Ferry.

War Department, May 25, 1862, 4:15 *P. M.*

If Banks reaches Martinsburg, is he any the better for it? Will not the enemy cut him off from thence to Harper's Ferry? Have you sent any thing to meet him, and assist him at Martinsburg? This is an inquiry, not an order. A. LINCOLN.

To Major-General McClellan.

Washington, May 25, 1862, 2 *P. M.*

The enemy is moving north in sufficient force to drive General Banks before him, precisely in what force we can not tell. He is also threatening Leesburg and Geary, on the Manassas Gap Railroad, from both north and south—in precisely what force we can not tell. I think the movement is a general and concerted one, such as would not be if he was acting upon the purpose of a very desperate defense of Richmond. I think the time is near when you must either attack Richmond, or give up the job, and come to the defense of Washington. Let me hear from you instantly. A. LINCOLN.

To MAJOR-GENERAL MCCLELLAN.

Washington, May 25, 1862.

Your dispatch received. General Banks was at Strasburg, with about 6,000 men, Shields having taken from him to swell a column for McDowell to aid you at Richmond, and the rest of his force scattered at various places. On the 23d, a rebel force of 7,000 to 10,000 fell upon one regiment and two companies, guarding the bridge at Front Royal, destroying it entirely, crossed the Shenandoah, and on the 24th (yesterday) pushed on to get north of Banks, on the road to Winchester. General Banks ran a race with them, beating them into Winchester yesterday evening.

This morning a battle ensued between the two forces, in which General Banks was beaten back into full retreat toward Martinsburg, and probably is broken up into a total rout. Geary, on the Manassas Gap Railroad, just now reports that Jackson is now near Front Royal, with 10,000 troops, following up and supporting, as I understand, the force now pursuing Banks. Also that another force of 10,000 is near Orleans, following on the same direction. Stripped bare, as we are here, I will do all we can to prevent them crossing the Potomac at Harper's Ferry or above. McDowell has about 20,000 of his forces moving back to the vicinity of Front Royal, and Fremont, who was at Franklin, is moving to Harrisonburg; both these movements intended to get in the enemy's rear.

One more of McDowell's brigades is ordered through here to Harper's Ferry, the rest of his force remain at present at Fredericksburg. We are sending such regiments and dribs from here and Baltimore as we can spare to Harper's Ferry, supplying their places in some sort, by calling in militia from the adjacent states. We also have eighteen cannon on the road to Harper's Ferry, of which arm there is not a single one at that point. This is now our situation.

If McDowell's force was now beyond our reach we should be entirely helpless. Apprehensions of something like this, and no unwillingness to sustain you, have always been my reasons for withholding McDowell's from you. Please understand this, and do the best you can with the forces you have.

A. LINCOLN.

To GENERAL SAXTON, HARPER'S FERRY.

War Department, May 25, 1862.

I fear you have mistaken me. I did not mean to question the correctness of your conduct; on the contrary, I approve what you have done. As the 2,500 reported by you seemed small to me, I feared some had got to Banks and been cut off with him. Please tell me the exact number you have in hand.

           A. LINCOLN.

To GENERAL SAXTON, HARPER'S FERRY.

War Department, May 25, 1862, 6:50 P. M.

One good six-gun battery, complete in its men and appointments, is now on its way to you from Baltimore. Eleven other guns, of different sorts, are on their way to you from here. Hope they will all reach you before morning. As you have 2,500 men at Harper's Ferry, where are the rest which were in that vicinity and which we have sent forward? Have any of them been cut off?   A. LINCOLN.

To SECRETARY CHASE, FREDERICKSBURG, VA.

War Department, May 25, 1862.

It now appears that Banks got safely into Winchester last night, and is this morning retreating on Harper's Ferry. This justified the inference that he is pressed by numbers superior to his own. I think it not improbable that Ewell, Jackson, and Johnson are pouring through the gap they made day before yesterday at Port Royal, making a dash northward. It will be a very valuable and very honorable service for General McDowell to cut them off. I hope he will put all possible energy and speed into the effort.

           A. LINCOLN.

To General McDowell, Manassas Junction.

Washington, May 28, 1862, 1 *P. M.*

General McClellan, at 6:30 P. M. yesterday, telegraphed that Fitz John Porter's division had fought and driven 13,000 of the enemy, under General Brand, from Hanover Court-House, and was driving them from a stand they had made on the railroad at the time the messenger left. Two hours later he telegraphed that Stoneman had captured an engine and six cars on the Virginia Central, which he at once sent to communicate with F. J. Porter. Nothing further from McClellan.

If Porter effects a lodgment on both railroads near Hanover Court-House, consider whether your forces in front of Fredericksburg should not push through and join him.   A. Lincoln.

Letter to General McClellan, May 28, 1862.

I am very glad of General F. J. Porter's victory; still, if it was a total rout of the enemy, I am puzzled to know why the Richmond and Fredericksburg Railroad was not seized again, as you say you have all the railroads but the Richmond and Fredericksburg. I am puzzled to see how, lacking that, you can have any, except the scrap from Richmond to West Point. The scrap of the Virginia Central, from Richmond to Hanover Junction, without more, is simply nothing.

That the whole of the enemy is concentrating on Richmond, I think can not be certainly known to you or me. Saxton, at Harper's Ferry, informs us that large forces, supposed to be Jackson's and Ewell's, forced his advance from Charlestown to-day. General King telegraphs us from Fredericksburg that contrabands give certain information that 15,000 left Hanover Junction Monday morning to reinforce Jackson.

I am painfully impressed with the importance of the struggle before you, and shall aid you all I can consistently with my view of the due regard to all points. A. LINCOLN.

To MAJOR-GENERAL FREMONT, MOOREFIELD, VA.

Washington, May 29, 1862, 12 M.

General McDowell's advance, if not checked by the enemy, should, and probably will, be at Front Royal at 12 (noon) to-morrow. His force, when up, will be about 20,000. Please have your force at Strasburg, or, if the route you are moving on does not lead to that point, as near Strasburg as the enemy may be by the same time. Your dispatch, No. 30, received and satisfactory. A. LINCOLN.

MESSAGE EXPLANATORY OF GOVERNMENT PURCHASES IN MAY, 1861.

May 29, 1862.

To the Senate and House of Representatives:—The insurrection which is yet existing in the United States, and aims at the overthrow of the Federal Constitution and the Union, was clandestinely prepared during the winter of 1860 and 1861, and assumed an open organization in the form of a treasonable provisional government at Montgomery, in

Alabama, on the 18th day of February, 1861. On the 12th day of April, 1861, the insurgents committed the flagrant act of civil war by the bombardment and capture of Fort Sumter, which cut off the hope of immediate conciliation. Immediately afterward all the roads and avenues to this city were obstructed, and the capital was put into the condition of a siege. The mails in every direction were stopped, and the lines of telegraph cut off by the insurgents; and military and naval forces, which had been called out by the government for the defense of Washington, were prevented from reaching the city by organized and combined treasonable resistance in the State of Maryland. There was no adequate and effective organization for the public defense. Congress had indefinitely adjourned. There was no time to convene them. It became necessary for me to choose whether, using only the existing means, agencies, and processes which Congress had provided, I should let the government fall at once into ruin, or whether, availing myself of the broader powers conferred by the Constitution in cases of insurrection, I would make an effort to save it, with all its blessings, for the present age and for posterity.

I thereupon summoned my constitutional advisers, the heads of all departments, to meet on Sunday, the 20th day of April, 1861, at the office of the Navy Department, and then and there, with their unanimous concurrence, I directed that an armed revenue cutter should proceed to sea, to afford protection to the commercial marine, and especially the California treasure ships then on their way to this coast. I also directed the commandant of the navy-yard at Boston to purchase or charter, and arm as quickly as possible, five steamships, for purposes of public defense. I directed the commandant of the navy-yard at Philadelphia to purchase, or charter and arm, an equal number for the same purpose. I directed the commandant at New York to purchase, or charter and arm, an equal number. I directed Commander Gillis to purchase, or charter and arm, and put to sea two other vessels. Similar directions were given to Commodore DuPont, with a view to the opening of passages by water to and from the capital. I directed the several officers to take the advice and obtain the aid and efficient services in the matter of his Excellency, Edwin D. Morgan, the governor of New York; or, in his absence, George D. Morgan, William M. Evarts, R. M. Blatchford, and Moses H. Grinnell, who were, by my directions, especially empowered by the Secretary of the Navy to act for his department in that crisis, in matters pertaining to the forwarding of troops and supplies for the public defense.

On the same occasion, I directed that Governor Morgan and Alexander Cummings, of the city of New York, should be authorized by the Secretary of War, Simon Cameron, to make all necessary arrangements for the transportation of troops and munitions of war, in aid and assistance of the officers of the army of the United States, until communication by mails and telegraph should be completely re-established between the cities of Washington and New York. No security was required to be given by them, and either of them was authorized to act in case of inability to consult with the others.

On the same occasion, I authorized and directed the Secretary of the Treasury to advance, without requiring security, two millions of dollars for public money to John A. Dix, George Opdyke, and Richard M. Blatchford, of New York, to be used by them in meeting such requisitions as should be directly consequent upon the military and naval measures necessary for the defense and support of the government, requiring them only to act without compensation, and to report their transactions when duly called upon. The several departments of the government at that time contained so large a number of disloyal persons that it would have been impossible to provide safely, through official agents only, for the performance of the duties thus confided to citizens favorably known for their ability, loyalty and patriotism.

The several orders issued upon these occurrences were transmitted by private messengers, who pursued a circuitous way to the seaboard cities, inland, across the States of Pennsylvania and Ohio and the northern lakes. I believe that by these and other similar measures taken in that crisis, some of which were without any authority of law, the government was saved from overthrow. I am not aware that a dollar of the public funds thus confided without authority of law, to unofficial persons was either lost or wasted, although apprehension of such misdirection occurred to me as objections to those extraordinary proceedings, and were necessarily overruled.

I recall these transactions now because my attention has been directed to a resolution which was passed by the House of Representatives on the 30th day of last month, which is in these words:

Resolved, That Simon Cameron, late Secretary of War, by investing Alexander Cummings with the control of large sums of the public money, and authority to purchase military supplies without restriction, without requiring from him any guarantee for the faithful performance of his duties, when the services of competent public officers were available, and by involving the government in a vast number of contracts with persons not legitimately engaged in the business pertaining to the subject-matter of such contracts, especially in the purchase of arms for future delivery, has adopted a policy highly injurious to the public service, and deserves the censure of the house.

Congress will see that I should be wanting equally in candor and in justice, if I should leave the censure expressed in this resolution to rest exclusively or chiefly upon Mr. Cameron. The same sentiment is unanimously entertained by the heads of departments, who participated in the proceedings which the House of Representatives has censured. It is due to Mr. Cameron to say that, although he fully approved the proceedings, they were not moved or suggested by himself, and that not only the President but all the other heads of departments were at least equally responsible with him for whatever error, wrong, or fault was committed in the premises.

ABRAHAM LINCOLN.

To Major-General McClellan.
Washington, May 31, 1862.

A circle whose circumference shall pass through Harper's Ferry, Front Royal and Strasburg, and whose center shall be a little north east of Winchester, almost certainly has within it this morning the forces of Jackson, Ewell and Edward Johnson. Quite certainly they were within it two days ago. Some part of their forces attacked Harper's Ferry at dark last evening, and are still in sight this morning. Shields, with McDowells advance, took Front Royal at 11 A. M. yesterday, with a dozen of our own prisoners taken there a week ago, 150 of the enemy, two locomotives and eleven cars, some other property and stores, and saved the bridge.

General Fremont, from the direction of Moorefield, promises to be at or near Strasburg at 5 P. M. to-day. General Banks at Williamsport with his old force, and his new force at Harper's Ferry, is directed to co-operate. Shields, at Front Royal, reports a rumor of still an additional force of the enemy, supposed to be at Anderson's, having entered the valley of Virginia. This last may or may not be true. Corinth is certainly in the hands of General Halleck. A. Lincoln.

To Major-General McClellan.
War Dep't, Washington City, June 1, 1862, 5 P. M.

Thanks for what you *could* and *did* say in your dispatch of noon to-day to the Secretary of War. If the enemy shall not have renewed the attack this afternoon, I think the hardest of your work is done.

Shields's advance came in collision with part of the enemy yesterday evening six miles from Front Royal, in a direction between Winchester and Strasburg, driving them back, capturing a few prisoners and one rifled cannon. Firing in that direction to-day heard both from Harper's Ferry and Front Royal, indicate a probability that Fremont has met the enemy.

We have concluded to send General Sigel to Harper's Ferry, so that what I telegraphed you about him this morning is revoked. Dix goes to Fort Monroe to-night. A. LINCOLN.

To MAJOR-GENERAL FREMONT.

Washington, June 9, 1862.

Halt at Harrisonburg, pursuing Jackson no farther. Get your force well in hand and stand on the defensive, guarding against a movement of the enemy back toward Strasburg or Franklin, and wait further orders, which will soon be sent you. A. LINCOLN.

To MAJOR-GENERAL FREMONT.

Washington, June 12, 1862.

Yours preferring Mount Jackson to Harrisonburg, is just received. On this point use your discretion, remembering that our object is to give such protection as you can to Western Virginia. Many thanks to yourself, officers, and men for the gallant battle of last Sunday. A. LINCOLN.

To MAJOR-GENERAL FREMONT.

Washington, June 13, 1862.

We can not afford to keep your force and Banks's and McDowell's engaged in keeping Jackson south of

Strasburg and Front Royal. You fought Jackson alone and worsted him. He can have no substantial re-inforcements so long as a battle is pending at Richmond. Surely you and Banks in supporting distance, are capable of keeping him from returning to Winchester. But if Sigel be sent forward to you and McDowell (as he must be put to other work), Jackson will break through at Front Royal again. He is already on the right side of the Shenandoah to do it, and on the wrong side of it to attack you. The orders already sent you and Banks place you and him in the proper position for the work assigned you. Jackson can not move his whole force on either of you before the other can learn of it and go to his assistance. He can not divide his force, sending part against each of you, because he will be too weak for either. Please do as I directed in the order of the 8th, and my dispatch of yesterday, the 12th, and neither you or Banks will be overwhelmed by Jackson. By proper scout lookouts, and beacons of smoke by day and fires by night, you can always have timely notice of the enemy's approach. I know not as to you, but by some this has been too much neglected. LINCOLN.

To MAJOR-GENERAL FREMONT.

War Dep't, Washington City, D. C., June 15, 1862.

My dear sir:—Your letter of the 12th, by Colonel Zagonyi, is just received. In answer to the principal part of it, I repeat the substance of an order of the 8th, and one or two telegraphic dispatches sent you since.

We have no indefinite power of sending reinforcements, so that we are compelled rather to consider the proper disposal of the forces we have than of those we could wish to have. We may be able to send you some dribs by degrees, but I do not believe we can do more. As you alone beat Jackson last Sunday, I argue that you are stronger than he is to-day, unless he has been reinforced, and that he can not have been materially reinforced, because such reinforcement could only have come from Richmond, and he is much more likely to go to Richmond than Richmond is to come to him. Neither is very likely. I think Jackson's game—his assigned work—now is to magnify the accounts of his number and reports of his movements, and thus, by constant alarms, to keep three or four times as many of our troops away from Richmond as his own force amounts to.

Thus he helps his friends at Richmond three or four times as much as if he were there. Our game is not to allow this. Accordingly, by the order of the 8th, I directed you to halt at Harrisonburg, rest your force, and get it well in hand, the object being to guard against Jackson's returning by the same route to the Upper Potomac, over which you have just driven him out, and at the same time give some protection against a raid into West Virginia. Already I have given you discretion to occupy Mount Jackson instead, if, on full consideration, you think best. I do not believe Jackson will attack you, but certainly he can not attack you by surprise; and if he comes upon you in superior force, you have but to notify us, fall back cautiously, and Banks will join you in due time. But, while we know not whether Jackson will move at all, or by what route, we can not safely put you and Banks both on the Strasburg line, and have no force on the Front Royal line, upon which he prosecuted his last raid. The true policy is to place one of you on one line, and the other on the other, in such position that you can unite on either, once you actually find Jackson moving upon it. And this is precisely what we are doing.

This protects that part of our frontier, so to speak, and liberates McDowell to go to the assistance of McClellan. I have arranged this, and am very unwilling to have it deranged. While you have only asked for Sigel, I have spoken only of Banks, and this because Sigel's force is now the principal part of Banks's force. About transferring General Schenck's command, the purchase of supplies, and the promotion and appointment of officers mentioned in your letter, I will consult with the Secretary of War to-morrow. Yours truly, A. LINCOLN.

To MAJOR-GENERAL FREMONT, MOUNT JACKSON, VA.

Washington, June 16, 1862.

Your dispatch of yesterday, reminding me of a supposed understanding that I would furnish you a corps of 35,000 men, and asking of me the "fulfillment of this understanding" is received. I am ready to come to a fair settlement of accounts with you on the fulfillment of understandings.

Early in March last, when I assigned you to the command of the Mountain Department, I did tell you I would give you all the force I could, and that I hoped to make it reach 35,000. You at the same time told me that within a reasonable time you would seize the railroad at or east of Knoxville, Tennessee, if you could. There was then in the department a force supposed to be 25,000, the exact number as well known to you as to me. After looking about two or days, you called, and distinctly told me that if I would add the Blenker division to the force already in the department, you would undertake the job. The Blenker division contained 10,000, and. at the expense of great dissatisfaction to General McClellan, I took it from his army, and gave it to you. My promise was literally fulfilled. I have given you all I could, and I have given you very nearly, if not quite, 35,000. Now for yours: On the 23d of May, largely over two months afterward, you were at Franklin, Virginia, not within 300 miles of Knoxville, nor within eighty miles of any part of the railroad east of it, and not moving forward, but telegraphing here that you could not move for lack of everything. Now, do not misunderstand me. I do not say you have not done all you could. I presume you met unexpected difficulties; and I beg you to believe that, as surely as you have done your best, so have I. I have not the power now to fill up your corps to 35,000. I am not demanding of you to do the work of 35,000. I am only asking of you to stand cautiously on the defensive, get your force in order, and give such protection as you can to the valley of the Shenandoah and to Western Virginia.

Have you received the orders, and will you act upon them?   A. LINCOLN.

To Brigadier-General Schurz, Mount Jackson, Va.
                    Washington, *June* 16, 1862.

Your long letter is received. The information you give is valuable. You say it is fortunate that Fremont did not intercept Jackson; that Jackson had a superior force, and would have overwhelmed him. If this is so, how happened it that Fremont fairly fought and routed him on the 8th? Or is the account that he did fight and rout him false and fabricated? Both General Fremont and you speak of Jackson having beaten Shields. By our accounts he did not beat Shields. He had no engagement with Shields. He did meet and drive back with disaster about 2,000 of Shields's advance till they were met by an additional brigade of Shields's, when Jackson himself turned and retreated. Shields himself and more than half his force were not nearer than twenty miles to any of it.   A. Lincoln.

To Major-General McClellan.
                    Washington City, June 20, 1862.

We have this morning sent you a dispatch of General Sigel, corroborative of the proposition that Jackson is being re-inforced from Richmond. This may be reality and yet may be only contrivance for deception, and to determine which, is perplexing. If we knew it was not true, we could send you some more force, but as the case stands we do not think we safely can. Still, we will watch the signs and do so if possible.

In regard to a contemplated execution of Captains

Sprigg and Triplett, the government has no information whatever, but will inquire and advise you.

A. LINCOLN.

To Major-General McClellan.

Washington, June 21, 1862, 6 *P. M.*

Your dispatch of yesterday (2 P. M.) was received this morning. If it would not divert too much of your time and attention from the army under your immediate command, I would be glad to have your views as to the present state of military affairs throughout the whole country, as you say you would be glad to give them. I would rather it should be by letter than by telegraph, because of the better chance of secrecy. As to the numbers and position of the troops not under your command in Virginia and elsewhere, even if I could do so with accuracy, which I can not, I would rather not transmit either by telegraph or letter, because of the chances of its reaching the enemy. I would be glad to talk with you, but you can not leave your camp and I can not well leave here. A. LINCOLN.

PRESIDENTIAL ORDERS.

Executive Mansion, Washington, June 22, 1862.

Ordered, First. The forces under Major-Generals Fremont, Banks, and McDowell, including the troops now under Brigadier-General Sturges at Washington, shall be consolidated and form one army, to be called the Army of Virginia.

Second. The command of the Army of Virginia

is specially assigned to Major-General John Pope, as commanding general. The troops of the Mountain Department, heretofore under command of General Fremont, shall constitute the First Army Corps, under the command of General Fremont; the troops of the Shenandoah Department, now under General Banks, shall constitute the Second Army Corps, and be commanded by him; the troops under the command of General McDowell, except those within the fortifications and city of Washington, shall form the Third Army Corps, and be under his command.

Third. The Army of Virginia shall operate in such manner as, while protecting Western Virginia and the National capital from danger or insult, it shall in the speediest manner attack and overcome the rebel forces under Jackson and Ewell, threaten the enemy in the direction of Charlottesville, and render the most effective aid to relieve General McClellan and capture Richmond.

Fourth. When the Army of the Potomac and the Army of Virginia shall be in a position to communicate and directly co-operate at or before Richmond, the chief command, while so co-operating together, shall be governed, as in like cases, by the Rules and Articles of War. A. LINCOLN

To GENERAL McCLELLAN.

June 26, 1862.

Your three dispatches of yesterday, in relation to the affair, ending with the statement that you completely succeeded in making your point, are very gratifying. The later one, of 6½ P. M., suggesting the probability of your being overwhelmed by two hundred thousand men, and talking of whom the responsibility will belong to, pains me very much. I give you all I can, and act on the presumption that you will do the best you can with what you have; while you continue, ungenerously, I think, to assume that I could give you more if I would. I have omitted, I shall omit, no opportunity to send you re-inforcements whenever I possibly can. A. LINCOLN.

To GENERAL MCCLELLAN.

June 28, 1862.

Save your army at all events. Will send re-inforcements as fast as we can. Of course, they can not reach you to-day, to-morrow or next day. I have not said that you were ungenerous for saying you needed re-inforcements. I thought you were ungenerous in assuming that I did not send them as fast as I could. I feel any misfortune to you and your army as keenly as you feel it yourself. If you have had a drawn battle or a repulse, it is the price we pay for the enemy not being in Washington. We protected Washington, and the enemy concentrated on you. Had we stripped Washington, he would have been upon us before the troops sent could have got to you. Less than a week ago you notified us that re-inforcements were leaving Richmond to come in front of us. It is the nature of the case, and neither you nor the government is to blame. A. LINCOLN.

Hon. William H. Seward, Astor House, New York.
War Department, June 29, 1862, 6 *P. M.*

Not much more than when you left. Fulton, of Baltimore American, is now with us. He left White House at 11 A. M. yesterday. He conversed fully with a paymaster, who was with Porter's force during the fight of Friday, and fell back to nearer McClellan's quarters just a little sooner than Porter did, seeing the whole of it. Staid on the Richmond side of the Chickahominy over night, and left for White House at five A. M. Saturday. He says Porter retired in perfect order under protection of guns arranged for the purpose, under orders, and not from necessity, and with all others of our forces, except what was left on purpose to go to White House, was safely in position over the Chickahominy before morning, and that there was heavy firing on the Richmond side, begun at 5 and ceased at 7 A. M., Saturday. On the whole, I think we have had the better of it up to that point of time. What has happened since we still know not, as we have no communication with General McClellan. A dispatch from Colonel Ingalls shows that he thinks McClellan is fighting with the enemy at Richmond to-day, and will be to-morrow.

We have no means of knowing upon what Colonel Ingalls founds his opinion. All confirmed about saving all property. Not a single unwounded straggler came back to the White House from the field, and the number of wounded reaching there up to 11 A. M., Saturday, was not large.   A. Lincoln.

Hon. William H. Seward, New York.
War Department, June 30, 1862.
We are yet without communication with General McClellan, and this absence of news is our point of anxiety.

Up to the latest period to which we are posted he effected every thing in such exact accordance with his plan, contingently announced to us before the battle began, that we feel justified to hope that he has not failed since.

He had a severe engagement in getting the part of his army on this side of the Chickahominy over to the other side, in which the enemy lost certainly as much as we did.

We are not dissatisfied with this, only that the loss of enemies does not compensate for the loss of friends. The enemy can not come below White House; certainly is not there now, and probably has abandoned the whole line.

Dix's pickets are at New Kent Court-house.

A. Lincoln.

Major-General Hunter.
Executive Mansion, Washington, June 30, 1862.
My Dear General:—I have just received your letter of the 25th of June.

I assure you, and you may feel authorized in stating, that the recent change of commanders in the Department of the South was made for no reasons which convey any imputation upon your known energy, efficiency and patriotism, but for causes which seemed sufficient, while they were in no degree incompatible with the respect and esteeem in which I have always held you as a man and an officer.

I can not, by giving my consent to a publication of whose details I know nothing, assume the responsibility of whatever you may write. In this matter your own sense of military propriety must be your guide, and the regulation of the service your rule of conduct. I am, very truly, your friend,

A. LINCOLN.

To Major-General Dix, Fort Monroe.

War Department, Washington City, June 30, 1862.

Is it not probable the enemy has abandoned the line between White House and McClellan's rear? He could have but little object to maintain it, and nothing to subsist upon. Would not Stoneman better move up and see about it? I think a telegraphic communication can at once be opened to White House from Williamsburg. The wires must be up still. A. LINCOLN.

To McClellan, July 1, 1862.

It is impossible to re-inforce you for your present emergency. If we had a million of men we could not get them to you in time. We have not the men to send. If you are not strong enough to face the enemy, you must find a place of security, and wait, rest and repair. Maintain your ground if you can, but save the army at all events, even if you fall back to Fort Monroe. We still have strength enough in the country, and will bring it out. A. LINCOLN.

Letter to McClellan, July 2, 1862.

Your dispatch of yesterday induces me to hope that your army is having some rest. In the hope, allow me to reason with you for a moment. When you ask for 50,000 men to be promptly sent you, you surely labor under some gross mistake of fact. Recently you sent papers showing your disposal of forces made last spring for the defense of Washington, and advising a return to that plan. I find it included, in and about Washington, 75,000 men.

Now, please be assured that I have not men enough to fill that very plan by 15,000. All of General Fremont's in the valley, all of General Banks', all of General McDowell's not with you, and all in Washington taken together, do not exceed, if they reach, 60,000.

With General Wool and General Dix added to those mentioned, I have not, outside of your army, 75,000 men east of the mountains. Thus, the idea of sending you 50,000, or any other considerable force promptly, is simply absurd. If, in your frequent mention of responsibility, you have the impression that I blame you for not doing more than you can, please be relieved of such impression. I only beg that in like manner, you will not ask impossibilities of me.

If you think you are not strong enough to take Richmond just now, I do not ask you to try just now. Save the army, material and *personnel*, and I will strengthen it for the offensive again as fast as I can.

The governors of eighteen states offer me a new levy of 300,000, which I accept. A. LINCOLN.

To MAJOR-GENERAL HALLECK, CORINTH, MISS.

War Department, July 2, 1862.

Your several dispatches of yesterday to Secretary of War and myself received. I did say, and now repeat, I would be exceedingly glad for some reinforcements from you; still, do not send a man if, in your judgment, it will endanger any point you deem important to hold, or will force you to give up or weaken or delay the Chattanooga expedition. Please tell me, could you make me a flying visit for consultation without endangering the service in your department?

A. LINCOLN.

To MAJOR-GENERAL GEORGE B. McCLELLAN.

War Department, Washington, July 3, 1862.

Yours of 5:30 yesterday is just received. I am satisfied that yourself, officers and men have done the best you could. All accounts say better fighting was never done. Ten thousand thanks for it.

On the 28th we sent General Burnside an order to send all the force he could spare to you. We then learned that you had requested him to go to Goldsborough; upon which we said to him our order was intended for your benefit, and we did not wish to be in conflict with your views. We hope you will have help from him soon. To-day we have ordered General Hunter to send you all he can spare. At last advice General Hunter thinks he can not send reinforcements without endangering all he has gained.

A. LINCOLN, *President.*

To Governor Morton.

July 3, 1862.

My Dear Sir:—I would not want the half of 300,000 new troops if I could have them now. If I had 50,000 additional troops here now I believe I could substantially close the war in two weeks; but time is every thing, and if I get the 50,000 new men in a month I shall have lost 20,000 old ones during that same month, having gained only 30,000, with the difference between old and new troops still against me. The quicker you raise the troops the fewer you will have to send, and time is every thing. Please act in view of this. The enemy having given up Corinth, it is not wonderful that he is thereby enabled to check us for a time at Richmond. A. LINCOLN.

Letter to General McClellan.

War Dep't, Washington City, July 4, 1862.

I understand your position as stated in your letter, and by General Marcy. To re-inforce you so as to enable you to resume the offensive within a month, or even six weeks, is impossible. In addition to that arrived and now arriving from the Potomac (about 10,000 men, I suppose), and about 10,000, I hope, you will have from Burnside very soon, and about 5,000 from Hunter a little later, I do not see how I can send you another man within a month. Under these circumstances, the defensive, for the present, must be your only care.

Save the army, first, where you are, if you *can;* and secondly, by removal if you must. You, on the ground, must be the judge as to which you will attempt, and of the means for effecting it. I but give it as my opinion, that with the aid of the gunboats and the re-inforcements mentioned above, you can hold your present position; provided, and so long as you can keep the James river open below you. If you are not tolerably confident you can keep the James river open you had better remove as soon as possible. I do not remember that you have expressed any apprehension as to the danger of having your communication cut on the river below you, yet I do not suppose it can have escaped your attention.

A. LINCOLN.

To Major-General Halleck, Corinth, Miss.
War Department, Washington, D. C., July 6, 1862.

My Dear Sir:—This introduces Governor William Sprague, of Rhode Island. He is now governor for the third time and senator elect of the United States. I know the object of his visit to you. He has my cheerful consent to go, but not my direction. He wishes to get you and part of your force, one or both, to come here. You already know I should be exceedingly glad of this, if in your judgment it could be, without endangering positions and operations in the south-west, and I now repeat what I have more than once said by telegraph on this point: "Do not come or send a man if in your judgment it will endanger any point you deem important to hold or endanger or delay the Chattanooga expedition." Still, please give my friend Governor Sprague a full and fair hearing.

Yours very truly, A. LINCOLN.

To Hon. Andrew Johnson.

War Department, July 11, 1862.

My Dear Sir:—Yours of yesterday is received. Do you not, my good friend, perceive that what you ask is simply to put you in command of the West? I do not suppose you desire this. You only wish to control in your own localities; but this you must know may derange all other posts.

Can you not, and will you not have a full conference with General Halleck? Telegraph him and meet him at such place as you and he can agree upon.

I telegraph him to meet you and confer fully with you. A. LINCOLN.

Address to the Senators and Representatives of the Border States.

July, 1862.

Gentlemen:—After the adjournment of Congress, now near, I shall have no opportunity of seeing you for several months. Believing that you of the border states hold more power for good than any other equal number of members, I feel it a duty which I can not justifiably waive to make this appeal to you.

I intend no reproach or complaint when I assure you that, in my opinion, if you all had voted for the resolution in the gradual emancipation message of last March, the war would now be substantially ended.

And the plan therein proposed is yet one of the most potent and swift means of ending it. Let the states which are in rebellion see definitely and certainly that in no event will the states you represent ever join

their proposed confederacy, and they can not much
longer maintain the contest. But you can not divest
them of their hope to ultimately have you with them,
as long as you show a determination to perpetuate
the institution within your own states; beat them at
election as you have overwhelmingly done and nothing
daunted, they still claim you as their own. You and
I know what the lever of their power is. Break that
lever before their faces, and they can shake you no
more forever. Most of you have treated me with
kindness and consideration; and I trust you will not
now think I improperly touch what is exclusively
your own, when for the sake of the whole country, I
ask, can you, for your states, do better than to take
the course I urge? Discarding punctilio and maxims
adapted to more manageable times, and looking only
to the unprecedently stern facts of our case, can you
do better in any possible event? You prefer that the
constitutional relation of the states to the nation shall
be practically restored without disturbance of the institution;
and if this were done, my whole duty, in this
respect, under the constitution and my oath of office,
would be performed. But it is not done, and we are
trying to accomplish it by war.

The incidents of the war can not be avoided. If
the war continues long, as it must if the object be not
sooner attained, the institution in your states, will be
extinguished by mere friction and abrasion—by the
mere incidents of the war. It will be gone, and you
will have nothing valuable in lieu of it. Much of its
value is gone already. How much better for you and
your people, to take the step which at once shortens

the war, and secures substantial compensation for that which is sure to be wholly lost in any other event. How much better to thus save the money which else we sink forever in the war. How much better to do it while we can, lest the war ere long render us pecuniarily unable to do it. How much better for you, as seller, and the nation, as buyer, to sell out and buy out, that without which the war never could have been, than to sink both the thing to be sold and the price of it in cutting one another's throats. I do not speak of emancipation at once, but of a decision at once to emancipate gradually.

Room in South America for colonization can be obtained cheaply, and in abundance; and when numbers shall be large enough to be company and encouragement for one another, the freed people will not be so reluctant to go.

I am pressed with a difficulty not yet mentioned, one which threatens division among those who, united, are none too strong. An instance of it is known to you. General Hunter is an honest man. He was, and I hope still is, my friend. I valued him none the less for his agreeing with me in the general wish that all men every-where could be free. He proclaimed all men free within certain states, and I repudiated the proclamation. He expected more good and less harm from the measure than I could believe would follow. Yet, in repudiating it, I gave dissatisfaction, if not offense, to many whose support the country can not afford to lose. And this is not the end of it. The pressure in this direction is still upon me, and is increasing. By conceding what I now ask, you can relieve me, and, much more, can relieve the country in this important point.

Upon these considerations I have again begged your attention to the message of March last.

Before leaving the capital, consider and discuss it among yourselves. You are patriots and statesmen, and as such, I pray you consider this proposition; and at the least, commend it to the consideration of your states and people. As you would perpetuate popular government, for the best people in the world, I beseech you that you do in no wise omit this.

Our common country is in great peril, demanding the loftiest views and boldest action, to bring a speedy relief. Once relieved, its form of government is saved to the world; its beloved history and cherished memories are vindicated; and its happy future fully assured, and rendered inconceivably grand. To you, more than to any others, the privilege is given to assure that happiness and swell that grandeur, and to link your own names therewith forever.

To McClellan, July 13, 1862.

My Dear Sir:—I am told that over 160,000 men have gone with your army to the Peninsula. When I was with you the other day, we made out 86,000 remaining, leaving 73,500 to be accounted for. I believe 23,500 will cover all the killed, wounded, and missing, in all your battles and skirmishes, leaving 50,000 who have left otherwise, and more than 5,000 of these have died, leaving 45,000 of your army still alive and not with it. I believe half or two-thirds of them are fit for duty to-day. Have you any more perfect knowledge of this than I have? If I am right, and you had these men with you, you could go into Richmond in the next three days. How can they be got to you, and how can they be prevented from getting away in such numbers for the future?

A. LINCOLN.

PRESIDENT'S NOMINATION, JULY 16, 1862.

The President of the United States of America to all who shall see these presents, greeting:

Know ye that, reposing special trust and confidence in the patriotism, valor, fidelity, and abilities of Fitz John Porter, I have nominated, and, by and with the advice and consent of the Senate, do appoint him major-general of volunteers in the service of the United States, to rank as such from the 4th day of July, 1862. He is, therefore, carefully and diligently to discharge the duty of major-general, by doing and performing all manner of things thereunto belonging. And I do strictly charge and require all officers and soldiers under his command to be obedient to his orders as major-general. And he is to observe and follow such orders and directions, from time to time, as he shall recieve from me, or the future President of the United States of America, or the general, or other superior officers set over him, according to the rules and discipline of war. This commission to continue in force during the pleasure of the President of the United States for the time being.

Given under my hand, at the city of Washington, this 16th day of July, in the year of our Lord one thousand eight hundred and sixty-two, and in the eighty-seventh year of the independence of the United States. ABRAHAM LINCOLN.

COMMUNICATION TO CONGRESS, JULY 17, 1862.

Fellow-Citizens of the Senate and House of Representatives:—Considering the bill for an act to suppress insurrection, to punish treason and rebellion, to seize and confiscate the property of the rebels and other purposes, and the joint resolution explanatory of said act as being substantially one, I have approved and signed both.

Before I was informed of the passage of the resolution, I had prepared the draft of a message stating objections to the bill becoming a law, a copy of which draft is herewith transmitted.

ABRAHAM LINCOLN.

Fellow-Citizens of the House of Representatives:—I herewith return to your honorable body, in which it originated, the bill for an act entitled An act to suppress treason and rebellion, to sieze and confiscate the property of the rebels, and for other purposes, together with my objections to its becoming a law. There is much in the bill to which I perceive no objection. It is wholly prospective, and it touches neither the person nor property of any loyal citizen, in which particular it is just and proper. The first and second sections provide for the conviction and punishment of persons who shall be guilty of treason, and the persons who shall incite, set on foot, assist, or engage in any rebellion or insurrection against the authority of the United States, or the laws thereof, or shall give aid or comfort to any such existing rebellion or insurrection.

By fair construction, the persons within these sections are not to be punished without regular trials in duly constituted courts under the forms and all the substantial provisions of law and of the Constitution applicable to their several cases. To this I perceive no objection, especially as such persons would be within the general pardoning power, and also within the special provision for pardon and amnesty contained in this act. It also provides that the slaves of persons confiscated under these sections shall be free. I think there is an unfortunate form of expression rather than a substantial objection in this. It is startling to say that Congress can free a slave within a state, and yet were it said that the ownership of a slave had first been transferred to the nation, and that Congress had then liberated him, the difficulty would vanish, and this is the real case. The traitor against the general government forfeits his slave, at least as justly as he does any other property, and he forfeits both to the government against which he offends.

The government, so far as there can be ownership, owns the forfeited slaves, and the question for Congress in regard to them is, shall they be made free or sold to new masters? I see no objection to Congress deciding in advance that they shall be free. To the high honor of Kentucky, as I am informed, she has been the owner of some slaves by escheat, and has sold none, but liberated all.

I hope the same is true of some other states. Indeed I do not believe it would be physically possible for the general government to return persons so circumstanced to actual slavery. I believe there would be physical resistance to it, which would never be turned aside by argument, nor driven away by force. In this view of it, I have no objection to this feature of the bill. Another matter, valued in these two sections, and running through other parts of the act, will be noticed hereafter.

I perceive no objection to the third and fourth sections. So far as I wish to notice the fifth and sixth sections, they may be considered together. That the enforcement of these sections would do no injustice to the persons embraced within them is clear. That those who make a causeless war should be compelled to pay the cost of it is too obviously just to be called into question. To give government protection to the property of persons who have abandoned it, and gone on a crusade to overthrow that same government, is absurd, if considered in the mere light of justice. The severest justice may not always be the best policy. The principle of seizing and appropriating the property of the persons embraced within these sections is certainly not very objectionable, but a justly discriminating application of it would be very difficult, and to a great extent impossible; and would it not be wise to place a power of remission somewhere, so that these persons may know that they have something to save by desisting?

I am not sure whether such power of remission is or is not within section thirteen, without a special act of Congress. I think our military commanders, when, in military phrase, they are within the enemy's country, should in an orderly manner seize and keep whatever of real or personal property may be necessary or convenient for their demands, and at the same time preserve in some way the evidence of what they do.

What I have said in regard to slaves, while commenting on the first and second sections, is applicable to the ninth, with the difference that no provision is made in the whole act for determining whether a particular individual slave does or does not fall within the class defined within that section. He is to be free upon certain conditions, but whether these conditions do or do not pertain to him, no mode of ascertaining is provided. This could be easily supplied.

To the tenth section I make no objection. The oath therein required seems to be proper, and the remainder of the section is substantially identical with a law already existing.

The eleventh section simply assumes to confer discretionary powers upon the Executive without the law. I have no hesitation to go as far in the direction indicated as I may at any time deem expedient, and I am ready to say now I think it is proper for our military commanders to employ as laborers as many persons of African descent as can be used to advantage.

The twelfth and thirteenth sections are something better—they are unobjectionable—and the fourteenth is entirely proper, if all other parts of the act shall stand.

That to which I chiefly object pervades most parts of the act, but more distinctly appears in the first, second, seventh, and eighth sections. It is the sum of those provisions which results in the divesting of title forever. For the causes of treason—the ingredients of treason, but amounting to the full crime—it declares forfeiture extending beyond the lives of the guilty parties, whereas the Constitution of the United States declares that no attainder of treason shall work corruption of blood or forfeiture, except during the life of the person attainted. True, there is to be no formal attainder in this case, still I think the greater punishment can not be constitutionally inflicted in a different form for the same offense. With great respect I am constrained to say I think this feature of the act is unconstitutional. It would not be difficult to modify it. I may remark that the provision of the Constitution, put in language borrowed from Great Britain, applies only in this country, as I understand, to real estate.

Again, this act, by proceedings *in rem*, forfeits property for the ingredients of treason without a conviction of the supposed criminal, or a personal hearing given him in any proceeding. That we may not touch property lying within our reach because we can not give personal notice to an owner who is absent endeavoring to destroy the government, is certainly not very satisfactory. Still the owner may not be thus engaged, and I think a reasonable time should be provided for such parties to appear and have personal hearings. Similar provisions are not uncommon in connection with proceedings *in rem*.

For the reason stated I return the bill to the house in which it originated.

To CUTHBERT BULLITT, ESQ., NEW ORLEANS, LA.

Washington, D. C., July 28, 1862.

Sir :—The copy of a letter addressed to yourself by Mr. Thomas J. Durant has been shown to me. The writer appears to be an able, a dispassionate and an entirely sincere man.

The first part of the letter is devoted to an effort to show that the secession ordinance of Louisiana was adopted against the will of the majority of the people. This is probable true, and in that fact may be found some instruction. Why did they allow the ordinance to go into effect? Why did they not exert themselves? Why stand passive and allow themselves to be trodden down by a minority? Why did they not hold popular meetings, and have a convention of their own to express and enforce the true sentiments of the state? If pre-organization were against them, then why not do this now that the United States army is present to protect them?

The paralysis—the dread palsy—of the government in the whole struggle is, that this class of men will do nothing for the government—nothing for themselves, except demanding that the government shall not strike its enemies, lest they be struck by accident. Mr. Durant complains, that in various ways, the relation of master and slave is disturbed by the presence of our army; and he considers it particularly vexatious that this, in part, is done under cover of an act of Congress, while constitutional guarantees are superseded on the pleas of military necessity.

The truth is, that what is done and omitted about slaves is done and omitted on the same military necessity. It is a military necessity to have men and money; and we can not get either in sufficient numbers or amounts, if we keep from or drive from our lines slaves coming to them. Mr. Durant can not be ignorant of the pressure in this direction, nor of my efforts to hold it within bounds, till he, and such as he, shall have time to help themselves. I am not posted to speak understandingly on the public regulations of which Mr. Durant complains. If experience shows any of them to be wrong, let them be set right. I think I can perceive in the freedom of trade which Mr. Durant urges, that he would relieve both friends and enemies from the pressure of the blockade. By this he would serve the enemy more effectively than the enemy is able to serve himself.

I do not say or believe that to serve the enemy is the purpose of Mr. Durant, or that he is conscious of any purposes other than national and patriotic ones. Still, if this were a class of men who, having no choice of sides in the contest, were anxious only to have quiet and comfort for themselves while it rages, and to fall in with the victorious side at the end of it, without loss to themselves, their advice as to the mode of conducting the contest would be precisely such as his.

He speaks of no duty, apparently thinks of none,

resting upon Union men. He even thinks it injurious to the Union cause that they should be restrained in trade and passages, without taking sides.

They are to touch neither a sail nor a pump line, merely passengers ("dead heads" at that)— be carried snug and dry throughout the storm and safely landed right side up. Nay, more—even a mutineer is to go untouched, lest these sacred passengers receive an accidental wound.

Of course the rebellion will never be suppressed in Louisiana, if the professed Union men there will neither help to do it, nor permit the government to do it without their help. Now, I think the remedy is very different from that suggested by Mr. Durant. It does not lie in rounding the rough angles of the war, but in removing the necessity for the war. The people of Louisiana, who wish protection to person and property, have but to reach forth their hands and take it. Let them in good faith re-inaugurate the national authority and set up a state government conforming thereto under the constitution. They know how to do it, and have the protection of the army while doing it. The army will be withdrawn as soon as such government can dispense with its presence, and the people of the state can then, upon the old terms, govern themselves to their liking. This is very simple and easy.

If they do not do this, if they prefer to hazard all for the sake of destroying the government, it is for them to consider whether it is probable I will surrender the government to save them from losing all.

If they decline what I suggest, you will scarcely need to ask what I will do. What would you do in my position? Would you drop the war where it is? Or would you prosecute it in future with elder-stalk squirts, charged with rose-water? Would you deal lighter blows rather than heavier ones? Would you give up the control leaving every available means unapplied? I am in no boastful mood. I shall not do more than I can, but I shall do all I can to save the government, which is my sworn duty as well as my personal inclination. I shall do nothing in malice. What I deal with is too vast for malicious dealing.

Yours truly, A. LINCOLN.

REMARKS AT A UNION MEETING IN WASHINGTON, AUGUST, 6, 1862.

Fellow-Citizens:—I believe there is no precedent for my appearing before you on this occasion, but it is also true that there is no precedent for your being here yourselves, and I offer, in justification of myself and of you, that, upon examination, I have found nothing in the constitution against it. I, however, have an impression that there are younger gentlemen who will entertain you better, and better address your understanding than I will or could, and therefore I propose to detain you but a moment longer.

I am very little inclined on any occasion to say anything unless I hope to produce some good by it. The only thing I think of just now not likely to be better said by some one else, is a matter in which we have heard some other persons blamed for what I did myself. There has been a very widespread attempt to have a quarrel between General McClellan and the Secretary of War. Now, I occupy a position that enables me to observe, that these two gentlemen are not nearly so deep in the quarrel as some pretending to be their friends. General McClellan's attitude is such that, in the very selfishness of his nature, he can not but wish to be successful, and I hope he will—and the Secretary of War is in precisely the same situation. If the military commanders in the field can not be successful, not only the Secretary of War, but myself, for the time being the master of them both, can not but be failures.

I know General McClellan wishes to be successful, and I know that he does not wish it any more than the Secretary of War for him, and both of them together not more than I wish it. Sometimes we have a dispute about how many men General McClellan has had, and those who would disparage him say that he has had a very large number, and those who would disparage the Secretary of War insist that General McClellan has had a very small number. The basis for this is, there is always a wide difference, and on this occasion, perhaps a wider one than usual, between the grand total on McClellan's rolls and the men actually fit for duty; and those who would disparage him talk of the grand total on paper, and those who would disparage the Secretary of War talk of those at present fit for duty.

General McClellan has sometimes asked for things

that the Secretary of War did not give him. General McClellan is not to blame for asking for what he wanted and needed, and the Secretary of War is not to blame for not giving when he had none to give. And I say here, as far as I know, the Secretary of War has withheld no one thing at any time in my power to give him. I have no accusation against him. I believe he is a brave and able man, and I stand here, as justice requires me to do, to take upon myself what has been charged on the Secretary of War, as withholding from him. I have talked longer than I expected to do, and now I avail myself of my privilege of saying no more.

THE PRESIDENT ON COLONIZATION, AUGUST 14, 1862.

Perhaps you have long been free, or all your lives. Your race is suffering, in my judgment, the greatest wrong inflicted on any people. But even when you cease to be slaves, you are yet far removed from being placed on an equality with the white race. You are cut off from many of the advantages which the other race enjoys. The aspiration of men is to enjoy equality with the best when free, but on this broad continent not a single man of your race is made the equal of a single man of ours. Go where you are treated the best, and the ban is still upon you. I do not propose to discuss this, but to present it as a fact, with which we have to deal. I can not alter it if I would. It is a fact about which we all think and feel alike, I and you. We look to our condition. Owing to the existence of the two races on this continent, I need not recount to you the effects upon white men, growing out of the institution of slavery. I believe in its general evil effects on the white race. See our present condition—the country engaged in war; our white men cutting one another's throats—none knowing how far it will extend—and then consider what we know to be the truth. But for your race among us there could not be war, although many men engaged on either side do not care for you one way or the other. Nevertheless, I repeat, without the institution of slavery, and the colored race as a basis, the war could not have an existence.

It is better for us both therefore to be separated. I know that there are free men among you who, even if they could better their condition, are not as much inclined to go out of the country as those who, being slaves, could obtain their freedom on this condition. I suppose one of the principal difficulties in the way of colonization is that the free colored man can not see that his comfort would be advanced by it. You may believe that you can live in Washington, or elsewhere in the United States, the remainder of your life; perhaps more so than you can in any foreign country, and hence you may come to the conclusion that you have nothing to do with the idea of going to a foreign country. This is (I speak in no unkind sense) an extremely selfish view of the case. But you ought to do something to help those who are not so fortunate as yourselves. There is an unwillingness on the part of our people, harsh as it may be, for you free colored people to remain with us. Now, if you could give a start to the white people you would open a wide door for many to be made free. If we deal with those who are not free at the beginning, and whose intellects are clouded by slavery, we have very poor material to start with. If intelligent colored men, such as are before me, would move in this matter, much might be accomplished. It is exceedingly important that we have men at the beginning capable of thinking as white men, and not those who have been systematically oppressed. There is much to encourage you. For the sake of your race you should sacrifice something of your present comfort for the purpose of being as grand in that respect as the white people. It is a cheering thought throughout life, that something can be done to ameliorate the condition of those who have been subject to the hard usages of the world. It is difficult to make a man miserable while he feels he is worthy of himself and claims kindred to the great God who made him. In the American Revolutionary war sacrifices were made by men engaged in it, but they were cheered by the future. General Washington himself endured greater physical hardships than if he had remained a British subject, yet he was a happy man, because he was engaged in benefiting his race, in doing something for the children of his neighbors, having none of his own.

The colony of Liberia has been in existence a long time. In a certain sense it is a success. The old President of Liberia, Roberts, has just been with me, the first time I ever saw him. He says they have within the bounds of that colony between three and four hundred thousand people, or more than in some of our old states, such as Rhode Island or Delaware, or in some of our newer states, and less than in some of our larger ones.

They are not all American colonists or their descendants. Something less than 12,000 have been sent thither from this country. Many of the original settlers have died, yet, like people elsewhere, their offspring outnumber those deceased. The question is, if the colored people are persuaded to go anywhere, why not there? One reason for unwillingness to do so is, that some of you would rather remain in reach of the country of your nativity. I do not know how much attachment you may have toward our race. It does not strike me that you have the greatest reason to love them. But still you are attached to them at all events. The place I am thinking about having for a colony is in Central America. It is nearer to us than Liberia, not much more than one-fourth as far as Liberia, and within seven days run by steamers. Unlike Liberia, it is a great line of travel, it is a highway. The country is a very excellent one for any people, and with great natural resources and advantages, and especially because of the similarity of climate with your native soil, thus being suited to your physical condition.

The particular place I have in view is to be a great highway from the Atlantic or Caribbean Sea to the Pacific Ocean, and this particular place has all the advantages for a colony. On both sides there are harbors among the finest in the world. Again, there is evidence of very rich coal mines. A certain amount of coal is valuable in any country. Why I attach so much importance to coal is it will afford an opportunity to the inhabitants for immediate employment till they get ready to settle permanently in their homes. If you take colonists where there is no good landing, there is a bad show; and so where there is nothing to cultivate, and of which to make a farm. But if something is started, so that you can get your daily bread as soon as you reach there, it is a great advantage. Coal land is the best thing I know of with which to commence an enterprise. To return, you have been talked to upon this subject, and told that a speculation is intended by gentlemen who have an interest in the country, including the coal mines. We have been mistaken all our lives if we do not know whites, as well as blacks, look to their self-interest. Unless among those deficient of intellect, every body you trade with makes something. You meet with these things here and every-where. If such persons have what will be an advantage to them, the question is, whether it can not be made of advantage to you? You are intelligent, and know that success does not as much depend on external help as on self-reliance. Much, therefore, depends upon yourselves. As to the coal mines, I think I see the means available for your self-reliance. I shall, if I get a sufficient number of you engaged, have provision made that you will not be wronged. If you will engage in the enterprise, I will spend some of the money intrusted to me. I am not sure you will succeed. The government may lose the money, but we can not succeed unless we try; but we think with care we can succeed. The political affairs in Central America are not in quite as satisfactory condition as I wish. There are contending factions in that quarter, but it is true all the factions are agreed alike on the subject of colonization, and want it, and are more generous than we are here. To your colored race they have no objection. Besides, I would endeavor to have you made equals, and have the best assurance that you should be the equals of the best. The practical thing I want to ascertain is, whether I can get a number of able-bodied men, with their wives and children, who are willing to go, when I present evidence, encouragement, and protection. Could I get a hundred tolerably intelligent men, with their wives and children, and able to "cut their own fodder," so to speak? Can I have fifty? If I could find twenty-five able-bodied men, with a mixture of women and children—good things in the family relation, I think—I could make a successful commencement. I want you to let me know whether this can be done or not. This is the practical part of my wish to see you. These are subjects of very great importance, worthy of a month's study, of a speech delivered in an hour. I ask you, then, to consider seriously, not pertaining to yourselves merely, nor for your race and ours for the present time, but as one of the things, if successfully managed, for the good of mankind, not confined to the present generation, but as

> "From age to age descends the lay
> To millions yet to be,
> Till far it's echoes roll away
> Into eternity."

LETTER TO HORACE GREELEY, AUG. 22, 1862.

Dear Sir:—I have just read yours of the 19th inst., addressed to myself through the New York Tribune. If there be in it any statements or assumptions of fact which I may know to be erroneous, I do not now and here controvert them. If there be any inferences which I may believe to be falsely drawn, I do not now and here argue against them. If there be perceptible in it an impatient and dictatorial tone, I waive it in deference to an old friend whose heart I have always supposed to be right.

As to the policy I "seem to be pursuing," as you say, I have not meant to leave any one in doubt. I would save the Union. I would save it in the shortest way under the Constitution. The sooner the national authority can be restored, the nearer the Union will be—the Union as it was. If there be those who would not save the Union unless they could at the same time save slavery, I do not agree with them.

If there be those who would not save the Union unless they could at the same time destroy slavery, I do not agree with them. My paramount object is to save the Union, and not either to save or destroy slavery.

If I could save the Union, without freeing any

slave, I would do it; if I could save it by freeing all the slaves, I would do it; and if I could do it by freeing some, and leaving others alone, I would also do that. What I do about slavery and the colored race, I do because I believe it helps to save this Union. And what I forbear, I forbear because I do not believe it would help to save the Union.

I shall do less whenever I shall believe what I am doing hurts the cause, and I shall do more whenever I believe doing more will help the cause.

I shall try to correct errors when shown to be errors, and I shall adopt new views so fast as they shall appear to be true views.

I have here stated my purpose according to my views of official duty, and I intend no modification of my oft-expressed personal wish that all men everywhere could be free. Yours, A. LINCOLN.

LETTER TO MAJ.-GEN. J. C. FREMONT, SEPT. 11, 1862.

Sir:—Yours of the 8th, in answer to mine of the 2d inst., was just received. Assuming that you, upon the ground, could better judge of the necessities of your position than I could at this distance, on seeing your proclamation of August 30th, I perceived no general objection to it; the particular clause, however, in relation to the confiscation of property and the liberation of slaves, appeared to me to be objectionable in its non-conformity to the act of Congress passed the 6th of last August upon the same subject, and hence I wrote you expressing my wish that the clause should be modified accordingly. Your answer, just received, expresses the preference on your part that I should make an open order for the modification, which I very cheerfully do.

It is therefore ordered that the said clause of said proclamation be so modified, held, and construed as to conform with and not to transcend the provisions on the same subject contained in the act of Congress, entitled "An act to confiscate property used for insurrectionary purposes, approved August 6, 1861," and that said act be published at length with this order. Your obedient servant, A. LINCOLN.

To HIS EXCELLENCY, ANDREW G. CURTIN, GOVERNOR OF PENNSYLVANIA, HARRISBURG, PA.

War Department, Washington, D. C., Sept. 11, 1862.

Sir:—The application made to me by your adjutant-general for authority to call out the militia of the State of Pennsylvania has received careful consideration. It is my anxious desire to afford, as far as possible, the means and power of the Federal Government to protect the State of Pennsylvania from invasion by the rebel force, and since, in your judgment, the militia of the state are required, and have been called upon by you to organize for home defense and protection, I sanction the call that you have made, and will receive them into the service and pay of the United States to the extent they can be armed, equipped, and usefully employed. The arms and equipments now belonging to the general government will be needed for the troops called out for the national armies, so that arms can only be furnished for the quota of militia furnished by the draft of nine months men, heretofore ordered. But, as arms may be supplied by the militia under your call, these, with the 30,000 in your arsenal, will probably be sufficient for the purpose contemplated by your call. You will be authorized to provide such equipments as may be required, according to the regulations of the United States service, which, upon being turned over to the United States Quartermaster's Department, will be paid for at regulation prices, or the rates allowed by the department for such articles. Railroad transportation will also be paid for, as in other cases. Such general officers will be supplied as the exigencies of the service will permit.

    Yours truly, Abraham Lincoln.

To Hon. Andrew G. Curtin, Harrisburg, Pa.
War Department, Washington, D. C.,
   September 12, 1862, 10:35 *A. M.*

Your dispatch, asking for 80,000 disciplined troops to be sent to Pennsylvania, is received. Please consider we have not to exceed 80,000 disciplined troops, properly so called, this side of the mountains, and most of them, with many of the new regiments, are now close in the rear of the enemy supposed to be invading Pennsylvania. Start half of them to Harrisburg, and the enemy will turn upon and beat the remaining half, and then reach Harrisburg before the part going there, and beat it, too, when it comes. The best possible security for Pennsylvania is putting the strongest force possible into the enemy's rear.

          A. Lincoln.

To Hon. Alexander Henry, Philadelphia.

War Department, Washington, D. C., Sept. 12, 1862.

Yours of to-day received—General Halleck has made the best provision he can for generals in Pennsylvania. Please do not be offended when I assure you that in my confident belief Philadelphia is in no danger. Governor Curtin has just telegraphed me. I have advices that Jackson is crossing the Potomac at Williamsport, and probably the whole rebel army will be drawn from Maryland. At all events, Philadelphia is more than a hundred and fifty miles from Hagerstown, and could not be reached by the rebel army in ten days, if no hindrance was interposed.   A. Lincoln.

Remarks Respecting the Issue of the Proclamation, September 13, 1862.

The President gave an audience to a deputation from all the religious denominations of Chicago, presenting a memorial for the immediate issue of an emancipation proclamation, which was enforced by some remarks by the chairman. The President replied:—The subject presented in the memorial is one upon which I have thought much for weeks past, and I may even say for months. I am approached with the most opposite opinions and advice, and that by religious men, who are equally certain that they represent the Divine will. I am sure that either the one or the other class is mistaken in that belief, and perhaps, in some respect, both. I hope it will not be irreverent for me to say that if it is probable that God would reveal his will to others, on a point so connected with my duty, it might be supposed He would reveal it directly to me; for, unless I am more deceived in myself than I often am, it is my earnest desire to know the will of Providence in this matter, and if I can learn what it is, I will do it. These are not, however, the days of miracles, and I suppose it will be granted that I am not to expect a direct revelation. I must study the plain physical facts of the case, ascertain what is possible, and learn what appears to be wise and right.

The subject is difficult, and good men do not agree. For instance, the other day four gentlemen of standing and intelligence from New York called as a delegation on business connected with the war, but before leaving, two of them earnestly besought me to proclaim general emancipation, upon which the other two at once attacked them. You know also that the last session of Congress had a decided majority of anti-slavery men, yet they could not unite on this policy. And the same is true of the religious people. Why, the rebel soldiers are praying with a great deal more earnestness, I fear, than our own troops, and expecting God to favor their side, for one of our soldiers, who had been taken prisoner, told Senator Wilson a few days since, that he met nothing so discouraging as the evident sincerity of those he was among in their prayers. But we will talk over the merits of the case.

What good would a proclamation of emancipation from me do, especially as we are now situated? I do not want to issue a document that the whole world will see must necessarily be inoperative, like the Pope's bull against the comet. Would my word free the slaves when I can not even enforce the Constitution in the rebel states? Is there a single court or magistrate, or individual, that would be influenced by it there? And what reason is there to think it would have any greater effect upon the slaves than the late law of Congress, which I approved, and which offers protection and freedom to the slaves of rebel masters who come within our lines? Yet I can not learn that that law has caused a single slave to come over to us. And suppose they could be induced by a proclamation of freedom from me to throw themselves upon us, what should we do with them? How can we feed and care for such a multitude? General Butler wrote me a few days since that he was issuing more rations to the slaves who have rushed to him, than to all the white troops under his command. They eat, and that is all, though it is true General Butler is feeding the whites also by the thousand, for it nearly amounts to a famine there. If now, the pressure of the war should call off our forces from New Orleans to defend some other point, what is to prevent the masters from reducing the blacks to slavery again, for I am told that whenever the rebels take any black prisoners, free or slave, they immediately auction them off. They did so with those they took from a boat that was aground in the Tennessee river a few days ago. And then I am very ungenerously attacked for it. For instance, when after the late battles at and near Bull Run, an expedition went out from Washington under a flag of truce, to bury the dead and bring in the wounded, and the rebels seized the blacks who went along to help, and sent them into slavery,

Horace Greeley said in his paper that the government would probably do nothing about it. What could I do?

Now, then, tell me, if you please, what possible result of good would follow the issuing of such a proclamation as you desire? Understand, I raise no objections against it on legal or constitutional grounds, for, as commander-in-chief of the army and navy, in time of war I suppose I have a right to take any measure which may best subdue the enemy; nor do I raise objections of a moral nature, in view of possible consequences of insurrection and massacre at the south. I view this matter as a practical war measure, to be decided on according to the advantages or disadvantages it may offer to the suppression of the rebellion.

I admit that slavery is at the root of the rebellion, or at least its *sine qua non*. The ambition of politicians may have instigated them to act, but they would have been impotent without slavery as their instrument. I will also concede that emancipation would help us in Europe, and convince them that we are incited by something more than ambition. I grant, further, that it would help somewhat at the North, though not so much, I fear, as you and those you represent imagine. Still, some additional strength would be added in that way to the war, and then, unquestionably, it would weaken the rebels by drawing off their laborers, which is of great importance; but I am not so sure we could do much with the blacks. If we were to arm them, I fear that in a few weeks the arms would be in the hands of the rebels; and, indeed, thus far, we have not had arms enough to equip our white troops. I will mention another thing, though it meet only your scorn and contempt. There are 50,000 bayonets in the Union army from the border slave states. It would be a serious matter if, in consequence of a proclamation such as you desire, they should go over to the rebels. I do not think they all would—not so many, indeed, as a year ago, or as six months ago—not so many to-day as yesterday.

Every day increases their Union feeling. They are also getting their pride enlisted, and want to beat the rebels. Let me say one thing more: I think you should admit that we already have an important principle to rally and unite the people, in the fact that constitutional government is at stake. This is a fundamental idea going down about as deep as any thing.

Do not misunderstand me because I have mentioned these objections. They indicate the difficulties that have thus far prevented my action in some such way as you desire. I have not decided against a proclamation of liberty to the slaves, but hold the matter under advisement. And I can assure you that the subject is on my mind, by day and night, more than any other. Whatever shall appear to be God's will I will do. I trust that in the freedom with which I have canvassed your views I have not in any respect injured your feelings.

Proclamation of Emancipation.

I, Abraham Lincoln, President of the United States of America, and commander-in-chief of the army and navy thereof, do hereby proclaim and declare that hereafter, as heretofore, the war will be prosecuted for the object of practically restoring the constitutional relation between the United States and each of the states, and the people thereof, in which states that relation is or may be suspended or disturbed.

That it is my purpose, upon the next meeting of Congress, to again recommend the adoption of a practical measure tendering pecuniary aid to the free acceptance or rejection of all slave states so called— the people whereof may not then be in rebellion against the United States, and which states may then have voluntarily adopted, or thereafter may voluntarily adopt, immediate or gradual abolishment of slavery within their respective limits; and that the effort to colonize persons of African descent, with their consent, upon this continent or elsewhere, with the previously obtained consent of the governments existing there, will be continued.

That on the first day of January, in the year of our Lord one thousand eight hundred and sixty-three, all persons held as slaves within any state, or designated part of a state, the people whereof shall then be in rebellion against the United States, shall be then, thenceforward, and forever free; and the Executive Department of the United States, including the military and naval authority thereof, will recognize and maintain the freedom of such persons, and will do no act or acts to repress such persons, or any of them, in any efforts they may make for their actual freedom.

That the Executive will, on the first day of January, by proclamation aforesaid, designate the states and parts of states, if any, in which the people thereof respectively shall then be in rebellion against the United State; and the fact that any state, or the people thereof, shall on that day be in good faith represented in the Congress of the United States, by members chosen thereto at election wherein a majority of the qualified voters of such state shall have participated, shall, in the absence of strong countervailing testimony, be deemed conclusive evidence that such state, and the people thereof, are not then in rebellion against the United States.

The attention is hereby called to an act of Congress, entitled:

"AN ACT to make an additional Article of War" approved March 13, 1862, and which act is in the words and figures following:

Be it enacted by the Senate and House of Representatives of the United States of America, in Congress assembled, That hereafter the following shall be promulgated as an additional article of war for the government of the army of the United States, and shall be obeyed and observed as such:

Article.—All officers or persons in the military or naval service of the United States are prohibited from employing any of the forces under their respective commands for the purpose of returning fugitives from service or labor who may have escaped from any persons to whom such service or labor is claimed to be due; and any officer who shall be found guilty by a court-martial of violating this article shall be dismissed from the service.

Sec. 2. *And be it further enacted*, That this act shall take effect from and after its passage.

Also, to the ninth and tenth sections of an act entitled "An act to Suppress Insurrection, to Punish Treason and Rebellion, to Seize and Confiscate Property of Rebels, and for Other Purposes," approved July 16, 1862, and which sections are in the words and figures following:

Sec. 9. *And be it further enacted*, That all slaves of persons who shall hereafter be engaged in rebellion against the Government of the United States, or who shall in any way give aid or comfort thereto, escaping from such persons and taking refuge within the lines of the army; and all slaves captured from such persons, or deserted by them and coming under the control of the Government of the United States; and all slaves of such persons found on [or] being within any place occupied by rebel forces and afterwards occupied by forces of the United States, shall be deemed captives of war, and shall be forever free of their servitude, and not again held as slaves.

Sec. 10. *And be it further enacted*, That no slave escaping into any state, territory, or the District of Columbia, from any other state, shall be delivered up, or in any way impeded or hindered of his liberty, except for crime, or some offense against the laws, unless the person claiming such fugitive shall first make oath that the person to whom the labor or service of such fugitive is alleged to be due is his lawful owner, and has not borne arms against the United States in the present rebellion, nor in any way given aid or comfort thereto; and no person engaged in the military or naval service of the United States shall, under any pretense whatever, assume to decide on the validity of the claim of any person to the service or labor of any other person, or surrender up any such person to the claimant, on pain of being dismissed from the service.

And I do hereby enjoin upon and order all persons engaged in the military or naval service of the United States to observe, obey, and enforce, within their respective spheres of service, the act and sections above recited.

And the Executive will in due time recommend that all citizens of the United States who shall have remained loyal thereto throughout the rebellion, shall (upon the restoration of the constitutional relation between the United States and their respective states and people, if that relation shall have been suspended or disturbed) be compensated for all losses by acts of the United States, including the loss of slaves.

In witness whereof, I have hereunto set my hand and caused the seal of the United States to be affixed.

Done at the City of Washington, this twenty-second day of September, in the year of our Lord one thousand eight hundred and sixty-two, and of the independence of the United States the eighty-seventh.

ABRAHAM LINCOLN.

SPEECH AT SERENADE IN HONOR OF THE EMANCIPATION PROCLAMATION, SEPTEMBER 24, 1862.

Fellow-citizens: — I appear before you to do little more than to acknowledge the courtesy you pay me, and to thank you for it. I have not been distinctly informed why it is on this occasion you appear to do me this honor, though I suppose it is because of the proclamation. I was about to say, I suppose I understand it. What I did, I did after very full deliberation, and under a very heavy and solemn sense of responsibility. I can only trust in God I have made no mistake. I shall make no attempt on this occasion to sustain what I have done or said by any comment. It is now for the country and the world to pass judgment upon it, and, may be, take action upon it. I will say no more upon this subject. In my position I am environed with difficulties. Yet they are scarcely so great as the difficulties of those who, upon the battle field, are endeavoring to purchase with their blood and their lives the future happiness and prosperity of the country. Let us never forget them. On the fourteenth and seventeenth days of the present month there have been battles bravely, skillfully, and successfully fought. We do not yet know the particulars. Let us be sure that in giving praise to particular individuals, we do no injustice to others. I only ask you at the conclusion of these few remarks to give three hearty cheers to all good and brave officers and men who fought these successful battles.

To Major John J. Key.

Executive Mansion, Washington, September 26, 1862.

Sir:—I am informed that in answer to the question, "Why was not the rebel army bagged immediately after the battle near Sharpsburg?" propounded to you by Major Levi C. Turner, Judge Advocate, etc., you answered: "That is not the game. The object is, that neither army shall get much advantage of the other; that both shall be kept in the field till they are exhausted, when we will make a compromise and save slavery."

I shall be very happy if you will, within twenty-four hours from the receipt of this, prove to me by Major Turner that you did not, either literally or in substance, make the answer stated. Yours,

A. LINCOLN.

At about eleven o'clock A. M., September 27, 1862, Major Key and Major Turner appeared before me. Major Turner says, "As I remember it, the conversation was: I asked the question, why we did not bag them after the battle of Sharpsburg. Major Key's reply was, That was not the game; that we should tire the rebels out and ourselves; that that was the only way the Union could be preserved; we come together fraternally, and slavery be saved."

On cross-examination Major Turner says he has frequently heard Major Key converse in regard to the present troubles, and never heard him utter a sentiment unfavorable to the maintenance of the Union. He has never uttered any thing which he, Major Turner, would call disloyalty. The particular conversation detailed was a private one.

A. LINCOLN.

INDORSED ON THE ABOVE.

In my view it is wholly inadmissible for any gentleman holding a military commission from the

United States to utter such sentiments as Major Key is within proved to have done. Therefore, let Major John J. Key be forthwith dismissed from the military service of the United States.   A. LINCOLN.

TO THOMAS H. CLAY, CINCINNATI, OHIO.

War Department, October 8, 1862.

You can not have reflected seriously when you ask that I shall order General Morgan's command to Kentucky as a favor because they have marched from Cumberland Gap. The precedent established by it would eventually break up the whole army. Buell's old troops now in pursuit of Bragg have done more hard marching recently; and, in fact, if you include marching and fighting, there are scarcely any old troops east or west of the mountains that have not done as hard service.

I sincerely wish war was an easier and pleasanter business than it is, but it does not admit of holidays. On Morgan's command, where it is now sent, as I understand, depends the question whether the enemy will get to the Ohio river in another place.

A. LINCOLN.

LETTER TO GENERAL MCCLELLAN, OCTOBER 13, 1862.

My Dear Sir.—You remember my speaking to you of what I called your over-cautiousness. Are you not over-cautious when you assume that you can not do what the enemy is constantly doing? Should you not claim to be at least his equal in prowess and act upon the claim?

As I understand you telegraphed General Halleck

that you can not subsist your army at Winchester, unless the railroad from Harper's Ferry to that point be put in working order. But the enemy does now subsist his army at Winchester at a distance nearly twice as great from railroad transportation as you would have to do without the railroad last named. He now wagons from Culpepper Court-house, which is just about twice as far as you would have to do from Harper's Ferry. He is certainly not more than half as well provided with wagons as you are. I certainly should be pleased for you to have the advantage of the railroad from Harper's Ferry to Winchester; but it wastes all the remainder of autumn to give it to you, and in fact ignores the question of *time*, which can not and must not be ignored. Again, one of the standard maxims of war, as you know, is " to operate upon the enemy's communications as much as possible without exposing your own." You seem to act as if this applies *against* you, but can not apply in your *favor*. Change positions with the enemy, and think you not he would break your communication with Richmond within the next twenty-four hours? You dread his going into Pennsylvania.

But if he does so in full force he gives up his communications to you absolutely, and you have nothing to do but to follow and ruin him; if he does so with less than full force, fall upon and beat what is left behind all the easier.

Exclusive of the water line, you are now nearer Richmond than the enemy is by the route that you *can*, and he *must* take.

Why can you not reach there before him, unless

you admit that he is more than your equal on a march. His route is the arc of a circle, while yours is the chord. The roads are as good on yours as on his.

You know I desired, but did not order, you to cross the Potomac below instead of above the Shenandoah and Blue Ridge.

My idea was, that this would at once menace the enemy's communications, which I would seize if he would permit. If he should move northward, I would follow him closely, holding his communications. If he should prevent our seizing his communications, and move toward Richmond, I would press closely to him, fight him if a favorable opportunity should present, and at least try to beat him to Richmond on the inside track. I say "try;" if we never try, we shall never succeed. If he make a stand at Winchester, moving neither north nor south, I would fight him there, on the idea that if we can not beat him, when he bears the wastage of coming to us, we never can when we bear the wastage of going to him. This proposition is a simple truth, and is too important to be lost sight of for a moment. In coming to us, he tenders us an advantage which we should not waive. We should not so operate as to merely drive him away. As we must beat him somewhere, or fail finally, we can do it, if at all, easier near to us than far away. If we can not beat the enemy where he now is, we never can, he again being within the intrenchments at Richmond. Recurring to the idea of going to Richmond on the inside track, the facility of supplying from the side away from the enemy, is remarkable, as it were, by the different spokes of a wheel, extending from the hub toward the rim, and this whether you move directly by the chord or on the inside arc, hugging the Blue Ridge more closely. The chord line, as you see, carries you by Aldie, Haymarket, and Fredericksburg, and you see how turnpikes, railroads, and finally the Potomac, by Aquia creek, meet you at all points from Washington. The same, only the lines lengthened a little, if you press closer to the Blue Ridge part of the way. The gaps through the Blue Ridge I understand to be about the following distances from Harper's Ferry, to wit: Vestals, five miles; Gregory's, thirteen; Snicker's, eighteen; Ashby's, twenty-eight; Manassas, thirty-eight; Chester, forty-five; and Thornton's, fifty-three. I should think it preferable to take the route nearest the enemy, disabling him to make an important move without your knowledge, and compelling him to keep his forces together for dread of you. The gaps would enable you to attack if you should wish. For a great part of the way you would be practically between the enemy and both Washington and Richmond, enabling us to spare you the greatest number of troops from here. When, at length, running for Richmond ahead of him, enables him to move this way; if he does so, turn and attack him in the rear. But I think he should be engaged long before such point is reached. It is all easy if your troops march as well as the enemy, and it is unmanly to say they can not do it. This letter is in no sense an order. Yours, truly, A. LINCOLN.

ORDER ESTABLISHING A PROVISIONAL COURT.

Executive Mansion, Washington, Oct. 20, 1862.

The insurrection which has for some time prevailed in several of the states in this Union, including Louisiana, having temporarily subverted and swept away the civil institutions of that state, including the judiciary and the judicial authorities of the Union, so that it has become necessary to hold the state in military occupation, and it being indispensably necessary that there shall be some judicial tribunal existing there capable of administering justice, I have therefore thought it proper to appoint, and I do hereby constitute a provisional court, which shall be a court of record for the State of Louisiana, and I do hereby appoint Charles A. Peabody, of New York, to be a provisional judge to hold such court, with authority to hear, try, and determine all causes, civil and criminal, including causes in law, equity, revenue, and admiralty, and particularly with all such powers and jurisdiction as belong to the district and circuit court of the United States, conforming his proceedings, as far as possible, to the course of proceedings and practice which has been customary in the courts of the United States and Louisiana—his judgment to be final and conclusive. And I do hereby authorize and empower the said judge to make and establish such rules and regulations as may be necessary for the exercise of his jurisdiction, and to appoint a prosecuting attorney, marshal and clerk of the said court, who shall perform the functions of attorney, marshal and clerk according to such proceedings and practice as before mentioned, and such rules and regulations as may be made and established by said judge. These appointments are to continue during the pleasure of the president, not extending beyond the military occupation of the city of New Orleans, or the restoration of the civil authority in that city and in the State of Louisiana. These officers shall be paid out of the contingent fund of the war department. ABRAHAM LINCOLN.

LETTER GIVEN TO THOMAS R. SMITH, OF BOLIVAR, TENN

October 31, 1862.

Major-General Grant, Governor Johnson, and all having military, naval and civil authorities under the United States within the State of Tennessee: The bearer of this, Thomas R. Smith, a citizen of Tennessee, goes to that state, seeking to have such of the people thereof as desire to avoid the unsatisfactory prospect before them, and to have peace again upon the old terms, under the Constitution of the United States, to manifest such desire by election of members to the Congress of the United States particularly, and perhaps a legislature, state officers, and a United States senator, friendly to their object. I shall be glad for you and each of you, to aid him, and all others acting for this object, as much as possible. In all available ways give the people a chance to express their wishes at these elections. Follow law and forms of law as far as convenient; but, at all events, get the expression of the largest number of people possible. All see how such an action will connect with and affect the proclamation of September 22. Of course the men elected should be gentlemen of character, willing to swear to support the constitution as of old, and known to be above reasonable suspicion of duplicity. Yours very respectfully, A. LINCOLN.

TO McCLELLAN, OCTOBER 25, 1862.

I have just read your dispatch about sore-tongue and fatigued horses. Will you pardon me for asking what the horses of your army have done since the battle of Antietam that fatigues any thing?

A. LINCOLN.

TO McCLELLAN, OCTOBER 26, 1862.

Yours in reply to mine about horses received. Of course you know the facts better than I. Still, two considerations remain; Stuart's cavalry outmarched ours, having certainly done more marked service on the peninsula and every where since. Secondly; will not a movement of our army be a relief to the cavalry, compelling the enemy to concentrate instead of "foraging" in squads every-where? But I am so rejoiced to learn from your dispatch to General Halleck that you began crossing the river this morning.

A. LINCOLN.

Executive Mansion, Washington, Nov. 1, 1862.
To whom it may concern:—Captain Derrickson, with his company, has been for some time keeping guard at my residence, now at the Soldiers' Retreat. He and his company are very agreeable to me, and while it is deemed proper for any guard to remain, none would be more satisfactory to me than Captain D— and his company. A. LINCOLN.

Letter to Governor Bradford, November, 2, 1863.

Sir:—Yours of the 31st ultimo was received yesterday about noon, and since then I have been giving most earnest attention to the subject-matter of it. At my call General Schenck has attended, and he assures me it is almost certain that violence will be used at some of the voting places on election day, unless prevented by his provost guards. He says that in some of those places the Union voters will not attend at all, or run a ticket, unless they have assurance of protection. This makes the Missouri case of my action, in regard to which you express your approval.

The remaining point of your letter is a protest against any person offering to vote being put to any test not found in the laws of Maryland. This brings us to a difference between Missouri and Maryland. With the same reason in both states, Missouri has, by law, provided a test for the voter with reference to the present rebellion, while Maryland has not. For example, General Trimble, captured fighting us at Gettysburg, is, without recanting his treason, a legal voter by the laws of Maryland. Even General Schenck's order admits him to vote, if he recants upon oath. I think that is cheap enough. My order in Missouri, which you approve, and General Schenck's order here, reach precisely the same end. Each assures the right of voting to all loyal men, and whether that man is loyal, each allows that man to fix by his own oath. Your suggestion that nearly all the candidates are loyal I do not think quite meets the case.

In this struggle for the nation's life, I can not so

confidently rely on those whose election may have depended upon disloyal votes. Such men, when elected, may prove true, but such votes are given them in expectation that they will prove false. Nor do I think that to keep the peace at the polls, and to prevent the persistently disloyal from voting, constitutes just cause of offense to Maryland. I think she has her own example for it. If I mistake not, it is precisely what General Dix did when your excellency was elected governor. I revoke the first of the three propositions in General Schenck's general order, No. 53, not that it is wrong in principle, but because the military being of necessity exclusive judges as to who shall be arrested, the provision is liable to abuse. For the revoked part I substitute the following:

That all provost marshals and other military officers do prevent all disturbance and violence at or about the polls, whether offered by such persons as above described, or by any other person or persons whatsoever.

The other two propositions of the order I allow to stand. General Schenck is fully determined, and has my strict order besides, that all loyal men may vote, and vote for whom they please.

Your obedient servant,   A. LINCOLN.

PRESIDENT'S ORDER RELIEVING GENERAL MCCLELLAN.

Executive Mansion, Washington, November 5, 1862.

By direction of the President, it is ordered that Major-General McClellan be relieved from the command of the Army of the Potomac, and that Major-General Burnside take command of that army. Also that Major-General Hunter take command of the corps in said army which is now commanded by General Burnside. That Major-General Fitz John Porter be relieved from the command of the corps he now commands in said army, and that Major-General Hooker take command of such corps.

The General-in-chief is authorized in (his) discretion, to issue an order substantially as the above, forthwith, or so soon as he may deem proper. A. LINCOLN.

PROCLAMATION.

Executive Mansion, Washington, Nov., 16, 1862.

The President, Commander-in-chief of the Army and Navy, desires and enjoins the orderly observance of the Sabbath by the officers and men in the military and naval service. The importance for man and beast of the prescribed weekly rest, the sacred rights of Christian soldiers and sailors, a becoming deference to the best sentiment of a Christian people, and a due regard for the Divine will, demand that Sunday labor in the army and navy be reduced to the measure of strict necessity.

The discipline and character of the national forces should not suffer, nor the cause they defend be imperiled, by the profanation of the day or the name of the Most High. "At the time of public distress," adopting the words of Washington in 1776, "men may find enough to do in the service of God and their country, without abandoning themselves to vice and immorality." The first general order issued by the Father of his Country, after the Declaration of Independence, indicates the spirit in which our institutions were founded, and should ever be defended. "The general hopes and trusts that every officer and man will endeavor to live and act as becomes a Christian soldier defending the dearest rights and liberties of his country." A. LINCOLN.

LETTER TO CARL SCHURZ, NOVEMBER 24, 1862.

I have just received and read your letter of the 20th. The purport of it is that we lost the late elections, and the administration is failing because the war is unsuccessful, and that I must not flatter myself that I am not justly to blame for it. I certainly know that if the war fails the administration fails, and that I will be blamed for it, whether I deserve it or not. And I ought to be blamed, if I could do better. You think I could do better, therefore you blame me already. I think I could not do better, therefore I blame you for blaming me. I understand you now to be willing to accept the help of men who are not Republicans, provided they have "heart in it." Agreed. I want no others. But who is to be the judge of hearts, or of "heart in it?" If I must discard my own judgment, and take yours, I must also take that of others; and by the time I should reject all I should be advised to reject, I should have none left, Republicans or others, not even yourself, for be assured, my dear sir, there are men who have "heart in it" that think you are performing your part as poorly as you think I am performing mine. I certainly have been dissatisfied with the slowness of Buell and McClellan, but be-

fore I relieved them I had great fears I should not
find successors to them who would do better; and I
am sorry to add that I have seen little since to relieve those fears. I do not clearly see the prospect
of any more rapid movements. I fear we shall at
last find out the difficulty is in our case rather than
in particular generals. I wish to disparage no one,
certainly not those who sympathize with me, but I
must say I need success more than I need sympathy,
and that I have not seen the so much greater evidence of getting success from my sympathizers than
from those who are denounced as the contrary. It
does seem to me that in the field the two classes
have been very much alike in what they have done
and what they have failed to do. In sealing their
faith with their blood, Baker, and Lyon, and Bohlen,
and Richardson, Republicans, did all that men could
do; but did they any more than Kearney, Stevens,
and Reno, and Mansfield, none of whom were Republicans, and some at least of whom have been bitterly
and repeatedly denounced to me as secession sympathizers? I will not perform the ungrateful task of
comparing cases of failure. In answer to your question, Has it not been publicly stated in the newspapers, and apparently proved as a fact, that from
the commencement of the war the enemy was continually supplied with information by some of the
confidential subordinates of as important an officer
as Adjutant-General Thomas? I must say, "No," as
far as my knowledge extends. And I add if you can
give any tangible evidence upon the subject, I will
thank you to come to this city and do so.

Second Annual Message, December 1, 1862.

Fellow-Citizens of the Senate and House of Representatives:—Since your last annual assembling another year of health and bountiful harvests has passed. And while it has not pleased the Almighty to bless us with a return of peace, we can but press on, guided by the best light He gives us, trusting that in His own good time and wise way all will yet be well.

The correspondence touching foreign affairs which has taken place during the last year is herewith submitted, in virtual compliance with a request to that effect made by the House of Representatives near the close of the last session of Congress.

If the condition of our relations with other nations is less gratifying than it has usually been at former periods, it is certainly more satisfactory than a nation so unhappily distracted as we are, might reasonably have apprehended. In the month of June last there were some grounds to expect that the maritime powers which, at the beginning of our domestic difficulties, so unwisely and unnecessarily, as we think, recognized the insurgents as a belligerant, would soon recede from that position, which has proved only less injurious to themselves than to our own country. But the temporary reverses which afterward befell the national arms, and which were exaggerated by our own disloyal citizens abroad, have hitherto delayed that act of simple justice.

The civil war, which has so radically changed, for the moment, the occupations and habits of the American people, has necessarily disturbed the social condition and affected very deeply the prosperity of the nations with which we have carried on a commerce that has been steadily increasing throughout a period of half a century. It has, at the same time, excited political ambitions and apprehensions which have produced a profound agitation throughout the civilized world. In this unusual agitation we have forborne from taking part in any controversy between foreign states, and between parties or factions in such states. We have attempted no propagandism, and acknowledged no revolution. But we have left to every nation the exclusive conduct and management of its own affairs. Our struggle has been, of course, contemplated by foreign nations with reference less to its own merits than to its supposed and often exaggerated effects and consequences resulting to those nations themselves. Nevertheless, complaint on the part of this government, even if it were just, would certainly be unwise.

The treaty with Great Britain for the suppression of the slave trade has been put into operation with a good prospect of complete success. It is an occasion of special pleasure to acknowledge that the execution of it, on the part of her majesty's government, has been marked with a jealous respect for the authority of the United States, and the rights of their moral and loyal citizens.

The convention with Hanover for the abolition of the state dues has been carried into full effect, under the act of Congress for that purpose.

A blockade of three thousand miles of sea-coast could not be established, and vigorously enforced, in a season of great commercial activity like the present, without committing occasional mistakes and inflicting unintentional injuries upon foreign nations and their subjects.

A civil war, occurring in a country where foreigners reside, and carry on trade under treaty stipulations, is necessarily fruitful of complaints of the violation of neutral rights. All such collisions tend to excite misapprehensions, and possibly to produce mutual reclamations between nations which have a common interest in preserving peace and friendship. In clear cases of these kinds, I have, so far as possible, heard and redressed complaints which have been presented by friendly powers. There is still, however, a large and an augmenting number of doubtful cases upon which the government is unable to agree with the government whose protection is demanded by the claimants.

There are, moreover, many cases in which the United States, or their citizens, suffer wrongs from the naval or military authorities of foreign nations, which the governments of those states are not at once prepared to redress.

I have proposed to some of the foreign states, thus interested, mutual conventions to examine and adjust such complaints. This proposition has been made especially to Great Britain, to France, to Spain, and to Prussia. In each case it has been kindly received, but has not yet been formally adopted.

Applications have been made to me by many free Americans of African descent to favor the emigration with a view to such colonization as was contemplated in recent acts of Congress. Other parties, at home and abroad—some from interested motives, others upon patriotic considerations, and still others influenced from philanthropic sentiments—have suggested similar measures. While, on the other hand, several of the Spanish-American republics have protested against the sending of such colonies to their respective territories. Under these circumstances, I have declined to move any such colony to any state, without first obtaining the consent of its government, with an agreement on its part to receive and protect such emigrants in all the rights of freemen; and I have, at the same time, offered to the several states situated within the tropics, or having colonies there, to negotiate with them, subject to the advice and consent of the Senate, to favor the voluntary emigration of persons of that class to their respective territories, upon conditions which shall be equal, just and humane. Liberia and Hayti are, as yet, the only countries to which colonists of African descent from here could go with certainty of being received and adopted as citizens; and I regret to say such persons, contemplating colonization, do not seem so willing to migrate to those countries as to some others, nor so willing as I think their interest demands. I believe, however, opinion among them in this respect is improving; and that, ere long, there will be an augmented and considerable migration to both those countries from the United States.

On the 22d day of September last, a proclamation was issued by the Executive, a copy of which is herewith submitted.

In accordance with the purpose expressed in the second paragraph of that paper, I now respectfully recall your attention to what may be called "compensated emancipation."

A nation may be said to consist of its territory, its people, and its laws. The territory is the only part which is of certain durability. "One generation passeth away, and another generation cometh, but the earth abideth forever." It is of the first importance to duly consider and estimate this ever enduring part. That portion of the earth's surface which is owned and inhabited by the people of the United States is well adapted to be the home of one national family, and it is not well adapted for two, or more. Its vast extent, and its variety of climate and productions, are of advantage, in this age, for one people, whatever they might have been in former ages. Steam, telegraphs, and intelligence have brought these to be an advantageous combination for one united people.

In the inaugural address, I briefly pointed out the total inadequacy of disunion as a remedy for the differences between the people and the two sections. There is no line, straight or crooked, suitable for a national boundary upon which to divide. Trace through, from east to west, upon the line between the free and slave country, and we shall find a little more than one-third of its length are rivers, easy to be crossed, and populated, or soon to be populated, thickly, upon both sides; while nearly all its remaining length are merely surveyors' lines, over which people may walk back and forth without any consciousness of their presence. No part of this line can be made any more difficult to pass by writing it down on paper or parchment as a national boundary. The fact of separation, if it comes, gives up, on the part of the seceding section, the fugitive slave cause, along with all other constitutional obligations upon the section seceded from, while I should expect no treaty stipulation would ever be made to take its place.

But there is another difficulty. The great interior region, bounded east by the Alleghanies, north by the British Dominions, west by the Rocky mountains, and south by the line along which the culture of corn and cotton meets, and which includes part of Virginia, part of Tennessee, all of Kentucky, Ohio, Indiana, Michigan, Wisconsin, Illinois, Missouri, Kansas, Iowa, Minnesota, and the territories of Dakota, Nebraska, and part of Colorado, already has above ten million people, and will have fifty million within fifty years, if not prevented by any political folly or mistake. It contains more than one-third of the country owned by the United States—certainly more than one million square miles. Once half as populous as Massachusetts already is, it would have more than seventy-five million people. A glance at the map shows that, territorially speaking, it is the great body of the republic.

The other parts are but marginal borders to it, the magnificent region sloping west from the Rocky mountains to the Pacific, being the deepest and also the richest in undeveloped resources. In the production of provisions, grains, grasses, and all which proceed from them, this great interior region is naturally one of the most important in the world. Ascertain from the statistics the small proportion of the region which has, as yet, been brought into cultivation, and also the large and rapidly increasing amount of its products, and we shall be overwhelmed with the magnitude of the prospect presented. And yet this region has no sea-coast; touches no ocean anywhere. As part of one nation, its people now find, and may forever find, their way to Europe by New York, to South America and Africa by New Orleans, and to Asia by San Francisco. But separate our common country into two nations, as designed by the present rebellion, and every man of this great interior region is thereby cut off from some one or more of these outlets, not, perhaps, by a physical barrier, but by embarassing and onerous trade regulations.

And this is true wherever a dividing or boundary line may be fixed. Place it between the now free and slave country, or place it south of Kentucky, or north of Ohio, and still the truth remains, that none south of it can trade to any port or place north of it, and none north of it can trade to any port or place south of it, except upon terms dictated by a government foreign to them. These outlets, east, west and south, are indispensable to the well-being of the people inhabiting, and to inhabit this vast interior region. *Which* of the three may be the best is no proper question. All are better than either; and all of right belong to that people, and to their successors forever. True to themselves, they will not ask *where* a line of separation shall be, but will vow rather that there shall be no such line. Nor are the marginal regions less interested in these communications to and through them, to the great outside world. They, too, and each of them, must have access to this Egypt of the west, without paying toll at the crossing of any national boundary.

Our national strife springs not from our permanent part; not from the land we inhabit; not from our national homestead. There is no possible severing of this, but would multiply, and not mitigate evils among us. In all its adaptations and aptitudes, it demands union, and abhors separation. In fact, it would, ere long, force reunion, however much of blood and treasure the separation might have cost.

Our strife pertains to ourselves—to the passing generations of men; and it can, without convulsion, be hushed forever with the passing of one generation.

In this view, I recommend the adoption of the following resolution and articles amendatory to the Constitution of the United States:

"*Resolved by the Senate and House of Representatives of the United States of America in Congress assembled* (two-thirds of both houses concurring), That the following articles be proposed to the legislature (or conventions) of the several states as amendments to the Constitution of the United States, all or any of which articles when ratified by three-fourths of the said legislature (or conventions), to be valid as part or parts of the said Constitution, namely:

"Article—Every state, wherein slavery now exists, which shall abolish the same therein, at any time, or times, before the first day of January, in the year of our Lord one thousand nine hundred, shall receive compensation from the United States, as follows, to wit:

The President of the United States shall deliver to every such state bonds of the United States, bearing interest at the rate of —— for each slave shown to have been therein by the eighth census of the United States, such bonds to be delivered to such states by installments, or in one parcel, at the completion of the abolishment, accordingly as the same shall have been gradual, or at one time, within such state; and interest shall begin to run upon any such bond only from the proper time of its delivery as aforesaid.

Any state having received bonds as aforesaid, and afterward reintroducing or tolerating slavery therein, shall refund to the United States the bonds so received, or the value thereof, and all interest paid thereon.

"Article—All slaves who shall have enjoyed actual freedom by the chances of the war at any time before the end of the rebellion, shall be forever free; but all owners of such, who shall not have been disloyal, shall be compensated for them, at the same rates as is provided for states adopting abolishment of slavery, but in such way that no slave shall be twice accounted for.

"Article—Congress may appropriate money and otherwise provide for colonizing free colored persons, with their own consent, at any place or places without the United States."

I beg indulgence to discuss these proposed articles at some length. Without slavery the rebellion could never have existed; without slavery it could not continue.

Among the friends of the Union there is great diversity of sentiment and of policy in regard to slavery and the African race among us. Some would perpetuate slavery; some would abolish it suddenly, and without compensation; some would abolish it gradually, and with compensation; some would remove the freed people from us, and some would retain them with us; and there are yet other minor diversities. Because of these diversities, we waste much strength in struggles among ourselves. By mutual concession we should harmonize and act together. This would be compromise, but it would be compromise among the friends, and not with the enemies of the Union. These articles are intended to embody a plan of such mutual concessions. If the plan shall be adopted, it is assumed that emancipation will follow, at least, in several of the states.

As to the first article, the main points are, first, the emancipation; secondly, the length of time for consummating it—thirty-seven years—and, thirdly, the compensation.

The emancipation will be unsatisfactory to the advocates of perpetual slavery; but the length of time should greatly mitigate their dissatisfaction. The time spares both races from the evils of sudden derangement—in fact, from the necessity of any derangement—while most of those whose habitual course of thought will be disturbed by the measure will have passed away before its consummation. They will never see it. Another class will hail the prospect of emancipation, but will deprecate the length of time. They will feel that it gives too little to the now living slaves. But it really gives them much. It saves them from the vagrant destitution which must largely attend immediate emancipation in localities where their numbers are very great; and it gives the inspiring assurance that their posterity shall be free forever. The plan leaves to each state, choosing to act under it, to abolish slavery now or at the end of the century, or at any intermediate time, or by degrees, extending over the whole or any part of the period; and it obliges no two states to proceed alike.

It also provides for compensation, and generally, the mode of making it. This, it would seem, must further mitigate the dissatisfaction of those who favor perpetual slavery, and especially of those who are to receive the compensation. Doubtless some of those who are to pay, and not to receive, will object. Yet the measure is both just and economical. In a certain sense, the liberation of slaves is the destruction of property—property acquired by descent, or by purchase, the same as any other property.

It is no less true for having been often said, that the people of the South are not more responsible for the original introduction of this property than are the people of the North; and when it is remembered how unhesitatingly we all use cotton and sugar, and share the profits of dealing in them, it may not be quite safe to say that the South has been more responsible than the North for its continuance.

If, then, for a common object, this property is to

be sacrificed, is it not just that it be done at a common charge?

And if, with less money, or money more easily paid, we can preserve the benefits of the Union by this means than we can by the war alone, is it not also economical to do it? Let us consider it then. Let us ascertain the sum we have expended in the war since compensated emancipation was proposed last March, and consider whether, if that measure had been promptly accepted, by even some of the slave states, the same sum would not have done more to close the war than has been otherwise done. If so, the measure would save money, and, in that view, would be a prudent and economical measure. Certainly it is not so easy to pay *something* as it is to pay *nothing*—but it is easier to pay a *large* sum than it is to pay a larger one. And it is easier to pay any sum when we are able, than it is to pay it *before* we are able. The war requires large sums, and requires them at once. The aggregate sum necessary for compensated emancipation, of course, would be large. But it would require no ready cash, nor the bonds even, any faster than the emancipation progresses. This might not, and probably would not, close before the end of the thirty-seven years.

At that time we shall probably have a hundred million people to share the burden instead of thirty-one millions as now. And not only so, but the increase of our population may be expected to continue for a long time after that period as rapidly as before; because our territory will not have become full. I do not state this inconsiderately. At the same ratio of increase which we have maintained, on an average, from our first national census in 1790, until that of 1860, we should, in 1900, have a population of 103,-208,415. And why may we not continue that ratio far beyond that period? Our abundant room—our broad national homestead—is our ample resource. Were our territory as limited as are the British Isles, very certainly our population could not expand as stated. Instead of receiving the foreign born, as now, we should be compelled to send part of the native born away.

But such is not our condition. We have two million nine hundred and sixty-three thousand square miles. Europe has three million and eight hundred thousand, with a population averaging seventy-three and one-third persons to the square mile. Why may not our country, at some time, average as many? Is it less fertile? Has it more waste surface by mountains, rivers, lakes, deserts, or other causes? Is it inferior to Europe in any natural advantage? If then we are at some time to be as populous as Europe, how soon? As to when this *may* be, we can judge by the past and the present; as to when it will be, if ever, depends much on whether we maintain the Union.

The proposed emancipation would shorten the war, perpetuate peace, insure this increase of population, and proportionately the wealth of the country. With these, we should pay all the emancipation would cost, together with our other debt, easier than we should pay our other debt without it. If we had allowed our old national debt to run at six per cent. per annum, simple interest, from the end of our revolutionary struggle until to-day, without paying any thing on either principal or interest, each man of us would owe less upon that debt now, than each man owed upon it then; and this because our increase of men through our whole period has been greater than six per cent., has run faster than the interest upon the debt. Thus, time alone relieves a debtor nation, so long as its population increases faster than its unpaid interest accumulates on its debt.

This fact would be no excuse for delaying payment of what is justly due, but, it shows the great importance of time in this connection—the great advantage of a policy by which we shall not have to pay until we number a hundred million, what, by a different policy, we would have to pay now, when we number but thirty-one millions. In a word, it shows that a dollar will be much harder to pay for the war than will be a dollar for emancipation on the proposed plan. And then the latter will cost no blood, no precious life. It will be a saving of both.

As to the second article, I think it would be impracticable to return to bondage the class of persons therein contemplated. Some of them, doubtless, in the property sense, belong to loyal owners, and hence provision is made in this article for compensating such.

The third article relates to the future of the freed people. It does not oblige, but merely authorizes, Congress to aid in colonizing such as may consent. This ought not to be regarded as objectionable on the one hand or on the other, insomuch as it comes to nothing, unless by the mutual consent of the people to be deported, and the American voters, through their representatives in Congress.

I can not make it better known than it already is, that I strongly favor colonization. And yet I wish to say there is an objection urged against free colored persons remaining in the country which is largely imaginary, if not some times malicious.

It is insisted that their presence would injure and despoil white labor and white laborers. If there ever could be a proper time for mere catch arguments, that time surely is not now.

In times like the present, men should utter nothing for which they would not willingly be responsible through time and eternity. Is it true, then, that colored people can displace any more white labor by being free than by remaining slaves? If they stay in their old places, they jostle no white laborers; if they leave their old places, they leave them open to white laborers. Logically, there is neither more or less of it. Emancipation, even without deportation, would probably enhance the wages of white labor, and very surely would not reduce them. Thus, the customary amount of labor would still have to be performed.

The freed people would surely not do more than their old proportion of it, and, very probably, for a time would do less, leaving an increased part to white laborers, bring their labor into greater demand, and consequently enhancing the wages of it. With deportation, even to a limited extent, enhanced wages to white labor is mathematically certain. Labor is like any other commodity in the market—increase the demand for it and you increase the price of it. Reduce the supply of black labor by colonizing the black labor out of the country, and by precisely so much you increase the demand for and wages of white labor.

But it is dreaded that the freed people will swarm forth, and cover the whole land. Are they not already in the land? Will liberation make them any more numerous? Equally distributed among the whites of the whole country, and there would be but one colored to seven whites. Could the one, in any way, greatly disturb the seven? There are many communities now, having more than one freed colored person to seven whites; and this, without any apparent consciousness of evil from it. The District of Columbia, and the states of Maryland and Delaware, are all in this condition. The district has more than one free colored to six whites; and yet, in its frequent petitions to Congress, I believe it has never presented the presence of free colored persons as one of its grievances. But why should emancipation south send the freed people north? People, of any color, seldom run, unless there be something to run from. *Heretofore*, colored people, to some extent, have fled north from bondage, and now, perhaps, from both bondage and destitution. But if gradual emancipation and deportation be adopted, they will have neither to flee from. Their old masters will give them wages, at least until new laborers can be procured; and the freed men, in turn, will gladly give their labor for the wages, till new homes can be found for them, in congenial climes, and with people of their own blood and race. This proposition can be trusted on the mutual interests involved. And, in any event, can not the north decide for itself whether to receive them?

Again, as practice proves more than theory, in any case, has there been any irruption of colored people northward because of the abolishment of slavery in this district last spring?

What I have said of the proportion of free colored persons to the whites in the district is from the census of 1860, having no reference to persons called contrabands, nor to those made free by the act of Congress abolishing slavery here.

The plan consisting of these articles is recommended, not but that a restoration of the national authority would be accepted without its adoption.

Nor will the war, nor proceedings under the proclamation of September 22, 1862, be stayed because of the *recommendation* of this plan. Its timely *adoption*, I doubt not, would bring restoration, and thereby stay both.

And, notwithstanding this plan, the recommendation that Congress provide by law for compensating any state which may adopt emancipation before this plan shall have been acted upon, is hereby earnestly renewed. Such would be only an advance part of the plan, and the same arguments apply to both.

This plan is recommended as a means, not in exclusion of but additional to all others for restoring and preserving the national authority throughout the Union. The subject is presented exclusively in its economical aspect. The plan would, I am confident,

secure peace more speedily, and maintain it more
permanently, than can be done by force alone; while
all it would cost, considering amounts, and manner of
payment, and times of payment, would be easier paid
than will be the additional cost of the war, if we rely
solely upon force. It is much, very much, that it
would cost no blood at all.

The plan is proposed as permanent constitutional
law. It can not become such without the concurrence
of, first, two-thirds of Congress, and afterward,
three-fourths of the states. The requisite three-
fourths of the states will necessarily include seven of
the slave states. Their concurrence, if obtained, will
give assurance of their severally adopting emancipation at no very distant day upon the new constitutional terms. This assurance would end the struggle
now, and save the Union forever.

I do not forget the gravity which should character-
ize a paper addressed to the Congress of the nation
by the chief magistrate of the nation. Nor do I
forget that some of you are my seniors, nor that
many of you have more experience than I in the
conduct of public affairs. Yet I trust that in view of
the great responsibility resting upon me, you will
perceive no want of respect to yourselves in any
undue earnestness I may seem to display.

Is it doubted, then, that the plan I propose, if
adopted, would shorten the war, and thus lessen its
expenditure of money and of blood? Is it doubted
that it would restore the national authority and
national prosperity, and perpetuate both indefinitely?
Is it doubted that we here—Congress and Executive

—can secure its adoption? Will not the good people respond to a united and earnest appeal from us? Can we, can they, by any other means, so certainly or so speedily assure these vital objects? We can succeed only by concert. It is not "can *any* of us *imagine* better," but "can we *all* do better?" Object whatsoever is possible, still the question recurs, "can we do better? The dogmas of the quiet past are inadequate to the stormy present. The occasion is piled high with difficulty, and we must rise with the occasion. As our case is new, so we must think anew and act anew. We must disenthrall ourselves, and then we shall save our country.

Fellow Citizens, we can not escape history. We of this Congress and this administration, will be remembered in spite of ourselves. No personal significance, or insignificance, can spare one or another of us. The fiery trial through which we pass will light us down, in honor or dishonor, to the latest generation. We say we are for the Union. The world will not forget that we say this. We know how to save the Union. The world knows we do know how to save it. We—even *we here*—hold the power and bear the responsibility. In *giving* freedom to the *slave* we *assure* freedom to the *free*—honorable alike in what we give and what we preserve. We shall nobly save, or meanly lose, the last best hope of earth. Other means may succeed; this could not fail. The way is plain, peaceful, generous, just—a way which, if followed, the world will forever applaud, and God must forever bless. A. LINCOLN.

Letter to Mr. Wood, December 12, 1862.

My Dear Sir:—Your letter of the 8th, with the accompanying note of same date, was received yesterday.

The most important paragraph in the letter, as I consider, is in these words: "On the 26th of November last I was advised by an authority which I deemed likely to be well informed, as well as reliable and truthful that the Southern states would send representatives to the next Congress, provided that a full and general amnesty should permit them to do so. No guarantee or terms were asked for other than the amnesty referred to."

I strongly suspect your information will prove to be groundless; nevertheless, I thank you for communicating it to me. Understanding the phrase in the paragraph above quoted—"the Southern states would send representatives to the next Congress"—to be substantially the same as that "the people of the Southern states would cease resistance, and would inaugurate, submit to, and maintain the national authority within the limits of such states, under the Constitution of the United States," I say that in such case the war would cease on the part of the United States, and that if, within a reasonable time, "a full and general amnesty" were necessary to such end, it would not be withheld.

I do not think it would be proper now to communicate this, formally or informally, to the people of the Southern states. My belief is that they already know it, and when they choose, if ever, they can communicate with me unequivocally. Nor do I think it proper now to suspend military operations to try any experiment of negotiation.

I should, nevertheless, receive with great pleasure the exact information you now have, and also such other as you may in any way obtain. Such information might be more valuable before the 1st of January than afterward.

While there is nothing in this letter which I shall dread to see in history, it is perhaps better for the present that its existence should not become public. I therefore have to request that you will regard it as confidential. Your obedient servant,

A. LINCOLN.

ADDRESS TO THE ARMY OF THE POTOMAC, DECEMBER 22, 1862.

I have just read your commanding general's preliminary report of the battle of Fredericksburg. Although you were not successful, the attempt was not an error, nor the failure other than an accident.

The courage with which you, in an open field, maintained the contest against an intrenched foe, and the consummate skill and success with which you crossed and re-crossed the river in the face of the enemy, show that you possess all the qualities of a great army, which will yet give victory to the cause of the country and of popular government.

Condoling with the mourners for the dead, and sympathizing with the severely wounded, I congratulate you that the number of both is comparatively so small. I tender to you, officers and soldiers, **the thanks of a nation.** A. LINCOLN.

FINAL EMANCIPATION PROCLAMATION, JANUARY 1, 1863.

WHEREAS, on the twenty-second day of September, in the year of our Lord one thousand eight hundred and sixty-two, a proclamation was issued by the President of the United States, containing, among other things, the following, to wit:

"That on the first day of January, in the year of our Lord one thousand eight hundred and sixty-three, all persons held as slaves within any state, or designated part of state, the people whereof shall then be in rebellion against the United States, shall be then, thenceforward, and forever free; and the Executive Government of the United States, including the military and naval authority thereof, will recognize and maintain the freedom of such persons, and will do no act or acts to suppress such persons, or any of them, in any efforts they may make for their actual freedom.

"That the Executive will, on the first day of January aforesaid, by proclamation, designate the states, and parts of states, if any, in which the people thereof respectively shall then be in rebellion against the United States; and the fact that any state or the people thereof shall on that day be in good faith represented in the Congress of the United States, by members chosen thereto at election wherein a majority of the qualified voters of such state shall have participated, shall, in the absence of strong countervailing testimony, be deemed conclusive evidence that such state, and the people thereof, are not then in rebellion against the United States."

Now, therefore, I, Abraham Lincoln, President of the United States, by virtue of the power in me vested as commander-in-chief of the army and navy of the United States in time of actual armed rebellion against the authority and government of the United States, and as a fit and necessary war measure for suppressing said rebellion, do, on the first day of January, in the year of our Lord one thousand eight hundred and sixty-three, and in accordance with my purpose so to do, publicly proclaimed for the full period of one hundred days from the day first above mentioned, order and designate, as the states and parts of states wherein the people thereof respectively are this day in rebellion against the United States the following, to wit: Arkansas, Texas, Louisiana (except the parishes of St. Bernard, Plaquemine, Jefferson, St. John, St. Charles, St. James, Ascension, Assumption, Terre Bonne, Lafourche, St. Marie, St. Martin, and Orleans, including the city of New Orleans), Mississippi, Alabama, Florida, Georgia, South Carolina, North Carolina, and Virginia (except the forty-eight counties designated as West Virginia, and also the counties of Berkely, Accomac, Northampton, Elizabeth City, York, Princess Anne, and Norfolk, including the cities of Norfolk and Portsmouth), and which excepted parts are for the present left precisely as if this proclamation were not issued. And, by virtue of the power and for the purpose aforesaid, I do order and declare that all persons held as slaves within said designated states and parts of states, are, and henceforward shall be free; and that the executive government of the United States, including the military and naval authorities thereof, will recognize and maintain the freedom of said persons. And I hereby enjoin upon the people so declared to be free, to abstain from all violence, unless in necessary self-defense; and I recommend to them, that in all cases, when allowed, they labor faithfully for reasonable wages. And I further declare and make known that such persons of suitable condition will be received into the armed service of the United States, to garrison forts, positions, stations, and other places, and to man vessels of all sorts in said service. And upon this act, sincerely believed to be an act of justice, warranted by the Constitution, upon military necessity, I invoke the considerate judgment of mankind and the gracious favor of Almighty God.

In testimony whereof I have hereunto set my name, and caused the seal of the United States to be affixed.

Done at the city of Washington this first day of January, in the year of our Lord one thousand eight hundred and sixty-three, and of the independence of the United States the eighty-seventh.

ABRAHAM LINCOLN.

LETTER TO MAJOR-GENERAL CURTIS, JANUARY 2, 1863.

My Dear Sir:—Yours of December 29th, by the hand of Mr. Strong, is just received. The day I telegraphed you suspending the order in relation to Dr. McPheeters, he, with Mr. Bates, the attorney-general, appeared before me and left with me a copy of the order mentioned. The doctor also showed me the copy of an oath which he said he had taken, which is indeed very strong and specific. He also verbally assured me that he had constantly prayed in church for the president and government, as he had always done before the present war. In looking over the recitals in your order, I do not see that this matter of the prayer, as he states it, is negatived; nor that any violation of his oath is charged, nor in fact that any thing specific is alleged against him. The charges are all general, that he has a rebel wife, and rebel relations; that he sympathises with rebels, and that he exercises rebel influence. Now after talking with him, I tell you frankly, I believe he does sympathize with the rebels; but the question remains whether such a man of unquestioned good moral character, who has taken such an oath as he has, and can not even be charged of violating it, and who can be charged with no other specific act or omission, can, with safety to this government, be exiled upon the suspicion of his secret sympathies. But I agree that this must be left to you who are on the spot; and if, after all, you think the public good requires his removal, my suspension of the order is withdrawn, only with this qualification, that the time during the suspension is not to be counted against him. I have promised him this.

But I must add that the United States Government must not, as by this order, undertake to run the churches. When an individual in a church, or out of it, becomes dangerous to the public interest, he must be checked; but let the churches, as such, take care of themselves.

It will not do for the United States to appoint trustees, supervisors, or other agents for the churches.

Yours very truly,   A. LINCOLN.

To General Burnside.

January 8, 1863.

I understand General Halleck has sent you a letter of which this is a copy. I deplore the want of concurrence with you in opinion by your general officers, but I do not see the remedy. Be cautious, and do not understand that the government or country is driving you. I do not yet see how I could profit by changing the command of the Army of the Potomac, and if I did, I should not wish to do it by accepting the resignation of your commission.   A. LINCOLN.

Message to Congress, January 19, 1863.

I have signed the joint resolution to provide for the immediate payment of the army and navy of the United States, passed by the House of Representatives on the 14th, and by the Senate on the 15th inst. The joint resolution is a simple authority amounting, however, under the existing circumstances, to a direction to the Secretary of the Treasury to make an additional issue of $100,000,000 United States notes, if so much money is needed for the payment of the army and navy. My approval is given in order that every possible facility may be afforded for the prompt discharge of all arrears in pay due to our soldiers and our sailors.

While giving this approval, however, I think it my

duty to express my sincere regret that it has been found necessary to authorize so large an additional issue of United States notes, when this circulation and that of the suspended banks together have become already so redundant as to increase prices beyond real values, thereby augmenting the cost of living, to the injury of labor, and the cost of supplying to the injury of the whole country.

It seems very plain that continued issues of United States notes without any check to the issues of suspended banks, and without adequate provision for the raising of money by loans, and for funding the issues so as to keep them within due limits, might soon produce disastrous consequences, and this matter appears to me so important that I feel bound to avail myself of this occasion to ask the special attention of Congress to it. That Congress has power to regulate the currency of the country can hardly admit of doubt, and that a judicious measure to prevent the deterioration of this currency by a reasonable taxation of bank circulation or otherwise is needed, seems equally clear. Independent of this general consideration, it would be unjust to the people at large to exempt banks enjoying the special privilege of circulation, from their just proportion of the public burdens. In order to raise money by way of loans most easily, and cheaply, it is clearly necessary to give every possible support to the public credit. To that end a uniform currency, in which taxes, subscriptions, loans, and all other ordinary public dues may be paid, is almost, if not quite indispensable.

Such a currency can be furnished by banks and

associations authorized under a general act of Congress, as suggested in my message at the beginning of the present session. The securing of this circulation by the pledge of the United States bonds, as herein suggested, would still further facilitate loans by increasing the present, and causing a future demand for such bonds. In view of the actual financial embarrassments of the government, and of the greater embarrassments sure to come, if the necessary means of relief be not afforded, I feel that I should not perform my duty by a simple announcement of my approval of the joint resolution, which proposes relief only by increasing the circulation, without expressing my earnest desire that measures, such in substance as those I have just referred to, may receive the early sanction of Congress. By such measures, in my opinion, will payment be most certainly secured, not only to the army and navy, but to honest creditors of the government, and satisfactory provisions made for future demands on the treasury. A. LINCOLN.

APPROVAL OF COURT MARTIAL PROCEEDINGS.

January 21, 1863.

The foregoing proceedings, findings, and sentence in the foregoing case of Major-General Fitz John Porter are approved and confirmed, and it is ordered that the said Fitz John Porter be, and he hereby is, cashiered and dismissed from the service of the United States as a Major-General of volunteers, and as Colonel and Brevet Brigadier-General in the regular service of the United States, and forever disqualified from holding any office of trust or profit under the Government of the United States. ABRAHAM LINCOLN.

To Major-General Hooker.

Executive Mansion, Washington, D. C., Jan. 26, 1863.

General:— I have placed you at the head of the Army of the Potomac. Of course I have done this upon what appears to me to be sufficient reasons; and yet I think it best for you to know that there are some things in regard to which I am not quite satisfied with you. I believe you to be a brave and skillful soldier—which, of course, I like. I also believe you do not mix politics with your profession—in which you are right. You have confidence in yourself—which is a valuable, if not an indispensable quality. You are ambitious—which, within reasonable bounds, does good rather than harm; but I think that, during General Burnside's command of the army, you have taken counsel of your ambition and thwarted him as much as you could, in which you did a great wrong to the country, and to a most meritorious and honorable brother officer. I have heard, in such way as to believe it, of your recently saying that both the army and the government needed a dictator. Of course, it was not for this, but in spite of it, that I have given you the command. Only those generals who gain successes can set up dictators. What I now ask of you is military success, and I will risk the dictatorship. The government will support you to the utmost of its ability—which is neither more nor less than it has done and will do for all commanders. I much fear that the spirit which you have aided to infuse into the army, of criticising their commander and withholding confidence from him, will now turn upon you.

I shall assist you as far as I can to put it down. Neither you nor Napoleon, if he were alive again, could get any good out of an army while such a spirit prevails in it. And now, beware of rashness. Beware of rashness, but, with energy and sleepless viligance, go forward and give us victories. Yours, very truly.

A. LINCOLN.

LETTER TO THE WORKINGMEN OF MANCHESTER, ENG., FEB. 9, 1863.

I have the honor to acknowledge the receipt of the address and resolutions which you sent me on the eve of the New Year. When I came, on the 4th of March, 1861, through a free and constitutional election, to preside in the Government of the United States, the country was found at the verge of civil war. Whatever might have been the cause, or whosoever at fault, one duty, paramount to all others, was before me, namely, to maintain and preserve at once the Constitution and the integrity of the Federal Republic. A conscientious purpose to perform this duty is the key to all the measures of administration which have been and to all which will hereafter be pursued. Under our form of government, and my official oath, I could not depart from the purpose if I would. It is not always in the power of governments to enlarge or restrict the scope of moral results which follow the politics that they may deem it necessary for the public safety from time to time to adopt.

I have understood well that the duty of self-preservation rests solely with the American people. But I have at the same time been aware that favor or disfavor of foreign nations might have a material influence in enlarging and prolonging the struggle with disloyal men in which the country is engaged. A fair examination of history has seemed to authorize a belief that the past action and influence of the United States were generally regarded as having been beneficial toward mankind. I have therefore reckoned upon the forbearance of nations.

Circumstances—to some of which you kindly allude—induced me especially to expect that, if justice and good faith should be practiced by the United States, they would encounter no hostile influences on the part of Great Britain. It is now a pleasant duty to acknowledge the demonstration you have given to your desire that a spirit of peace and amity toward this country may prevail in the councils of your queen, who is respected and esteemed in your own country no more than she is by the kindred nation which has its home on this side of the Atlantic. I know and deeply deplore the sufferings which the workmen at Manchester and in all Europe are called to endure in this crisis. It has been often and studiously represented that the attempt to overthrow this government, which was built upon the foundation of human rights, and to substitute for it one which should rest exclusively on the basis of human slavery, was likely to obtain the favor of Europe.

Through the action of our disloyal citizens, the workingmen of Europe have been subjected to severe trial, for the purpose of forcing their sanction to that attempt. Under these circumstances, I can not but regard your decisive utterances upon the question as an instance of sublime Christian heroism, which has not been surpassed in any age or in any country. It is indeed an energetic and re-inspiring assurance of the inherent power of truth, and of the ultimate and universal triumph of justice, humanity, and freedom. And I do not doubt that the sentiments you have expressed will be sustained by your great nation. And, on the other hand, I have no hesitation in assuring you that they will incite admiration, esteem, and the other reciprocal feelings of friendship among the American people. I hail this interchange of sentiment, therefore, as an augury that whatever else may happen, whatever misfortune may befall your country or my own, the peace and friendship which now exist between the two nations will be, as it shall be my desire to make them, perpetual. ABRAHAM LINCOLN.

To REV. ALEXANDER REED.

Executive Mansion, February 22, 1863.

My Dear Sir:—Your note, by which you, as general superintendent of the U. S. Christian Commission, invite me to preside at a meeting to be held this day, at the hall of the House of Representatives in the city, is received.

While, for reasons which I deem sufficient, I must

decline to preside, I can not withhold my approval of the meeting and its worthy objects.

Whatever shall be, sincerely and in God's name, devised for the good of the soldiers and seamen in their hard spheres of duty, can scarcely fail to be blessed; and whatever shall tend to turn our thoughts from the unreasoning and uncharitable passions, prejudices, and jealousies incident to a great national trouble such as ours, and to fix them on the vast and long enduring consequences, for weal or for woe, which are to result from the struggle, and especially to strengthen our reliance on the Supreme Being for the final triumph of the right, can not but be well for us all.

The birthday of Washington and the Christian Sabbath coinciding this year, and suggesting together the highest interests of this life and of that to come, is most propitious for the meeting proposed.

Yours obedient servant, A. LINCOLN.

REPLY REGARDING THOMAS W. KNOX, CORRESPONDENT N. Y. HERALD.

Executive Mansion, Washington, May 20, 1863.

To whom it may concern:—Whereas, it appears to my satisfaction that Thomas W. Knox, a correspondent of the New York Herald, has been, by the sentence of a court-martial, excluded from the military department under command of Major-General Grant, and also that General Thayer, president of the court-martial which rendered the sentence, and Major-General McClernand, in command of a corps of that department, and many other respectable persons, are of opinion that Mr. Knox's offense was technical rather than willfully wrong, and that the sentence should be revoked; now therefore said sentence is hereby so far revoked as to allow Mr. Knox to return to General Grant's head-quarters, and to remain if General Grant shall not refuse such assent.

A. LINCOLN.

INTERNAL AND COASTWISE INTERCOURSE, BY THE PRESIDENT OF THE UNITED STATES OF AMERICA.

Proclamation, March 31, 1863.

Whereas, in pursuance of the act of Congress, approved July 13, 1861, I did by proclamation, dated August 16, 1861, declare that the inhabitants of the States of Georgia, South Carolina, Virginia, North Carolina, Tennessee, Alabama, Louisiana, Texas, Arkansas, Mississippi, and Florida (except the inhabitants of that part of Virginia lying west of the Alleghany Mountains, and of such other parts of that state, and the other states hereinbefore named, as might maintain a loyal adhesion to the Union and the constitution, or might be from time to time occupied and controlled by forces of the United States engaged in the dispersion of said insurgents) were in a state of insurrection against the United States, and that all commercial intercourse between the same and the inhabitants thereof, with the exceptions aforesaid, and the citizens of other states and other parts of the United States was unlawful, and would remain unlawful until such insurrection should cease or be suppressed, and that all goods and chattels, wares and merchandise, coming from any of said states, with the exceptions aforesaid, into other parts of the United States, without the license and permission of the President, through the Secretary of the Treasury, or proceeding to any of said states, with the exceptions aforesaid, by land or water, together with the vessel or vehicle conveying the same to or from said states, with the exceptions aforesaid, would be forfeited to the United States.

And, whereas, experience has shown that the exceptions made in and by said proclamation embarrass the due enforcement of said act of July 13, 1861, and the proper regulation of the commercial intercourse authorized by said act with the loyal citizens of said states—

Now, therefore, I, Abraham Lincoln, President of the United States, do hereby revoke the said exceptions, and declare that the inhabitants of the States of Georgia, South Carolina, North Carolina, Tennessee, Alabama, Louisiana, Texas, Arkansas, Mississippi, Florida, and Virginia (except the forty-eight counties of Virginia designated as West Virginia, and except also the ports of New Orleans, Key West, Port Royal, and Beaufort in North Carolina) are in a state of insurrection against the United States, and that all commercial intercourse, not licensed and conducted as provided in said act, between the said states and the inhabitants thereof, with the exceptions aforesaid, and the citizens of other states and other parts of the United States, is unlawful, and will remain unlawful until such insurrection shall cease or has been suppressed, and notice thereof has been duly given by proclamation; and all cotton, tobacco, and other products, and all other goods and chattels, wares, and merchandise coming from said states, with the exceptions aforesaid, into other parts of the United States, or proceeding to any of said states, with the exceptions aforesaid, without the license or permission of the President, through the Secretary of the Treasury, will, together with the vessel or vehicle conveying the same, be forfeited to the United States.

In witness whereof, I have hereunto set my hand and caused the seal of the United States to be affixed. Done at the City of Washington, this 31st day of March. A. D. 1863, and of the independence of the United States of America the eighty-seventh.

A. LINCOLN.

To GENERAL HUNTER AND ADMIRAL DUPONT.

Executive Mansion, Washington, April 14, 1863.

This is intended to clear up an apparent inconsistency between the recent order to continue operations before Charleston and the former one to remove to another point in a certain emergency. No censure upon you or either of you is intended.

We still hope that by cordial and judicious co-operation you can take the batteries on Morris Island and Sullivan's Island and Fort Sumter. But whether you can or not, we wish the demonstration kept up for a time for a collateral and very important object. We wish the attempt to be a real one (though not a desperate one), if it affords any considerable chance of success. But if prosecuted as a demonstration only this must not become public, or the whole effect will be lost. Once again before Charleston do not leave till further orders from here. Of course this is not intended to force you to leave unduly exposed Hilton's Head or other near points in your charge. Yours, truly, A. LINCOLN.

TO MAJOR-GENERAL HOOKER.

Executive Mansion, Washington, April 15, 1863.

It is now 10:15 P. M. An hour ago I received your letter of this morning, and a few minutes later your dispatch of this evening. The later gives me considerable uneasiness. The rain and mud, of course, were to be calculated upon. General S. is not moving rapidly enough to make the expedition come to any thing. He has now been out three days, two of which were unusually fair weather, and all three without hindrance from the enemy, and yet he is not twenty-five miles from where he started. To reach his point he has still sixty to go, another river (the Rapidan) to cross, and will be hindered by the enemy. By arithmetic, how many days will it take him to do it? I do not know that any better can be done, but I greatly fear it is another failure already. Write me often. I am very anxious.

Yours, truly, A. LINCOLN.

TO GOVERNOR CURTIN, HARRISBURG, PA.

Executive Mansion, May 1, 1863.

The whole disposable force at Baltimore and elsewhere in reach have already been sent after the enemy which alarms you. The worst thing the enemy could do for himself would be to weaken himself before Hooker, and therefore it is safe to believe he is not doing it, and the best thing he could do for himself would be to get us so scared as to bring part of Hooker's force away, and that is just what he is trying to do.

I will telegraph you in the morning about calling out the militia.   A. LINCOLN.

TO GOVERNOR CURTIN, HARRISBURG, PA.

Executive Mansion, May 2, 1863.

General Halleck tells me that he has a dispatch from General Schenck this morning informing him that our forces have joined, and that the enemy menacing Pennsylvania will have to fight or run to-day. I hope I am not less anxious to do my duty to Pennsylvania than yourself, but I really do not yet see the justification for incurring the trouble and expense of calling out the militia. I shall keep watch and try to do my duty.   A. LINCOLN.

P. S.—Our forces are exactly between the enemy and Pennsylvania.

TO GENERAL HOOKER.

Washington, D. C., May 6, 1863, 12:30 *P. M.*

Just as I had telegraphed you contents of Richmond papers, showing that our cavalry has not failed, I received General Butterfield's of 11 A. M. yesterday. This, with the great rain of yesterday and last night, securing your right flank, I think, puts a new phase upon your case, but you must be the judge.

    A. LINCOLN.

To Major-General Hooker.

Washington, D. C., May 6, 1863, 12:25 P. M.

We have, through General Dix, the contents of Richmond paper of the 5th. General Dix's dispatch in full is going to you, by Captain Fox, of the navy. The substance is General Lee's dispatch of the 3d (Sunday), claiming that he had beaten you, and that you were then retreating across the Rappahannock, distinctly stating that two of Longstreet's divisions fought you on Saturday, and that General (E. F.) Paxton was killed, Stonewall Jackson severely wounded, and Generals Heth and A. P. Hill slightly wounded. The Richmond papers also stated, upon what authority not mentioned, that our cavalry have been at Ashland, Hanover Court-House, and other points, destroying several locomotives and a good deal of other property, and all the railroad bridges to within five miles of Richmond. A. LINCOLN.

To Major-General Hooker.

Head-quarters Army of the Potomac, May 7, 1863.

My Dear Sir:—The recent movement of your army is ended without effecting its object, except, perhaps, some important breakings of the enemy's communications. What next? If possible, I would be very glad of another movement early enough to give us some benefit from the fact of the enemy's communication being broken; but neither for this reason nor any other do I wish any thing done in desperation or rashness. An early movement would also help to supersede the bad moral effect of the recent one, which is said to be considerably injurious.

Have you already in your mind a plan wholly or partially formed? If you have, prosecute it without interference from me. If you have not, please inform me, so that I, incompetent as I may be, can try and assist in the formation of some plan for the army.

Yours, as ever,   A. LINCOLN.

TO GENERAL HOOKER.

Washington, 2 P. M., *May* 8, 1863.

The news is here of the capture by our forces of Grand Gulf, *a large and very important thing*. General Willich, an exchanged prisoner just from Richmond, has talked with me this morning. He was there when our cavalry cut the roads in that vicinity. He says there was not a sound pair of legs in Richmond, and that our men, had they known it, could have safely gone in and burnt every thing and brought Jeff. Davis. captured and paroled three or four hundred men. He says as he came to City Point there was an army three miles long — Longstreet, he thought, moving toward Richmond. Milroy has captured a dispatch of General Lee, in which he says his loss was fearful in his late battle with you.

A. LINCOLN.

TO MAJOR-GENERAL DIX.

War Department, May 9, 1863.

It is very important for Hooker to know exactly what damage is done to the railroads at all points between Fredericksburg and Richmond. As yet we have no word as to whether the crossings of the North and South Anna, or any of them, have been touched. There are four of these crossings; that is, one on each road or each stream. You readily perceive why this information is desired. I suppose Kilpatrick or Davis can tell. Please ascertain fully what was done, and what is the present condition, as near as you can, and advise me at once. A. LINCOLN.

To Major-General Hooker.

Executive Mansion, Washington, May 14, 1863.

My Dear Sir:—When I wrote on the 7th, I had an impression that possibly, by an early movement, you could get some advantage, from the supposed facts that the enemy's communications were disturbed, and that he was somewhat deranged in position. The idea has now passed away, the enemy having re-established his communications, regained his positions, and actually received reinforcements. It does not now appear to me probable that you can gain any thing by an early renewal of the attempt to cross the Rappahannock. I therefore shall not complain if you do no more for a time than to keep the enemy at bay, and out of other mischief, by menaces and occasional cavalry raids, if practicable, and to put your own army in good condition again. Still, if, in your own clear judgment, you can renew the attack successfully, I do not mean to restrain you. Bearing upon this last point I must tell you I have some painful intimations that some of your corps and division commanders are not giving you their entire confidence. This would be ruinous if true, and you should, therefore, first of all, ascertain the real facts beyond all possibility of doubt. Yours truly,

A. LINCOLN.

To Major-General Hurlbert, Memphis, Tenn.

Washington, May 22, 1863.

We have news here in the Richmond newspapers of the 20th and 21st, including a dispatch from General Joe Johnston himself, that on the 15th or 16th—a little confusion as to the day—Grant beat Pemberton and (W. W.) Loring near Edwards Station, at the end of a nine hours fight, driving Pemberton over the Big Black, and cutting Loring off and driving him south to Crystal Springs, twenty-five miles below Jackson.

Joe Johnston telegraphed all this, except about Loring, from his camp between Brownsville and Lexington, on the 18th. Another dispatch indicates that Grant was moving against Johnston on the 18th.

A. LINCOLN.

Letter to General J. M. Schofield.

Executive Mansion, Washington, May 27, 1863.

Dear Sir:—Having removed General Curtis and assigned you to the command of the Department of the Missouri, I think it may be of some advantage to me to state to you why I did it.

I did not remove General Curtis because of my full conviction that he had done wrong by commission or omission. I did it because of a conviction in my mind that the Union men of Missouri, constituting, when uniting, a vast majority of the people, have entered into a pestilent, factious quarrel, among themselves, General Curtis, perhaps not of choice, being the head of one faction, and Governor Gamble that of the other.

After months of labor to reconcile the difficulty, it seemed to grow worse and worse, until I felt it my duty to break it up some how, and as I could not remove Governor Gamble, I had to remove General Curtis. Now that you are in the position, I wish you to undo nothing merely because General Curtis or Governor Gamble did it, but to exercise your judgment and do right for the public interest. Let your military measures be strong enough to repel the invaders and keep the peace, and not so strong as to unnecessarily harass and persecute the people. It is a difficult *role*, and so much greater will be the honor if you perform it well.

If both factions, or neither, shall abuse you, you will probably be about right. Beware of being assailed by one and praised by the other.

Yours truly,   A. LINCOLN.

LETTER TO GENERAL HOOKER, JUNE 5, 1863.

Yours of to-day was received an hour ago. So much of professional military skill is requisite to answer it that I turned the task over to General Halleck. He promises to perform it with his utmost care. I have but one idea which I think worth suggesting to you, and that is in case you find Lee coming to the north of the Rappahannock, I would by no means cross to the south of it. If he should leave a rear force at Fredricksburg, tempting you to fall upon it, would fight in intrenchments and have you at disadvantage, and so man for man worst you at that point, while his main force would in some way be getting the advantage of you northward. In one word, I would not take any risk of being entangled upon the river like an ox jumped half over a fence and liable to be torn by dogs front and rear without a fair chance to gore one way or kick the other.

If Lee would come to my side of the river, I would keep on the same side and fight him, or act on the defensive, according as might be my estimate of his strength relatively to my own. But these are mere suggestions which I desire to be controlled by the judgment of yourself and General Halleck.

A. LINCOLN.

To MAJOR-GENERAL HOOKER.

Washington, D. C., June 10, 1863.

Your long dispatch of to-day is just received. If left to me, I would not go south of the Rappahannock upon Lee's moving north of it. If you had Richmond invested to-day you would not be able to take it in twenty days; meanwhile your communications, and with them your army, would be ruined. I think Lee's army, and not Richmond, is your objective point. If he comes toward the Upper Potomac, follow on his flank, and on the inside track, shortening your lines, while he lengthens his. Fight him, too, when opportunity offers. If he stay where he is, *fret him and fret him.*

A. LINCOLN.

Reply to New York Democrats, June 12, 1863.

Hon. Erastus Corning and others: Gentlemen—Your letter of May 19th, inclosing the resolutions of a public meeting held at Albany, N. Y., on the 16th of the same month, was received several days ago.

The resolutions, as I understand them, are resolvable into two propositions—first, the expression of a purpose to sustain the cause of the Union, to secure peace through victory, and to support the administration in every constitutional and lawful measure to suppress the rebellion; and, secondly, a declaration of censure upon the administration for supposed unconstitutional action, such as the making of military arrests. And, from the two propositions, a third is deduced, which is, that the gentlemen composing the meeting are resolved on doing their part to maintain our common government and country, despite the folly or wickedness, as they may conceive, of any administration. This position is eminently patriotic, and, as such, I thank the meeting, and congratulate the nation for it. My own purpose is the same, so that the meeting and myself have a common object, and can have no difference, except in the choice of means or measures for effecting that object.

And here I ought to close this paper, and would close it, if there were no apprehension that more injurious consequences than any merely personal to myself might follow the censures systematically cast upon me for doing what, in my view of duty, I could not forbear. The resolutions promise to support me in every constitutional and lawful measure to suppress the rebellion, and I have not knowingly employed, nor shall knowingly employ, any other. But the meeting, by their resolutions, assert and argue that certain military arrests, and proceedings following them, for which I am ultimately responsible, are unconstitutional. I think they are not. The resolutions quote from the Constitution the definition of treason, and also the limiting safeguards and guarantees therein provided for the citizen on trials of treason; and on his being held to answer for capital or otherwise infamous crimes; and, in criminal prosecutions, his right to a speedy and public trial by an impartial jury. They proceed to resolve that these safeguards of the rights of the citizen against the pretensions of arbitrary power were intended more *especially* for his protection in times of civil commotion. And, apparently to demonstrate the proposition, the resolutions proceed: "They were secured substantially to the English people *after* years of protracted civil war, and were adopted into our Constitution at the *close* of the revolution." Would not the demonstration have been better if it could have been truly said that these safeguards had been adopted and applied *during* the civil wars and *during* our revolution, instead of *after* the one and at the *close* of the other? I, too, am devotedly for them *after* civil war, and *before* civil war, and at all times, "except when, in cases of rebellion or invasion, the public safety may require" their suspension.

The resolutions proceed to tell us that these safeguards "have stood the test of seventy-six years of trial, under our republican system, under circumstances that show that while they constitute the foundation of all free government, they are the elements of the enduring stability of the republic."

No one denies that they have so stood the test up to the beginning of the present rebellion, if we except a certain occurrence at New Orleans; nor does any one question that they will stand the same test much longer after the rebellion closes. But these provisions of the Constitution have no application to the case we have in hand, because the arrests complained of were not made for treason—that is, not for the treason defined in the Constitution, and upon the conviction of which the punishment is death—nor yet were they made to hold persons to answer for any capital or otherwise infamous crimes; nor were the proceedings following, in any constitutional or legal sense, "criminal prosecutions." The arrests were made on totally different grounds, and the proceedings following accorded with the grounds of the arrest. Let us consider the real case with which we are dealing, and apply to it the parts of the Constitution plainly made for such cases. Prior to my installation here it had been inculcated that any state had a lawful right to secede from the National Union, and that it would be expedient to exercise the right whenever the devotees of the doctrine should fail to elect a president to their own liking. I was elected contrary to their liking, and, accordingly, so far as it was legally possible, they had taken seven states out of the Union, had seized many of the United States forts, and had fired upon the United States flag, all before I was inaugurated; and, of course, before I had done any official act whatever. The rebellion thus begun, soon ran into the present civil war, and, in certain respects, it began on very unequal terms between the parties. The insurgents had been preparing for it more than thirty years, while the government had taken no steps to resist them. The former had carefully considered all the means which could be turned to their account.

It undoubtedly was a well pondered reliance with them that in their own unrestricted efforts to destroy Union, Constitution, and law, all together, the government would, in great degree, be restrained by the same Constitution and law from arresting their progress. Their sympathizers pervaded all departments of the government and nearly all communities of the people. From this material, under cover of "liberty of speech," "liberty of the press," and "habeas corpus," they hoped to keep on foot amongst us a most efficient corps of spies, informers, suppliers, and aiders and abettors of their cause in a thousand ways.

They knew that in times such as they were inaugurating, by the Constitution itself, the "habeas corpus" might be suspended; but they also knew they had friends who would make a question as to who was to suspend it; meanwhile their spies and others might remain at large to help on their cause. Or if, as has happened, the execution should suspend the writ, without ruinous waste of time, instances of arresting innocent persons might occur, as are always likely to occur in such cases; and then a clamor could be raised in regard to this, which might be, at least, of some service to the insurgent cause. It needed no very keen perception to discover this part of the enemy's programme, so soon as by open hostilities their machinery was fairly put in motion. Yet, thoroughly imbued with a reverence for the guaranteed rights of individuals, I was slow to adopt the strong measures which by degrees I have been forced to regard as being within the exceptions of the Constitution, and as indispensable to the public safety.

Nothing is better known to history than that courts of justice are utterly incompetent to such cases. Civil courts are organized chiefly for trials of individuals, or, at most, a few individuals acting in concert; and this in quiet times, and on charges of crimes well defined in the law. Even in times of peace, bands of horse-thieves and robbers frequently grow too numerous and powerful for ordinary courts of justice. But what comparison, in numbers, have such bands ever borne to the insurgent sympathizers even in many of the loyal states? Again, a jury too frequently has at least one member more ready to hang the panel than to hang the traitor. And yet, again, he who dissuades one man from volunteering, or induces one soldier **to desert**, weakens the Union cause as much as he who kills a Union soldier in battle. Yet this dissuasion or inducement may be so conducted as to be no defined crime of which any civil court would take cognizance.

Ours is a case of rebellion—so called by the resolutions before me—in fact, a clear, flagrant and gigantic case of rebellion; and the provision of the Constitution that " the privilege of the writ of habeas corpus shall not be suspended, unless when in cases of rebellion or invasion the public safety may require it," is the provision which specially applies to our present case. This provision plainly attests the understanding of those who made the Constitution, that ordinary courts of justice are inadequate to " cases of rebellion" —attests their purpose that, in such cases, men may be held in custody whom the courts, acting on ordinary rules, would discharge. Habeas corpus does not discharge men who are proved to be guilty of defined crime; and its suspension is allowed by the Constitution on purpose that men may be arrested and held who can not be proved to be guilty of defined crime, " when, in cases of rebellion or invasion, the public safety may require it."

This is precisely our present case—a case of rebellion, wherein the public safety does require the suspension. Indeed, arrests by process of courts, and arrests in cases of rebellion do not proceed altogether upon the same basis. The former is directed at the small percentage of ordinary and continuous perpetration of crime, while the latter is directed at sudden and extensive uprisings against the government, which, at most, will succeed or fail at no great length of time. In the latter case, arrests are made, not so much for what has been done, as for what probably would be done. The latter is more for the preventive and less for the vindictive than the former. In such cases the purposes of men are much more easily understood than in cases of ordinary crime.

The man who stands by and says nothing when the peril of his government is discussed, can not be misunderstood. If not hindered he is sure to help the enemy; much more, if he talks ambiguously—talks for his country with " buts " and " ifs " and " ands." Of how little value the constitutional provisions I have quoted will be rendered, if arrests shall never be made until defined crimes shall have been committed, may be illustrated by a few notable examples. General John C. Breckenridge, General Robert E. Lee, General Joseph E. Johnston, General John B. Magruder, General William B. Preston, General Simon B. Buckner, and Commodore Franklin Buchanan, now occupying the very highest places in the rebel war service, were all within the power of the government since the rebellion began, and were nearly as well known to be traitors then as now. Unquestionably if we had seized and held them, the insurgent cause would be much weaker. But no one of them had then committed any crime defined in the law. Every one of them, if arrested, would have been discharged on habeas corpus were the writ allowed to operate.

In view of these and similar cases, I think the time not unlikely to come when I shall be blamed for having made too few arrests rather than too many.

By the third resolution the meeting indicate their opinion that military arrests may be constitutional in localities where rebellion actually exists, but that such arrests are unconstitutional in localities where rebellion or insurrection does not actually exist. They insist that such arrests shall not be made " outside of the lines of necessary military occupation and the scenes of insurrection." Inasmuch, however, as the Constitution itself makes no such distinction, I am unable to believe that there is any such constitutional distinction. I concede that the class of arrests complained of can be constitutional only when, in cases of rebellion or invasion, the public safety may require them; and I insist that in such cases they are constitutional, whereas the public safety does require them, as well in places to which they may prevent the rebellion extending as in those where it may be already prevailing; as well where they may restrain mischievous interference with the raising and supplying of armies to suppress the rebellion, as where the rebellion may actually be; as well where they may restrain the enticing men out of the army, as where they would prevent mutiny in the army; equally constitutional at all places where they will conduce to the public safety, as against the dangers of rebellion or invasion.

Take the peculiar case mentioned by the meeting. It is asserted, in substance, that Mr. Vallandigham was, by a military commander, seized and tried, "for no other reason than words addressed to a public meeting, in criticism of the course of the administration, and in condemnation of the military orders of the general." Now if there be no mistake about this, if this assertion is the truth and the whole truth, if there was no other reason for the arrest, then I concede that the arrest was wrong.

But the arrest, as I understand, was made for a very different reason. Mr. Vallandigham avows his hostility to the war on the part of the Union; and his arrest was made because he was laboring, with some effect, to prevent the raising of troops; to encourage desertion from the army; and to leave the rebellion without an adequate military force to suppress it. He was not arrested because he was damaging the political prospects of the administration, or the personal interests of the commanding general, but because he was damaging the army, upon the existence and vigor of which the life of the Nation depends.

He was warring upon the military, and this gave the military constitutional jurisdiction to lay hands upon him. If Mr. Vallandigham was not damaging the military power of the country, then his arrest was made on mistake of fact, which I would be glad to correct, on reasonably satisfactory evidence.

I understand the meeting, whose resolutions I am considering, to be in favor of suppressing the rebellion by military force, by armies. Long experience has shown that armies can not be maintained unless desertion shall be punished by the severe penalty of death.

The case requires, and the law and the Constitution sanction, this punishment. Must I shoot a simple-minded soldier boy who deserts, while I must not touch a hair of a wily agitator who induces him to desert? This is none the less injurious when effected by getting a father, or brother, or friend, into a public meeting, and there working upon his feelings until he is persuaded to write the soldier boy that he is fighting in a bad cause, for a wicked administration of a contemptible government, too weak to arrest and punish him if he shall desert. I think that, in such a case, to silence the agitator, and save the boy, is not only constitutional, but withal a great mercy. If I be wrong on this question of constitutional power, my error lies in believing that certain proceedings are constitutional when, in cases of rebellion or invasion, the public safety requires them, which would not be constitutional, in absence of rebellion or invasion, the public safety does not require them; in other words, that the Constitution is not in its application in all respects the same, in cases of rebellion or invasion involving the public safety, as it is in times of profound peace and public security. The Constitution itself makes the distinction, and I can no more be persuaded that the government can constitutionally take no strong measures in time of rebellion, because it can be shown that the same could not be lawfully taken in time of peace, then I can be persuaded that a particular drug is not good medicine for a sick man because it can be shown to not be good food for a well one. Nor am I able to appreciate the danger apprehended by the meeting that the American people will, by means of military arrests during the rebellion, lose the right of public discussion, the liberty of speech and the press, the laws of evidence, trial by jury, and habeas corpus, throughout the indefinite peaceful future, which I trust lies before them, any more than I am able to believe that a man could contract so strong an appetite for emetics during temporary illness as to persist in feeding upon them during the remainder of his healthful life.

In giving the resolutions that earnest consideration which you request of me, I can not overlook the fact that the meeting speak as " Democrats." Nor can I, with full respect for their known intelligence, and the fairly presumed deliberation with which they prepared their resolutions, be permitted to suppose that this occurred by accident, or in any way other than that they preferred to designate themselves " Democrats" rather than American citizens. In this time of national peril, I would have preferred to meet you on a level one step higher than any party platform; because I am sure that, from such more elevated position, we could do better battle for the country we all love than we possibly can from those lower ones, where, from the force of habit, the prejudices of the past, and selfish hopes of the future, we are sure to expend much of our ingenuity and strength in finding fault with, and aiming blows at, each other. But, since you have denied me this, I will yet be thankful, for the country's sake, that not all Democrats have done so.

He on whose discretionary judgment Mr. Vallandigham was arrested and tried is a Democrat, having no old party affinity with me; and the judge who rejected the constitutional view expressed in these resolutions, by refusing to discharge Mr. Vallandigham on habeas corpus is a Democrat of better days than these, having received his judicial mantle at the hands of President Jackson. And still more, of all those Democrats who are nobly exposing their lives and shedding their blood on the battle field, I have learned that many approve the course taken with Mr. Vallandigham, while I have not heard of a single one condemning it. I can not assert that there are none such. And the name of President Jackson recalls an instance of pertinent history. After the battle of New Orleans, and while the fact that the treaty of peace had been concluded was well known in the city, but before official knowledge of it had arrived, General Jackson still maintained martial or military law. Now that it could be said the war was over, the clamor against martial law, which had existed from the first, grew more furious. Among other things, a Mr. Lonaillier published a denunciatory newspaper article. General Jackson arrested him. A lawyer by the name of Morel procured the United States Judge, Hall, to order a writ of habeas corpus to relieve Mr. Lonaillier. General Jackson arrested both the lawyer and the judge. A Mr. Hollander ventured to say of some part of the matter that "it was a dirty trick." General Jackson arrested him. When the officer undertook to serve the writ of habeas corpus, General Jackson took it from him, and sent him away with a copy. Holding the judge in custody a few days, the general sent him beyond the limits of his encampment, and set him at liberty, with an order to remain till the ratification of peace should be regularly announced, or until the British should have left the southern coast. A day or two more elapsed, the ratification of the treaty of peace was regularly announced, and the judge and others were fully liberated. A few days more, and the judge called General Jackson into court, and fined him $1,000 for having arrested him and the others named. The general paid the fine, and there the matter rested for nearly thirty years, when Congress refunded principal and interest. The late Senator Douglas, when in the House of Representatives, took a leading part in the debates, in which the constitutional question was much discussed. I am not prepared to say whom the journals would show to have voted for the measure.

It may be remarked: First, that we had the same Constitution then as now; secondly, that we then had a case of invasion, and now we have a case of rebellion; and, thirdly, that the permanent right of the people to public discussion, the liberty of speech and of the press, the trial by jury, the law of evidence, and the habeas corpus, suffered no detriment whatever by that conduct of General Jackson, or its subsequent approval by the American Congress.

And yet, let me say, that in my own discretion, I do not know whether I would have ordered the arrest of Mr. Vallandigham. While I can not shift the responsibility from myself, I hold that, as a general rule, the commander in the field is the better judge of the necessity in any particular case.

Of course, I must practice a general directory and revisory power in the matter.

One of the resolutions expresses the opinion of the meeting that arbitrary arrests will have the effect to divide and distract those who should be united in suppressing the rebellion, and I am specifically called on to discharge Mr. Vallandigham. I regard this as, at least, a fair appeal to me on the expediency of exercising a constitutional power which I think exists. In response to such appeal, I have to say, it gave me pain when I learned that Mr. Vallandigham had been arrested; that is, I was pained that there should have seemed to be a necessity for arresting him, and that it will afford me great pleasure to discharge him so soon as I can by any means, believe the public safety will not suffer by it.

I further say that as the war progresses, it appears to me opinion and action, which were in great confusion at first, take shape and fall into more regular channels, so that the necessity for strong dealing with them gradually decreases. I have every reason to desire that it shall cease altogether, and far from the least is my regard for the opinion and wishes of those who like the meeting at Albany, declare their purpose to sustain the government in every constitutional and lawful measure to suppress the rebellion. Still, I must continue to do so much as may seem to be required by the public safety.   A. LINCOLN.

To GENERAL HOOKER.

June 14, 1863, 5:50 *P. M.*

So far as we can make out here, the enemy have Milroy surrounded at Winchester, and Tyler at Martinsburg. If they could hold out a few days, could you help them? If the head of Lee's army is at Martinsburg and the tail of it on the plank-road between Fredericksburg and Chancellorsville, the animal must be very slim somewhere. Could you not break him?   A. LINCOLN.

To GENERAL HOOKER.

June 14, 1863, 11:55 *P. M.*

Yours of 11:30 just received. You have nearly all the elements for forming an opinion whether Winchester is surrounded that I have. I really fear, almost believe, it is. No communication has been had with it during the day either at Martinsburg or Harper's Ferry. At 7 P. M. we also lost communication with Martinsburg. The enemy had also appeared there some hours before. At nine P. M. Harper's Ferry said the enemy was also reported at Berryville and Smithfield. If I could know that, and Ewell moved in that direction so long ago as you stated in your last, then I should feel sure that Winchester is strongly invested. It is quite certain that a considerable force of the enemy is thereabout, and I fear it is an overwhelming one compared with Milroy's. I am unable to give any more certain opinion.   A. LINCOLN.

A Proclamation by the President of the United States of America.

War Department, June 15, 1863.

Whereas, the armed insurrectionary combinations now existing in several of the states are threatening to make inroads into the states of Maryland, West Virginia, Pennsylvania, and Ohio, requiring immediately an additional force for the service of the United States,

Now, therefore, I, Abraham Lincoln, President of the United States, and commander-in-chief of the army and navy thereof, and of the militia of the several states when called into actual service, do hereby call into the service of the United States 100,000 militia from the states following, namely: From the State of Maryland, 10,000; from the State of Pennsylvania, 50,000; from the State of Ohio, 30,000; from the State of West Virginia, 10,000, to be mustered into the service of the United States forthwith, and to serve for the period of six months from the date of such muster into said service, unless sooner discharged; to be mustered in as infantry, artillery, and cavalry, in proportions which will be made known through the War Department, which department will also designate the several places of rendezvous. These militia to be organized according to the rules and regulations of the volunteer service, and such orders as may hereafter be issued. The states aforesaid will be respectively under the enrollment act for the militia service rendered under this proclamation.

In testimony whereof, I have hereunto set my hand, and caused the seal of the United States to be affixed.

Done at the City of Washington, this fifteenth day of June, in the year of our Lord one thousand eight hundred and sixty-three, and of the independence of the United States the eighty-seventh. A. LINCOLN.

To MAJOR-GENERAL HOOKER.

Washington, June 16, 1863, 10 *A. M.*

To remove all misunderstanding, I now place you in the strict military relation to General Halleck of a commander of one of the armies to the general-in-chief of all the armies.

I have not intended differently, but, as it seems to be differently understood, I shall direct him to give you orders and you to obey them. A. LINCOLN.

To Hon. J. K. Moorehead, Pittsburg, Pa.

Washington, June 18, 1863, 10:40 *A. M.*

If General Brooks, now in command at Pittsburg, finds any person or persons injuriously affecting his military operations, he is authorized to arrest him or them at once, if the case is urgent. If not urgent, let him communicate the particulars to me. General Brooks is the man to now manage the matter at Pittsburg. Please show this to him.

A. Lincoln.

To General John M. Schofield.

Executive Mansion, Washington, June 22, 1863.

My Dear Sir:— Your dispatch, asking in substance whether, in case Missouri shall adopt gradual emancipation, the General Government will protect slave owners in that species of property during the short time it shall be permitted by the state to exist within it, has been received. Desirous as I am that emancipation shall be adopted by Missouri, and believing as I do that *gradual* can be made better than *immediate* for both black and white, except when military necessity changes the case, my impulse is to say that such protection would be given. I can not know exactly what shape an act of emancipation may take. If the period from the initiation to the final end should be comparatively short, and the act should prevent persons being sold during that period into more lasting slavery, the whole would be easier.

I do not wish to pledge the general government to the affirmative support of even temporary slavery beyond what can be fairly claimed under the Constitution.

I suppose, however, this is not desired, but that it is desired for the military force of the United States, while in Missouri, to not be used in subverting the temporarily reserved legal rights in slaves during the progress of emancipation. This I would desire also. I have very earnestly urged the slave states to adopt emancipation; and it ought to be, and is, an object with me not to overthrow or thwart what any of them may, in good faith, do to that end. You are, therefore, authorized to act in the spirit of this letter in conjunction with what may appear to be the military necessities of your department.

Although this letter will become public at some time, it is not intended to be made so now.

Yours, truly,   A. LINCOLN.

THE PRESIDENT'S ANNOUNCEMENT OF THE SUCCESS OF THE ARMY OF THE POTOMAC.

July 4, 1863.

The President announces to the country that news from the Army of the Potomac, up to ten P. M. of the 3d, is such as to cover that army with the highest honor; to promise a great success to the cause of the Union, and to claim the condolence of all for the many gallant fallen; and that for this, he especially desires that on this day He whose will, not ours, should ever be done, be every-where remembered and reverenced with the profoundest gratitude.

ABRAHAM LINCOLN.

Response to a Serenade, July, 1863.

Fellow-citizens:—I am very glad indeed to see you to-night, and yet I will not say I thank you for this call; but I do most sincerely thank Almighty God for the occasion on which you have called. How long ago is it—eighty odd years since on the Fourth of July, for the first time in the history of the world, a nation, by its representatives, assembled and declared as a self-evident truth that "all men are created equal." That was the birthday of the United States of America. Since then the Fourth of July has had several very peculiar recognitions. The two men most distinguished in the framing and the support of the declaration were Thomas Jefferson and John Adams—the one having penned it, and the other sustained it the most forcibly in debate—the only two of the fifty-five who signed it, and were elected President of the United States. Precisely fifty years after they put their hands to the paper, it pleased Almighty God to take both from this stage of action. This was indeed an extraordinary and remarkable event in our history. Another President, five years after, was called from this stage of existence on the same day and month of the year; and now on this last Fourth of July, just passed, when we have a gigantic rebellion, at the bottom of which is an effort to overthrow the principle that all men were created equal, we have the surrender of a most powerful position and army on that very day. And not only so, but in a succession of battles in

Pennsylvania, near to us, through three days, so rapidly fought that they might be called one great battle, on the first, second and third of the month of July; and on the fourth the cohorts of those who opposed the declaration that all men are created equal "turned tail" and run. Gentlemen, this is a glorious theme, and the occasion for a speech, but I am not prepared to make one worthy of the occasion. I would like to speak in terms of praise due to the many brave officers and soldiers who have fought in the cause of the Union and liberties of their country from the beginning of the war. These are trying occasions, not only in success, but for the want of success. I dislike to mention the name of one single officer, lest I might do wrong to those I might forget. Recent events bring up glorious names, and particularly prominent ones; but these I will not mention. Having said this much, I will now take the music.

To Major-General Curtis.

Executive Mansion, Washington, July 5, 1863.

My Dear Sir:—I am having a good deal of trouble with Missouri matters, and I now sit down to write you particularly about it. One class of friends believe in greater severity, and another in greater leniency in regard to arrests, banishments and assessments.

As usual in such cases, each questions the other's motives. On the one hand, it is insisted that Governor Gamble's unionism at most, is not better than a secondary spring of action; that hunkerism and a wish for political influence stand before unionism with him. On the other hand, it is urged that arrests, banishments, and assessments, are made more for private malice, revenge, and pecuniary interest than for the public good.

This morning I was told by a gentleman, who I have no doubt believes what he says, that in one case of assessments for $10,000, the different persons who paid, compared receipts, and found they had paid $30,000. If this be true, the inference is that the collecting agents pocketed the odd $20,000.

And true or not in this instance, nothing but the sternest necessity can justify the making and maintaining of a system so liable to such abuses. Doubtless the necessity for the making of the system in Missouri did exist, and whether it continues for the maintenance of it is now a practical and very important question.

Some days ago Governor Gamble telegraphed me, asking that the assessments outside of St. Louis county might be suspended, as they already have been within it, and this morning all the members of Congress here from Missouri but one laid a paper before me asking the same thing. Now, my belief is that Governor Gamble is an honest and true man, not less so than yourself; that you and he could confer together on this and other Missouri questions, with great advantage to the public; that each knows something which the other does not, and that acting together you could about double your stock of pertinent information. May I not hope that you and he will attempt this? I could at once safely do (or you could safely do **without** me) whatever you and he agree upon. There is absolutely no reason why you should not agree. Yours, as ever, A. LINCOLN.

P. S. I forgot to say that Hon. James S. Rollins, member of Congress from one of the Missouri districts, wishes that, upon his personal responsibility, Rev. John M. Robinson, of Columbia, Mo., James L. Mathews, of Boone county, Missouri, and James L. Stevens, also of Boone county, Missouri, may be allowed to return to their respective homes. Major Rollins leaves with me very strong papers from the neighbors of these men, whom he says he knows to be true men. He also says he has many constituents who he thinks are rightly exiled, but that he thinks these three should be allowed to return.

Please look into the case, and oblige Major Rollins, if you consistently can. Yours truly, A. LINCOLN.

To Major-General Halleck.

Soldiers' Home [*Washington*], *July* 6, 1863, 7 P. M.
I left the telegraph office a good deal dissatisfied. You know I did not like the phrase in order No. 68, I believe, " Drive the invaders from our soil." Since that, I see a dispatch from General French, saying the enemy is crossing his wounded over the river in flats, without saying why he does not stop it, or even insinuating a thought that it ought to be stopped. Still later, another dispatch from General Pleasonton, by direction of General Meade, to General French, stating that the main army is halted because it is believed the rebels are concentrating " on the road toward Hagerstown, beyond Fairfield," and is not to move

until it is ascertained that the rebels intend to evacuate Cumberland Valley.

These things all appear to me to be connected with a purpose to cover Baltimore and Washington, and to get the enemy across the river again without a further collision, and they do not appear connected with a purpose to prevent his crossing, and to destroy him. I do fear the former purpose is acted upon, and the latter is rejected.

If you are satisfied the latter purpose is entertained and is judiciously pursued, I am content. If you are not so satisfied, please look to it. Yours truly,
A. LINCOLN.

TO GENERAL LORENZO THOMAS, HARRISBURG, PA.

War Dep't., Washington, July 8, 1863, 12:30 P. M.

Your dispatch of this morning to the Secretary of War is before me.

The forces you speak of will be of no imaginable service if they can not go forward with a little more expedition.

Lee is now passing the Potomac faster than the forces you mention are passing Carlisle.

Forces now beyond Carlisle to be joined by regiments still at Harrisburg, and the united force to to again join Pierce somewhere, and the whole to move down the Cumberland Valley, will, in my unprofessional opinion, be quite as likely to capture the "man in the moon" as any part of Lee's army.
A. LINCOLN.

To Hon. J. K. Dubois, Springfield, Ill.

Washington, D. C., July 11, 1863. 9 *A. M.*

It is certain that after three days fighting at Gettysburg, Lee withdrew and made for the Potomac; that he found the river so swollen as to prevent his crossing; that he is still this side, near Hagerstown and Williamsport, preparing to defend himself; and that Meade is close upon him, and preparing to attack him, heavy skirmishing having occurred nearly all day yesterday. I am more than satisfied with what has happened north of the Potomac so far, and am anxious and hopeful for what is to come.

A. Lincoln.

Letter to General Grant, July 13, 1863.

My Dear General:—I do not remember that you and I ever met personally. I write this now as a grateful acknowledgment for the almost inestimable services you have done the country.

I wish to say a word further. When you reached the vicinity of Vicksburg, I thought you should do what you finally did—march the troops across the neck, run the batteries with the transports, and thus go below; and I never had any faith, except in a general hope, that you knew better than I, that the Yazoo Pass expedition and the like would succeed.

When you got below and took Fort Gibson, Grand Gulf, and vicinity, I thought you should go down the river and join General Banks; and when you turned northward, east of the Big Black, I feared it was a mistake. I now wish to make a personal acknowledgment that you were right and I was wrong.

A. LINCOLN.

CALL FOR A DAY OF THANKSGIVING AND PRAYER, SUMMER OF 1863.

After Gettysburg and Vicksburg President Lincoln called upon the people as follows:

"To set apart a time in the near future, to be observed as a day for national thanksgiving, praise and prayer to Almighty God, for the wonderful things he had done in the nation's behalf, and to invoke the influence of his Holy Spirit to subdue the anger which has produced and so long sustained a needless and cruel rebellion, to change the hearts of the insurgents, to guide the councils of the government with wisdom adequate to so great a national emergency; and to visit with tender care and consolation throughout the length and breadth of our land, all those who, through the vicissitudes and marches, voyages, battles, and sieges, had been brought to suffer in mind, body, or estate, and finally, to lead the whole nation, through paths of repentance and submission to the Divine will, back to the perfect enjoyment of Union and fraternal peace."

A PROCLAMATION. JULY 15, 1863.

It has pleased Almighty God to hearken to the supplications and prayers of an afflicted people, and to vouchsafe to the army and navy of the United States, on the land and on the sea, victories so signal and so effective as to furnish reasonable grounds for

augmented confidence that the Union of these states
will be maintained, their constitution preserved, and
their peace and prosperity permanently secured; but
these victories have been accorded, not without sacrifice of life, limb, and liberty, incurred by brave,
patriotic, and loyal citizens. Domestic affliction in
every part of the country follows in the train of these
fearful bereavements.

It is meet and right to recognize and confess the
presence of the Almighty Father, and the power
of his hand equally in these triumphs and these
sorrows.

Now, therefore, be it known, that I do set apart
Thursday, the sixth day of August next, to be observed as a day for national thanksgiving, praise,
and prayer; and I invite the people of the United
States to assemble on that occasion in their customary
places of worship, and in the form approved by their
own conscience, render the homage due to the Divine
Majesty, for the wonderful things He has done in
the nation's behalf, and invoke the influence of his
Holy Spirit, to subdue the anger which has produced and so long sustained a needless and cruel rebellion, to change the hearts of the insurgents, to
guide the councils of the government with wisdom
adequate to so great a national emergency, and to
visit with tender care and consolation, throughout
the length and breadth of our land, all those who,
through the vicissitudes of marches, voyages, battles,
and seiges, have been brought to suffer in mind,
body, or estate, and finally, to lead the whole nation
through paths of repentance and submission to the

Divine will, back to the perfect enjoyment of Union and fraternal peace.

In witness whereof, I have hereunto set my hand and caused the seal of the United States to be affixed.

Done at the City of Washington, this 15th day of July, in the year of our Lord one thousand eight hundred and sixty-three, and of the independence of the United States of America the eighty-eighth.

Abraham Lincoln.

Letter to Governor Seymour, July, 1863.

I do not object to abide the decision of the United States Supreme Court, or of the judges thereof, on the consitutionality of the draft law. In fact, I should be willing to facilitate the obtaining of it. But I can not consent to lose the time-while it is being obtained. We are contending with an enemy who, as I understand, drives every able bodied man he can reach into his ranks, very much as a butcher drives bullocks into a slaughter pen. No time is wasted, no argument is used. This produces an army which will soon turn upon our now victorious soldiers already in the field, if they shall not be sustained by recruits as they should be. It produces an army with a rapidity not to be matched on our side, if we first waste time to re-experiment with a volunteer system, already deemed by Congress, and palpably, in fact, so far exhausted as to be inadequate; and then more time to obtain a court decision, as to whether a law is constitutional which requires a part of those not now in service to go to the aid of those who are already in it; and still more time to determine with absolute certainty that we get those who are to go in the precisely legal proportion to those who are not to go. My purpose is to be in my action just and constitutional, and yet practical in performing the important duty with which I am charged, of maintaining the unity and the free principles of our common country.   A. LINCOLN.

TO HIS EXCELLENCY, JOEL PARKER, GOVERNOR OF NEW JERSEY.

Executive Mansion, Washington, July 20, 1863.

Dear Sir:—Yours of the 17th has been received and considered by the Secretary of War and myself. I was pained to be informed this morning, by the provost marshal general, that New Jersey is now behind twelve thousand, irrespective of the draft. I did not have time to ascertain by what rule this was made out; and I shall be very glad if it shall, by any means, prove to be incorrect. He also tells me that eight thousand will be the quota of New Jersey on the first draft; and the Secretary of War says the first draft in that state would not be made for some time, in any event. As every man obtained otherwise lessens the draft so much, and thus may supersede it altogether, I hope you will push forward your volunteer regiments as fast as possible. It is a very delicate matter to postpone the draft of one state, because of the argument it furnishes others to have postponement also. If we could have a reason in one case which would be good if presented in all cases, we could act upon it. I will thank you therefore to inform me, if you can, by what day, as the earliest, you can promise to have ready to be mustered into the United States service the eight thousand men. If you can make a reliable promise (I mean one on which you can yourself rely), of this sort, it will be of great value, if the day is not too remote.

I beg you to be assured I wish to avoid the difficulties you dread, as much as yourself.

Your obedient servant, A. LINCOLN.

To HON. POSTMASTER-GENERAL.

Executive Mansion, Washington, July 24, 1863.

Yesterday little indorsements of mine went to you in two cases of postmasterships sought for widows whose husbands have fallen in the battles of this war. These cases occurring on the same day, brought me to reflect more attentively than I had before done as to what is fairly due from us here in the dispensing of patronage toward the men who, by fighting our battles, bear the chief burden of saving our country. My conclusion is, that other claims and qualifications being equal, they have the better right, and this is especially applicable to the disabled soldier and the deceased soldier's family.

Your obedient servant, A. LINCOLN.

To HIS EXCELLENCY, GOVERNOR JOEL PARKER.

Executive Mansion, Washington, July 25, 1863.

Sir:—Yours of the 21st is received, and I have taken time and considered and discussed the subject with Secretary of War and provost marshal general, in order, if possible, to make you a more favorable answer that I finally find myself able to do.

It is a vital point with us to not have a special stipulation with the governor of any one state, because it would breed trouble in many, if not all other states; and my idea was, when I wrote you, as it still is, to get a point of time to which we could wait, on the reason that we were not ready ourselves to proceed, and which might enable you to raise the quota of your state, in whole, or in large part, without the draft. The points of time you fix are much further off than I had hoped. We might have got along in the way I have indicated for twenty, or possibly thirty days. As it stands, the best I can say is that every volunteer you will present us within thirty days from the date, fit and ready to be mustered into the United States service, on the usual terms, shall be *pro tanto*, an abatement of your quota of the draft. That quota I can now state at eight thousand, seven hundred and eighty-three (8,783). No draft from New Jersey, other than for the above quota, will be made before an additional draft, common to all the states, shall be required; and I may add, that if we get well through with this draft, I entertain a strong hope that any further one may never be needed. This expression of hope, however, must not be construed into a promise.

As to conducting the draft by townships, I find it would require such a waste of labor already done, and such an additional amount of it, and such a loss of time as to make it, I fear, inadvisable.

P. S.—Since writing the above, getting additional

information, I am enabled to say that the draft may be made in sub-districts, as the enrollment has been made, or is now in process of making. This will amount practically to drafting by townships, as the enrollment sub-districts are generally about the extent of townships. Your obedient servant,

A. LINCOLN.

TO MAJOR-GENERAL BURNSIDE, CINCINNATI, O.

War Department, Washington, July 27, 1863.

Let me explain. In General Grant's first dispatch after the fall of Vicksburg, he said, among other things, he would send the ninth corps to you.

Thinking it would be pleasant news to you, I asked the Secretary of War to telegraph you the news. For some reasons never mentioned to us by General Grant, they have not been sent, though we have seen outside intimations, that they took part in the expedition against Jackson.

General Grant is a copious worker and fighter, but a very meager writer or telegrapher. No doubt he changed his purpose in regard to the ninth corps for some sufficient reason, but has forgotten to notify us of it.

A. LINCOLN.

TO MAJOR-GENERAL HALLECK.

Executive Mansion, July 29, 1863.

Seeing General Meade's dispatch of yesterday to yourself, causes me to fear that he supposes the government here is demanding of him to bring on a general engagement with Lee as soon as possible. I am claiming no such thing of him. In fact, my judgment is against it, which judgment, of course, I will yield if yours and his are the contrary. If he could not safely engage Lee at Williamsport, it seems absured to suppose he can safely engage him now, when he has scarcely more than two-thirds of the force he had at Williamsport, while, it must be that Lee has been re-inforced. True, I desired General Meade to pursue Lee across the Potomac, hoping, as it proved true, that he would thereby clear the Baltimore and Ohio Railroad, and get some advantage by harassing him on his retreat. These being past, I am unwilling he should now get into a general engagement on the impression that we here are pressing him, and I shall be glad for you to so inform him, unless your own judgment is against it. Yours, truly,

A. LINCOLN.

REPLY TO LETTER FROM OHIO DEMOCRATS.

July 29, 1863.

The resolution of the Ohio Democratic State Convention, which you present me, together with your introductory and closing remarks, being in position and argument mainly the same as the resolutions of the Democratic meeting at Albany, N. Y., I refer you to my response to the later as meeting most of the points in the former. This response you evidently used in preparing you remarks, and I desire no more than that it be used with accuracy. In a single reading of your remarks, I only discovered one inaccuracy in matter which I suppose you took from that paper. It is where you say, the undersigned are unable to agree with you in the opinion you have expressed that the

Constitution is different in time of insurrection or invasion from what it is in the time of peace and public security.

A recurrence to the paper will show you that I have not expressed the opinion you suppose.

I expressed the opinion that the Constitution is different in its *application* in cases of rebellion or invasion, involving the public safety, from what it is in times of profound peace and public security; and this opinion I adhere to, simply because by the Constitution itself things may be done in the one case which may not be done in the other.

I dislike to waste a word on a merely personal point, but I must respectfully assure you that you will find yourselves at fault should you ever seek for evidence to prove your assumption that I "opposed in discussions before the people the policy of the Mexican war."

You say: "Expunge from the Constitution this limitation upon the power of Congress to suspend the writ of habeas corpus, and yet the other guarantees of personal liberty would remain unchanged." Doubtless if this clause of the Constitution, improperly called, as I think, a limitation upon the power of Congress, were expunged, the other guarantees would remain the same; but the question is, not how those guarantees would stand with that clause *out* of the Constitution, but how they stand with that clause remaining in it, in case of rebellion or invasion, involving the public safety. If the liberty could be indulged in expunging that clause, letter and spirit, I really think the constitutional argument would be with you.

My general view on this question was stated in the

Albany response, and hence I do not state it now. I
only add that, as seems to me, the benefit of the writ
of habeas corpus is the great means through which
the guarantees of personal liberty are conserved and
made available in the last resort; and corroborative
of this view is the fact that Mr. Vallandigham, in the
very case in question, under the advice of able lawyers,
saw not where else to go but to the habeas corpus.
But by the Constitution the benefits of the writ of
habeas corpus itself, may be suspended, when, in case
of rebellion or invasion the public safety may require it.

You ask, in substance, whether I really claim that
I may override all the guaranteed rights of individuals,
on the plea of conserving the public safety—when I
may choose to say the public safety requires it. This
question, divested of the phraseology calculated to represent me as struggling for an arbitrary personal
prerogative, is either simply a question *who* shall
decide, or an affirmation that *nobody* shall decide,
what the public safety does require in cases of rebellion or invasion. The Constitution contemplates the
question as likely to occur for decision, but it does
not expressly declare who is to decide it. By necessary implication, when rebellion or invasion comes,
the decision is to be made, from time to time, and I
think the man whom, for the time, the people have,
under the Constitution, made the commander-in-chief
of the army and navy, is the man who holds the
power and bears the responsibility of making it. If
he uses the power justly, the same people will probably justify him; if he abuses it, he is in their hands,
to be dealt with by all the modes they have reserved

to themselves in the Constitution. The earnestness with which you insist that persons can only, in times of rebellion, be lawfully dealt with, in accordance with the rules for criminal trials and punishments in times of peace, induces me to add a word to what I said on that point in the Albany response. You claim that men may, if they choose, embarrass those whose duty it is to combat a giant rebellion, and then be dealt with only in turn as if there were no rebellion. The Constitution itself rejects this view.

The military arrests and detentions which have been made, including those of Mr. Vallandigham, which are not different in principle from the other, have been for *prevention*, and not for *punishment*—as injunctions to stay injury, as proceedings to keep the peace—and hence like proceedings in such cases and for like reasons, they have not been accompanied with indictments, or trials by juries, nor in a single case by any punishment whatever beyond what is purely incidental to the prevention. The original sentence of imprisonment in Mr. Vallandigham's case was to prevent injury to the military service only, and the modification of it was made as a less disagreeable mode to him of securing the same prevention. I am unable to perceive an insult to Ohio in the case of Mr. Vallandigham. Quite surely nothing of this sort was or is intended. I was wholly unaware that Mr. Vallandigham was, at the time of his arrest, a candidate for the Democratic nomination for governor, until so informed by your reading to me the resolutions of the convention. I am grateful to the State of Ohio for many things, especially for the brave soldiers and officers she has given in the present national trial to the armies of the Union. You claim, as I understand, that, according to my position in the Albany response, Mr. Vallandigham should be released, and this because, as you claim, he has not damaged the military service by discouraging enlistments, encouraging desertions, or otherwise, and that if he had he should be turned over to the civil authorities under the recent acts of Congress. I certainly do not *know* that Mr. Vallandigham has specifically and by direct language advised against enlistments and in favor of desertion and resistance to drafting. We all know that combinations, armed in some instances to resist the arrest of deserters, began several months ago, that more recently the like has appeared in resistance to the enrollment preparatory to a draft, and that quite a number of assassinations have occurred from the same animus. These had to be met by military force, and this again has led to bloodshed and death. And now, under the sense of responsibility more weighty and enduring than any which is merely official, I solemnly declare my belief that this hindrance of the military, including maiming and murder, is due to the course in which Mr. Vallandigham has been engaged, in a greater degree than to any other cause, and it is due to him personally in a greater degree than to any other man.

These things have been notorious, known to all, and of course known to Mr. Vallandigham. Perhaps I would not be wrong to say they originated with his especial friends and adherents. With perfect knowledge of them he has frequently, if not constantly, made speeches in Congress and before popular assemblies; and if it can be shown that, with these things staring him in the face, he has ever uttered a word of rebuke or counsel against them, it will be a fact greatly in his favor with me, and one of which, as yet, I am totally ignorant.

When it is known that the whole burden of his speeches has been to stir up men against the prosecution of the war, and that in the midst of resistance to it he has not been known in any instance to counsel against such resistance, it is next to impossible to repel the inference that he has counseled directly in favor of it. With all this before their eyes, the convention you represent have nominated Mr. Vallandigham for governor of Ohio, and both they and you have declared the purpose to sustain the National Union by all constitutional means. But, of course, they and you, in common, reserve to yourselves to decide what are constitutional means, and, unlike the Albany meeting, you omit to state or intimate that, in your opinion, an army is a constitutional means of saving the Union against a rebellion, or even to intimate that you are conscious of an existing rebellion being in progress with the avowed object of destroying that very Union.

At the same time, your nominee for governor, in whose behalf you appeal, is known to you and to the world to declare against the use of an army to suppress the rebellion. Your own attitude, therefore, encourages desertion, resistance to the draft, and the like, because it teaches those who incline to desert and to escape the draft to believe it is your purpose to protect them and to hope that you will become strong enough to do so. After a short personal intercourse with you, gentlemen of the committee, I can not say I think you desire this effect to follow your attitude, but I assure you that both friends and enemies of the Union look upon it in this light. It is a substantial hope, and by consequence a real strength to the enemy. It is a false hope, and one which you would willingly dispel. I will make the way exceedingly easy. I send you duplicates of this letter, in order that you, or a majority, may, if you choose, indorse your names upon one of them and return it thus indorsed to me, with the understanding that those signing are hereby committed to the following propositions, and to nothing else:

1. That there is now a rebellion in the United States, the object and tendency of which is to destroy the national Union, and that in your opinion an army and navy are constitutional means for suppressing that rebellion. 2. That no one of you will do any thing which in his own judgment will tend to hinder the increase or favor the decrease or lessen the efficiency of the army and navy, while engaged in the effort to suppress that rebellion; and, 3. That each of you will, in his sphere, do all he can to have the officers, soldiers, and seamen of the army and navy, while engaged in the effort to suppress the rebellion, paid, fed, clad, and otherwise well provided for and supported.

And with the further understanding that upon receiving the letter and names thus indorsed, I will cause them to be published, which publication shall be within itself a revocation of the order in relation to Mr. Vallandigham.

It will not escape observation that I consent to the release of Mr. Vallandigham upon terms not embracing any pledge from him or from others as to what he will or will not do. I do this because he is not present to speak for himself, or to authorize others to speak for him; and hence I shall expect that on returning he would not put himself practically in antagonism with his friends. But I do it chiefly because I thereby prevail on other influential gentlemen of Ohio to so define their position as to be of immense value to the army—thus more than compensating for the consequence of any mistake in allowing Mr. Vallandigham to return, so that, on the whole, the public safety will not have suffered by it. Still, in regard to Mr. Vallandigham and all others, I must hereafter, as heretofore, do so much as the public service may seem to require.

I have the honor to be, respectfully yours, etc.,

A. LINCOLN.

WAR BULLETIN—OFFICIAL.

Executive Mansion, Washington, July 31, 1863.

It is the duty of every government to give protection to the citizens, of whatever class, color, or condition, and especially to those who are duly organized as soldiers in the public service. The law of nations, and the usages and customs of war, as carried on by civilized powers, permit no distinction as to color in the treatment of prisoners of war or public enemies. To sell or enslave any captured person, on account of his color, and for no offense against the laws of war, is a relapse into barbarism, and a crime against the civilization of the age.

The government of the United States will give the same protection to all its soldiers, and if the enemy shall sell or enslave any one because of his color, the offense shall be punished by retaliation upon the enemy's prisoners in our possession. It is therefore ordered that for every soldier of the United States killed in violation of the laws of war, a rebel soldier shall be executed, and for every one enslaved by the enemy or sold into slavery, a rebel soldier shall be placed at hard labor on the public works, and continued at such labor until the other shall be released, and receive the treatment due to a prisoner of war.

A. LINCOLN.

LETTER TO GENERAL BANKS, AUGUST 5, 1863.

My Dear General Banks:—While I very well know what I would be glad for Louisiana to do, it is quite a different thing for me to assume direction of the matter. I would be glad for her to make a new Constitution, recognizing the Emancipation Proclamation, and adopting emancipation in those parts of the state to which the proclamation does not apply. And while she is at it, I think it would not be objectionable for her to adopt some practical system by which the two races could gradually live themselves out of their old relations to each other, and both come out better prepared for the new. Education for young blacks should be included in the plan. After all, the power of element of "contract" may be sufficient for this probationary period, and by its simplicity and flexibility may be better. As an anti-slavery man, I have a motive to desire emancipation which proslavery men do not have; but even they have strong enough reason to thus place themselves again under the shield of the Union, and to thus perpetually pledge against the recurrence of the scenes through which we are now passing. Governor Shepley has informed me that Mr. Durant is now taking a registry, with a view to the election of a constitutional convention in Louisiana. This, to me, appears proper. If such convention were to ask my views, I could present little else than what I now say to you. I think the thing should be pushed forward so that, if possible, its mature work may reach here by the meeting of Congress. For my own part, I think I shall not, in any event, retract the Emancipation Proclamation; nor, as Executive, ever return to slavery any person who is free by the terms of that proclamation, or by any of the acts of Congress. If Louisiana shall send members to Congress, their admission to seats will depend, as you know, upon the respective houses, and not upon the President.

Yours, very truly, A. LINCOLN.

TO HIS EXCELLENCY, HORATIO SEYMOUR, GOVERNOR OF NEW YORK.

Executive Mansion, Washington, August 7, 1863.

Your communication of the third instant has been received and attentively considered.

I can not consent to suspend the draft in New York, as you request, because, among other reasons, *time* is important. By the figures you send, which I presume are correct, the twelve districts represented fall in two classes of eight and four respectively. The disparity of the quotas for the draft in these two classes is certainly very striking, being the difference between the average of 2,200 in one class, and 4,864 in the other.

Assuming that the districts are equal, one to another, an entire population, as required by the plan on which they were made, this disparity is such as to require attention. Much of it, however, I suppose will be accounted for by the fact that so many more persons fit for soldiers are in the city than are in the country, who have too recently arrived from other parts of the United States and from Europe to be either included in the census of 1860, or to have voted in 1862. Still, making due allowance for this, I am yet unwilling to stand upon it as an entirely sufficient explanation of the great disparity.

I shall direct the draft to proceed in all the districts, drawing, however, at first from each of the four districts, to wit: the second, fourth, sixth, and eighth—only 2,200 being the average quota of the other class. After the drawing, these four districts, and also the seventeenth and twenty-ninth, shall be carefully re-enrolled; and, if you please, agents of yours may witness every step of the process.

Any deficiency which may appear by the new enrollment will be supplied by special draft for that object, allowing due credit for volunteers who may be obtained from these districts respectively during the interval; and at all points, so far as consistent with practical convenience, due credit shall be given for volunteers, and your Excellency shall be notified of the time fixed for commencing a draft in each district. A. LINCOLN.

LETTER TO GENERAL GRANT, AUGUST 9, 1863.

General Thomas has gone again to the Mississippi valley, with the view of raising colored troops. I have no doubt that you are doing what you reasonably can upon the same subject. I believe it a resource which, if rigorously applied now, will soon close this contest. It works doubly, weakening the enemy and strengthening us. We were not fully ripe for it until the river was opened. Now, I think, at least one hundred thousand can, and ought to be, organized along its shores, relieving all the white troops to serve elsewhere.

Mr. Davis understands you as believing that the emancipation proclamation has helped some of your military operations, and I am very glad if this is so.
A. LINCOLN.

LETTER TO THE ILLINOIS CONVENTION.

Executive Mansion, Washington, Aug. 26, 1863.

Hon. James C. Conkling: My Dear Sir—Your letter inviting me to attend a mass meeting of unconditional Union men, to be held at the capital of Illinois, on the 3d day of September, has been received. It would be very agreeable for me thus to meet my old friends at my own home, but I can not just now be absent from here as long as a visit there would require.

The meeting is to be of all those who maintain unconditional devotion to the Union, and I am sure my old political friends will thank me for tendering, as I do, the nation's gratitude to those other noble men whom no partisan malice or partisan hope can make false to the nation's life.

There are those who are dissatisfied with me. To such I would say, you desire peace, and you blame me that we do not have it. But how can we attain it? There are but three conceivable ways: First, to suppress the rebellion by force of arms. This I am trying to do. Are you for it? If you are, so far we are agreed. If you are not for it, a second way, is to give up the Union. I am against this. Are you for it? If you are, you should say so plainly. If you are not for *force*, nor yet for *dissolution*, there only remains some imaginable *compromise*.

I do not believe that any compromise embracing the maintenance of the Union is now possible. All that I learn leads to a directly opposite belief. The strength of the rebellion is its military, its army. That army dominates all the country and all the people within its range. Any offer of terms made by any man or men within that range, in opposition to that army, is simply nothing for the present; because such man or men have no power whatever to enforce their side of a compromise, if one were made with them.

To illustrate: Suppose refugees from the South and peace men of the North get together in convention, and frame and proclaim a compromise embracing a restoration of the Union. In what way can that compromise be used to keep Lee's army out of Pennsylvania? Meade's army can keep Lee's army out of Pennsylvania, and, I think, can ultimately drive it out of existence. But no paper compromise to which the controllers of Lee's army are not agreed can at all affect that army. In an effort at such compromise we would waste time, which the enemy would improve to our disadvantage, and that would be all.

A compromise, to be effective, must be made either with those who control the rebel army, or with the people, first liberated from the domination of that army by the success of our own army. Now, allow me to assure you that no word or intimation from that rebel army, or from any of the men controlling it, in relation to any peace compromise, has ever come to my knowledge or belief. All charges and insinuations to the contrary are deceptive and groundless. And I promise you that if any such proposition shall hereafter come, it shall not be rejected and kept a secret from you. I freely acknowledge myself to be the servant of the people, according to the bond of service, the United States Constitution; and that, as such, I am responsible to them. But, to be plain, you are dissatisfied with me about the negro. Quite likely there is a difference of opinion between you and myself upon that subject. I certainly wish that all men could be free, while you, I suppose, do not. Yet I have neither adopted nor proposed any measure which is not consistent with even your views, provided that you are for the Union. I suggested compensated emancipation, to which you replied you wished not to be taxed to buy negroes. But I had not asked you to be taxed to buy negroes, except in such a way as to save you from greater taxation to save the Union exclusively by other means.

You dislike the emancipation proclamation, and perhaps would have it retracted. You say it is unconstitutional. I think differently. I think the Constitution invests its commander-in-chief with the law of war in time of war. The most that can be said if so much, is, that slaves are property. Is there, has there ever been, any question that by the law of war, property, both of enemies and friends, may be taken when needed? And is it not needed whenever it helps us and hurts the enemy? Armies, the world over, destroy enemies' property when they can not use it, and even destroy their own to keep it from the enemy.

Civilized belligerents do all in their power to help themselves, or hurt the enemy, except a few things regarded as barbarous or cruel. Among the exceptions are the massacre of vanquished foes and non-combatants, male and female.

But the proclamation, as law, either is valid or is not valid. If it is not valid it needs no retraction. If it is valid, it can not be retracted, any more than the dead can be brought to life. Some of you profess to think its retraction would operate favorably for the Union. Why better after the retraction than before the issue? There was more than a year and a half of trial to suppress the rebellion before the proclamation was issued, the last one hundred days of which passed under an explicit notice that it was coming, unless averted by those in revolt returning to their allegiance. The war has certainly progressed as favorably for us since the issue of the proclamation as before. I know as fully as one can know the opinion of others that some of the commanders of our armies in the field, who have given us our most important victories, believe the emancipation policy and the use of colored troops constitute the heaviest blows yet dealt to the rebellion, and that at least one of those important successes could not have been achieved when it was but for the aid of black soldiers.

Among the commanders who hold these views are some who have never had an affinity with what is called "abolitionism," or with "Republican party politics," but who held them purely as military opinions. I submit their opinions as entitled to some weight against the objections often urged that emancipation and arming the blacks are unwise as military measures, and were not adopted as such in good faith.

You say that you will not fight to free negroes. Some of them seem willing to fight for you; but no matter. Fight you then, exclusively to save the Union. I issued the proclamation on purpose to aid you in saving the Union. Whenever you shall have conquered all resistance to the Union, if I shall urge you to continue fighting, it will be an apt time then for you to declare you will not fight to free negroes. I thought that, in your struggle for the Union, to whatever extent the negroes should cease helping the enemy, to that extent it weakened the enemy in his resistance to you. Do you think differently?

I thought that whatever negroes can be got to do as soldiers, leaves just so much less for white soldiers to do in saving the Union. Does it appear otherwise to you? But negroes, like other people, act upon motives. Why should they do any thing for us, if we will do nothing for them? If they stake their lives for us, they must be prompted by the strongest motive, even the promise of freedom. And the promise being made, must be kept. The signs look better. The Father of Waters again goes unvexed to the sea. Thanks to the great north-west for it; nor yet wholly to them. Three hundred miles up they met New England, Empire, Keystone and Jersey, hewing their way right and left.

The sunny South, too, in more colors than one, also lent a helping hand. On the spot their part of the history was jotted down in black and white. The job was a great national one, and let none be slighted who bore an honorable part in it. And while those who have cleared the great river may well be proud, even that is not all. It is hard to say that any thing has been more bravely or well done than at Antietam, Murfreesboro, Gettysburg, and on many fields of less note. Nor must Uncle Sam's web-feet be forgotten. At all the watery margins they have been present, not only on the deep sea, the broad bay, and the rapid river, but also up the narrow muddy bayou, and wherever the ground was a little damp, they have been and made their tracks. Thanks to all. For the great republic—for the principle it lives by and keeps alive—for man's vast future—thanks to all.

Peace does not appear so distant as it did. I hope it will come soon, and come to stay, and so come as to be worth the keeping in all future time. It will then have been proved that among free men, there can be no successful appeal from the ballot to the bullet, and that they who take such appeal are sure to lose their case and pay the cost. And there will be some black men who can remember that with silent tongue, and clinched teeth, and steady eye, and well poised bayonet, they have helped mankind on to this great consummation; while I fear there will be some white men unable to forget that with malignant and deceitful speech they have striven to hinder it.

Still, let us not be over-sanguine of a speedy final triumph. Let us be quite sober. Let us diligently apply the means, never doubting that a just God, in his own good time, will give us the rightful result.

Yours very truly, A. LINCOLN.

INSTRUCTIONS TO GENERAL SCHOFIELD.

Executive Mansion, Washington, Oct. 1, 1863.

General John M. Schofield:—There is no organized military force in avowed opposition to the general government now in Missouri, and if any shall reappear, your duty in regard to it will be too plain to require any special instruction. Still, the condition of things, both there and elsewhere, is such as to render it indispensable to maintain, for a time, the United States military establishment in that state, as well as to rely upon it for a fair contribution of support to that establishment generally. Your immediate duty in regard to Missouri now is to advance the efficiency of that establishment, and to use it, as far as practicable to compel the excited people there to let one another alone.

Under your recent order, which I have approved,

you will only arrest individuals, and suppress assemblies or newspapers, when they may be working *palpable* injury to the military in your charge; and in no other case will you interfere with the expression of opinion in any form, or allow it to be interfered with violently by others. In this you have a discretion to exercise with great caution, calmness and forbearance.

With the matter of removing the inhabitants of certain counties *en masse*, and of removing certain individuals from time to time, who are supposed to be mischievous, I am not now interfering, but am leaving to your own discretion.

Nor am I interfering with what may still seem to you to be necessary restrictions upon trade and intercourse. I think proper, however, to enjoin upon you the following: Allow no part of the military under your command to be engaged in either returning fugitive slaves, or in forcing or enticing slaves from their homes; and, as far as practicable, enforce the same forbearance upon the people.

Report to me your opinion upon the availability for good of the enrolled militia of the state. Allow no one to enlist colored troops, except upon orders from you, or from here through you.

Allow no one to assume the functions of confiscating property, under the law of Congress, or otherwise, except upon orders from here.

At elections see that those, and only those, are allowed to vote, who are entitled to do so by the laws of Missouri, including as of those laws the restrictions laid by the Missouri convention upon those who may have participated in the rebellion.

So far as practicable, you will, by means of your military force, expel guerrillas, marauders and murderers, and all who are known to harbor, aid, or abet them. But in like manner you will repress assumptions of unauthorized individuals to perform the same service, because under pretense of doing this they become marauders and murderers themselves.

To now restore peace, let the military obey orders; and those not of the military leave each other alone, thus not breaking the peace themselves.

In giving the above directions, it is not intended to restrain you in other expedient and necessary matters not falling within their range.

Your obedient servant, A. LINCOLN.

PROCLAMATION, OCTOBER 3, 1863.

The year that is drawing toward its close has been filled with the blessings of fruitful fields and healthful skies.

To these bounties, which are so constantly enjoyed that we are prone to forget the source from which they come, others have been added which are of so extraordinary a nature that they can not fail to penetrate and soften even the heart which is habitually insensible to the ever watchful Providence of Almighty God.

In the midst of a civil war of unparalleled magnitude and severity, which has sometimes seemed to invite and provoke the aggressions of foreign states, peace has been preserved with all nations, order has been maintained, the laws have been respected and obeyed, and harmony has prevailed every-where except in the theater of military conflict, while that theater has been greatly contracting by the advancing armies and navies of the Union.

The needful diversion of wealth and strength from the fields of peaceful industry to the national defense, has not arrested the plow, the shuttle, or the ship.

The ax has enlarged the borders of our settlements, and the mines, as well of iron and coal as of the precious metals, have yielded even more abundantly than heretofore. Population has steadily increased, notwithstanding the waste that has been made in the camp, the seige, and the battle field ; and the country, rejoicing in the consciousness of augmented strength and vigor, is permitted to expect a continuance of years, with large increase of freedom.

No human council hath devised, nor hath any mortal hand worked out these great things. They are the gracious gifts of the most High God, who, while dealing with us in anger for our sins, hath nevertheless remembered mercy.

It has seemed to me fit and proper that they should be solemnly, reverently, and gratefully acknowledged, as with one heart and voice, by the whole American people. I do, therefore, invite my fellow-citizens in every part of the United States, and also those who are at sea, and those who are sojourning in foreign lands, to set apart and observe the last Thursday of November next as a day of thanksgiving and prayer to our beneficent Father, who dwelleth in the heavens ; and I recommend to them that while offering up the ascriptions justly due to Him, for such singular deliverances and blessings, they do also, with humble penitence for our national perverseness and disobedience, commend to His tender care all those who have become widows, orphans, mourners, or sufferers in the lamentable civil strife in which we are unavoidably engaged, and fervently implore the interposition of the Almighty hand to heal the wounds of the nation, and to restore it, as soon as may be consistent with the Divine purposes, to the full enjoyment of peace, harmony, tranquillity, and union.

In testimony whereof, I have hereunto set my hand, and caused the seal of the United States to be affixed.

Done at the City of Washington, this third day of October, in the year of our Lord eighteen hundred and sixty-three, and of the independence of the United States the eighty-eighth. A. LINCOLN.

TO GENERAL ROSECRANS.

October 4, 1863.

Yours of yesterday received. If we can hold Chattanooga and East Tennessee, I think the rebellion must dwindle and die. I think you and Burnside can do this, and hence doing so is your main object. Of course, to greatly damage or destroy the enemy in your front would be a greater object, because it would include the former, and more; but it is not so certainly within your power. I understand the main body of the enemy is very near you—so near that you could "board at home," so to speak, and menace or attack him any day. Would not the doing of this be your best mode of counteracting his raids on your communications?

But this is not an order. I intend doing something like what you suggest whenever the case shall appear ripe enough to have it accepted in the true understanding, rather than as a confession of weakness and fear. A. LINCOLN.

To HON. CHARLES DRAKE AND OTHERS, COMMITTEE.

Executive Mansion, Washington, October 5, 1863.

Gentlemen:—Your original address, presented on the 30th ult., and the four supplementary ones, presented on the 3d inst., have been carefully considered. I hope you will regard the other duties claiming my attention, together with the great length and importance of these documents, as constituting a sufficient apology for my not having responded sooner.

These papers, framed for a common object, consist of the things demanded, and the reasons for demanding them. The things demanded are:

First—That General Schofield shall be relieved and General Butler be appointed as commander of the Military Department of Missouri;

Second—That the system of enrolled militia in Missouri may be broken up, and national forces be substituted for it; and,

Third—That at elections persons may not be allowed to vote who are not entitled by law to do so.

Among the reasons given, enough of suffering and wrong to Union men is certainly, and I suppose truly, stated. Yet the whole case, as presented, fails to convince me that General Schofield, or the enrolled militia, is responsible for that suffering and wrong.

The whole can be explained on a more charitable, and, as I think, a more rational, hypothesis.

We are in civil war. In such cases there always is a main question; but in this case that question is a perplexing compound—Union and slavery. It thus becomes a question, not of two sides merely, but of at least four sides, even among those who are for the Union, saying nothing of those who are against it. Thus, those who are for the Union *with* but not *without slavery;* those for it *without* but not *with;* those for it *with* or *without,* but prefer it *with;* and those for it *with* or *without,* but prefer it *without.*

Among these, again, is a subdivision of those who are for *gradual* but not for *immediate,* and those who are for *immediate* but not for *gradual,* extinction of slavery. It is easy to conceive that all these shades of opinion, and even more, may be sincerely entertained by honest and truthful men. Yet, all being for the Union, by reason of these differences each will prefer a different way of sustaining the Union. At once sincerity is questioned and motives are assailed. Actual war coming, blood grows hot and blood is spilled. Thought is forced from old channels into confusion. Deception breeds and thrives. Confidence dies, and universal suspicion reigns. Each man feels an impulse to kill his neighbor, lest he be killed by him. Revenge and retaliation follow. And all this, as before said, may be among honest men only. But this is not all. Every foul bird comes abroad, and every dirty reptile rises up. These add crime to confusion. Strong measures, deemed indispensable but harsh at best, such men make worse by mal-administration. Murders for old grudges and murders for pelf proceed under any cloak that will best serve for the occasion.

These causes amply account for what has occurred in Missouri, without ascribing it to the weakness or wickedness of any general. The newspaper files, those chroniclers of current events, will show that the evils now complained of were quite as prevalent under Fremont, Hunter, Halleck, and Curtis, as under Schofield. If the former had greater force opposed to them, they also had greater force with which to meet it. When the organized rebel army left the state, the main Federal force had to go also, leaving the department commander at home relatively no stronger than before. Without disparaging any, I affirm with confidence that no commander of that department has, in proportion to his means, done better than General Schofield.

The first specific charge against General Schofield is, that the enrolled militia was placed under his command, whereas it had not been placed under the command of General Curtis. The fact is, I believe, true; but you do not point out, nor can I conceive, how that did, or could, injure loyal men or the Union cause. You charge that General Curtis being superseded by General Schofield, Franklin A. Dick was superseded by James O. Brodhead as provost-marshal-general. No very specific showing is made as to how this did or could injure the Union cause. It recalls, however, the condition of things, as presented to me, which led to a change of commander of that department.

To restrain contraband intelligence and trade, a system of searches, seizures, permits, and passes had been introduced, I think, by General Fremont. When General Halleck came, he found and continued the system, and added an order, applicable to some parts of the state, to levy and collect contributions from noted rebels, to compensate losses and relieve destitution caused by the rebellion. The action of General Fremont and General Halleck, as stated, contributed a sort of system which General Curtis found in full operation when he took command of the department. That there was a necessity for something of the sort was clear; but that it could only be justified by stern necessity, and that it was liable to great abuse in administration, was equally clear. Agents to execute it, contrary to the great prayer, were led into temptation. Some might, while others would not, resist that temptation. It was not possible to hold any to a very strict accountability; and those yielding to the temptation would sell permits and passes to those who would pay most and most readily for them, and would seize property and collect levies in the aptest way to fill their own pockets. Money being the object, the man having money, whether loyal or disloyal, would be a victim. This practice doubtless existed to some extent, and it was a real additional evil that it could be, and was plausibly charged to exist in greater extent than it did.

When General Curtis took command of the department, Mr. Dick, against whom I never knew any thing to allege, had general charge of this system.

A controversy in regard to it rapidly grew into almost unmanageable proportions. One side ignored the *necessity*, and magnified the evils of the system, while the other ignored the evils, and magnified the necessity; and each bitterly assailed the other. I could not fail to see that the controversy enlarged in the same proportion as the professed Union men there distinctly took sides in two opposing political parties. I exhausted my wits, and very nearly my patience also, in efforts to convince both that the evils they charged on each other were inherent in the case, and could not be cured by giving either party a victory over the other.

Plainly, the irritating system was not to be perpetual; and it was plausibly urged that it could be modified at once with advantage. The case could scarcely be worse, and whether it could be made better could only be determined by a trial. In this view, and not to ban or brand General Curtis, or to give a victory to any party, I made the change of commander for the department. I now learn that soon after this change Mr. Dick was removed, and that Mr. Brodhead, a gentleman of no less good character, was put in the place. The mere fact of this change is more distinctly complained of than is any conduct of the new officer, or other consequence of the change.

I gave the new commander no instructions as to the administration of the system mentioned, beyond what is contained in the private letter afterward surreptitiously published, in which I directed him to act solely for the public good, and independently of both parties.

Neither any thing you have presented me, nor any thing I have otherwise learned, has convinced me that he has been unfaithful to this charge.

Imbecility is urged as one cause for removing General Schofield, and the late massacre at Lawrence, Kansas, is pressed as an evidence of that imbecility. To my mind, that fact scarcely tends to prove the proposition. That massacre is only an example of what Grierson, John Morgan, and many others, might have repeatedly done on their respective raids, had they chosen to incur the personal hazard, and possessed the fiendish hearts to do it.

The charge is made that General Schofield, on purpose to protect the Lawrence murderers, would not allow them to be pursued into Missouri. While no punishment could be too sudden or too severe for those murderers, I am well satisfied that the preventing of the threatened remedial raid into Missouri was the only way to avoid an indiscriminate massacre there, including probably more innocent than guilty. Instead of condemning, I therefore approve what I understand General Schofield did in that respect.

The charge that General Schofield has purposely withheld protection from loyal people, and purposely facilitated the objects of the disloyal, are altogether beyond my belief. I do not arraign the veracity of gentlemen as to the facts complained of, but I do more than question the judgment which would infer that these facts occurred in accordance with the purposes of General Schofield.

With my present views, I must decline to remove General Schofield. In this I decide nothing against General Butler. I sincerely wish it were convenient to assign him a suitable command.

In order to meet some existing evils, I have addressed a letter of instruction to General Schofield, a copy of which I inclose you. As to the "enrolled militia," I shall endeavor to ascertain, better than I now know, what is its exact value. Let me say now, however, that your proposal to substitute national force for the "enrolled militia" implies that, in your judgment, the latter is doing something which needs to be done; and if so, the proposition to throw that force away, to supply its place by bringing other forces from the field, where they are urgently needed, seems to me very extraordinary. Whence shall they come? Shall they be withdrawn from Banks, or Grant, or Steele, or Rosecrans?

Few things have been so grateful to my anxious feelings as when, in June last, the local force in Missouri aided General Schofield to so promptly send a large general force to the relief of General Grant, then investing Vicksburg, and menaced from without by General Johnston. Was this all wrong? Should the enrolled militia then have been broken up, and General Heron kept from Grant to police Missouri? So far from finding cause to object, I confess to a sympathy for whatever relieves our general force in Missouri, and allows it to serve elsewhere. I therefore, as at present advised, can not attempt the destruction of the enrolled militia of Missouri.

I may add, that the force being under the national

military control, it is also within the proclamation with regard to the habeas corpus. I concur in the propriety of your request, in regard to elections, and have, as you see, directed General Schofield accordingly.

I do not feel justified to enter upon the broad field you present, in regard to the political differences between radicals and conservatives. From time to time I have done and said what appeared to me proper to do and say. The public knows it well. It obliges nobody to follow me, and I trust it obliges me to follow nobody. The radicals and conservatives each agree with me in some things and disagree in others. I could wish both to agree with me in all things; for then they would agree with each other, and would be too strong for any foe from any quarter. They, however, choose to do otherwise; and I do not question their right. I too shall do what seems to be my duty. I hold whoever commands in Missouri or elsewhere responsible to me, and not to either radicals or conservatives. It is my duty to hear all; but, at last, I must within my sphere, judge what to do and what to forbear. Your obedient servant,   A. LINCOLN.

THE PRESIDENT TO THURLOW WEED.

Washington, October 14, 1863.

Dear Sir:—I have been brought to fear recently that somehow, by commission or omission, I have caused you some degree of pain. I have never entertained an unkind feeling or a disparaging thought toward you; and if I have said or done any thing which has been construed into such unkindness or disparagement, it has been misconstrued.

I am sure if we could meet we would not part with any unpleasant impression on either side.

Yours truly,   A. LINCOLN.

Washington, D. C., October 27, 1863.

In June last, a division was substantially lost at, and near Winchester, Va. At the time, it was under General Milroy as immediate commander in the field, General Schenck as department commander at Baltimore, and General Halleck as General-in-Chief, at Washington.

General Milroy, as immediate commander, was put in arrest, and subsequently a court of inquiry examined chiefly with reference to disobedience of orders, and reported the evidence.

The foregoing is a synoptical statement of the evidence, together with the Judge-Advocate-General's conclusions. The disaster, when it came, was a surprise to all. It was very well known to Generals Schenck and Milroy for some time, before that, General Halleck thought the division was in great danger of a surprise at Winchester; that it was of no service commensurate with the risk it incurred, and that it ought to be withdrawn; but, although, he more than once advised its withdrawel, he never positively ordered it. General Schenck, on the contrary, believed the service of the force at Winchester was worth the hazard, and so did not positively order its withdrawal until it was so late that, the enemy cut the wire and prevented the order reaching General Milroy. General

Milroy seems to have concurred with General Schenck in the opinion that the force should be kept at Winchester, at least until the approach of danger, but he disobeyed no order upon the subject.

Some question can be made whether some of General Halleck's dispatches to General Schenck should not have been construed to be orders to withdraw the force and obeyed accordingly; but, no such question can be made against General Milroy. In fact, the last order he received was to be prepared to withdraw, but not to actually withdraw until further orders, which further order never reached him.

Serious blame is not necessarily due to any serious disaster, and I can not say that in this case, any of the officers are deserving of serious blame.

No court-martial is deemed necessary or proper in this case. A. LINCOLN.

PRIVATE AND CONFIDENTIAL.

Executive Mansion, Washington, Oct. 28, 1863.

General John M. Schofield:—There have recently reached the War Department, and thence been laid before me, from Missouri, three communications, all similar in import and identical in object.

One of them addressed to nobody and without place or date, but having the signature of (apparently) the writer, is a letter of eight closely written foolscap pages. The other two are written by a different person, at St. Joseph, Mo., and of the dates, respectively, October 12 and 13, 1863, and each inclosing a large number of affidavits. The general statement of the whole are that the Federal and state authorities are arming the disloyal and disarming the loyal, and that the latter will all be killed and driven out of the state unless there shall be a change. In particular, no loyal man who has been disarmed is named, but the affidavits show by name forty-two persons as disloyal who have been armed.

A majority of these are shown to have been in the rebel service. I believe it could be shown that the government here has deliberately armed more than ten times as many captured at Gettysburg, to say nothing of similar operations in East Tennessee.

These papers contain altogether thirty-one manuscript pages, and one newspaper *in extenso*, and yet I do not find it anywhere charged in them that any loyal man has been harmed by reason of being disarmed, or that any disloyal one has harmed anybody by reason of being armed by the Federal or state government. Of course, I have not had time to carefully examine all, but I have had most of them examined and briefed by others, and the result is as stated. The remarkable fact that the actual evil is yet only anticipated—inferred—induces me to suppose I understand the case; but I do not state my impression, because I might be mistaken, and because your duty and mine is plain in any event. The locality of nearly all this seems to be St. Joseph and Buchanan county.

I wish you to give special attention to this region, particularly on election day. Prevent violence from whatever quarter, and see that the soldiers themselves do no wrong. Yours truly,

A. LINCOLN.

Reply of President Lincoln on the Re-Admission of Louisiana.

Fall of 1863.

Messrs. E. E. Motriol, Bradit, Johnston, and Thomas Gottsman: Gentlemen—Since receiving the letter, reliable information has reached me that a respectable portion of the Louisiana people desire to amend their state constitution, and contemplate holding a convention for that object. This fact alone, as it seems to me, is a sufficient reason why the general government should not give the committee the authority you seek to act under the existing state constitution. I may add that while I do not perceive how such a committee could facilitate our military operations in Louisiana, I really apprehend it might be so used as to embarrass them.

As to an election to be held in November, there is abundant time without any order or proclamation from me just now. The people of Louisiana shall not lack an opportunity for a fair election for both Federal and state officers by want of any thing within my power to give them.

Your obedient servant, A. LINCOLN.

To the Honorable House of Representatives.

In compliance with the request contained in your resolution of the 29th ultimo, a copy of which resolution is herewith returned, I have the honor to transmit the following:

Executive Mansion, Washington, Nov. 2, 1863.
Hon. Montgomery Blair: My Dear Sir—Some days

ago I understood you to say that your brother, General Frank Blair, desired to be guided by my wishes as to whether he will occupy his seat in Congress or remain in the field.

My wish, then, is compounded of what I believe will be best for the country; and it is that he will come here, put his military commission in my hands, take his seat, go into caucus with our friends, abide the nominations, help elect the nominees, and thus aid to organize a House of Representatives which will really support the government in the war.

If the result shall be the election of himself as speaker, let him serve in that position. If not, let him retake his commission and return to the army for the benefit of the country. This will heal a dangerous schism for him. It will relieve him from a dangerous position or a misunderstanding, as I think he is in danger of being permanently separated from those with whom only he can ever have a real sympathy—the sincere opponents of slavery.

It will be a mistake if he shall allow the provocation offered him by insincere time-servers to drive him from the house of his own building. He is young yet. He has abundant talents—quite enough to occupy all his time without devoting any to temper. He is rising in military skill and usefulness. His recent appointment to the command of a corps, by one so competent to judge as General Sherman, proves this.

In that line he can serve both the country and himself more profitably than he could as a member of Congress upon the floor. The foregoing is what I would say if Frank Blair was my brother instead of yours. A. LINCOLN.

Address at the Dedication of Gettysburg Cemetery, November 19, 1863.

Fourscore and seven years ago our fathers brought forth upon this continent a new nation, conceived in liberty, and dedicated to the proposition that all men are created free and equal. Now we are engaged in a great civil war, testing whether that nation, or any nation so conceived and so dedicated, can long endure. We are met on a great battle field of that war. We have come to dedicate a portion of that field as a final resting-place for those who here gave their lives that that nation might live. It is altogether fitting and proper that we should do this. But in a larger sense we can not dedicate, we can not consecrate, we can not hallow, this ground. The brave men, living and dead, who struggled here, have consecrated it far above our power to add or detract. The world will little note, nor long remember, what we say here, but it can never forget what they did here. It is for us, the living, rather to be dedicated here to the unfinished work which they who fought here have thus far so nobly advanced. It is rather for us to be here dedicated to the great task remaining before us, that from these honored dead we take increased devotion to that cause for which they gave the last full measure of devotion; that we here highly resolve that these dead shall not have died in vain, that this nation, under God, shall have a new birth of freedom, and that the government of the people, by the people, and for the people, shall not perish from the earth.

This finds an echo in the following ever-to-be-remembered words of Daniel Webster, in his reply to Hayne, in the United States Senate, January 26, 1830:

"When my eyes turn to behold for the last time the sun in heaven, may they not see him shining on the broken and dishonored fragments of a once glorious Union; on states dissevered, discordant, belligerent; on a land rent with civil feuds; or drenched, it may be, in fraternal blood. Let their last feeble and lingering glance rather behold the gorgeous ensign of the republic, now known and honored throughout the earth, still full high advanced; its arms and trophies streaming in all their original luster; not a stripe erased or polluted; not a single star obscured; bearing for its motto no such miserable interrogatory as 'What is all this worth?' nor those other words of delusion and folly, of liberty first and union afterward, but every-where, spread all over in characters of living light, and blazing on all its ample folds, as they float over the sea and over the land, and in every wind under the whole heavens, that other sentiment dear to every American heart—' Liberty AND Union—now and forever—one and inseparable.'"

PRESIDENT LINCOLN'S THIRD ANNUAL MESSAGE.

December 8, 1863.

Fellow-citizens of the Senate and House of Representatives:—Another year of health and of sufficiently abundant harvests has passed. For these, and especially for the improved condition of our national affairs, our renewed and profoundest gratitude to God is due.

We remain in peace and friendship with foreign powers.

The efforts of disloyal citizens of the United States to involve us in foreign wars, to aid an inexcusable insurrection, have been unavailing. Her Britannic Majesty's government, as was justly expected, have exercised their authority to prevent the departure of new hostile expeditions from British ports. The Emperor of France has, by a like proceeding, promptly vindicated the neutrality which he proclaimed at the beginning of the contest. Questions of great intricacy and importance have arisen out of the blockade and other belligerent operations, between the government and several of the maritime powers, but they have been discussed, and, as far as possible, accommodated in a spirit of frankness, justice, and mutual good-will. It is especially gratifying that our prize courts, by the impartiality of their adjudications, have commanded the respect and confidence of maritime powers. . . .

Incidents occurring in the progress of our civil war have forced upon my attention the uncertain state of international questions touching the rights of foreigners in this country and of United States citizens abroad. In regard to some governments, these rights are at least partially defined by treaties. In no instance, however, is it expressly stipulated that in the event of civil war a foreigner residing in this country, within the lines of the insurgents, is to be exempted from the rule which classes him as a belligerent, in whose behalf the government of his country can not expect any privileges or immunities distinct from that character. I regret to say, however, that such claims have been put forward, and, in some instances, in behalf of foreigners who have lived in the United States the greater part of their lives. . . .

When Congress assembled a year ago the war had already lasted nearly twenty months, and there had been many conflicts on both land and sea, with varying results.

The rebellion had been pushed back into reduced limits; yet the tone of public feeling and opinion, at home and abroad, was not satisfactory. With other signs, the popular elections, then just past, indicated uneasiness among ourselves, while amid much that was cold and menacing, the kindest words coming from Europe were uttered in accents of pity, that we were too blind to surrender a hopeless cause.

Our commerce was suffering greatly by a few armed vessels built upon and furnished from foreign shores, and we were threatened with such additions from the same quarter as would sweep our trade from the sea and raise our blockade. We had failed to elicit from European governments any thing hopeful upon this subject. The preliminary emancipation proclamation, issued in September, was running its assigned period to the beginning of the new year. A month later the final proclamation came, including the announcement that colored men of suitable condition would be received into the war service. The policy of emancipation, and of employing black soldiers, gave to the future a new aspect, about which hope, and fear, and doubt contended in uncertain conflict. According to our political system, as a matter of civil administration, the general government had no lawful power to effect emancipation in any state, and for a long time it had been hoped that the rebellion could be suppressed without resorting to it as a military measure. It was all the while deemed possible that the necessity for it might come, and that if it should, the crisis of the contest would then be presented. It came, and, as was anticipated, it was followed by dark and doubtful days. Eleven months have now passed, we are permitted to take another view. The rebel borders are pressed still further back, and by the complete opening of the Mississippi, the country dominated by the rebellion is divided into distinct parts, with no practical communication between them. Tennessee and Arkansas have been substantially cleared of insurgent control, and influential citizens in each, owners of slaves and advocates of slavery at the beginning of the rebellion, now declare openly for emancipation in their respective states.

Of those states not included in the emancipation proclamation, Maryland and Missouri, neither of which three years ago would tolerate any restraint upon the extension of slavery, into new territories, only dispute now as to the best mode of removing it within their own limits.

Of those who were slaves at the beginning of the rebellion, full one hundred thousand are now in the United States military service, about one half of which number actually bear arms in the ranks, thus giving the double advantage of taking so much labor from the insurgent cause, and supplying the places which otherwise must be filled with so many white men. So far as tested, it is difficult to say they are not as good soldiers as any. No servile insurrection or tendency to violence or cruelty, has marked the measures of emancipation and arming the blacks. These measures have been much discussed, in foreign countries, and contemporary with such discussion the tone of public sentiment there is much improved. At home the same measures have been fully discussed, supported, criticised and denounced, and the annual elections following are highly encouraging to those whose official duty it is to bear the country through this great trial. Thus we have the new reckoning. The crisis which threatened to divide the friends of the Union is past.

Looking now at the present and future, and with reference to a resumption of the national authority within the states wherein that authority has been suspended, I have thought fit to issue a proclamation, a copy of which is herewith transmitted. On examination of this proclamation it will appear, as is believed, that nothing will be attempted beyond what is simply justified by the Constitution. True, the form of an oath is given, but no man is coerced to take it. The man is only promised a pardon in case he voluntarily takes the oath. The Constitution authorizes the Executive to grant or withhold the pardon at his own absolute discretion, and this includes the power to grant on terms, as is fully established by judicial and other authorities. It is also proffered that if, in any of the states named, a state government shall be, in the mode prescribed, set up, such government shall be recognized and guaranteed by the United States, and that under it the state shall, on constitutional conditions, be protected against invasion and domestic violence. The constitutional obligation of the United States, to guarantee to every state in the Union a republican form of government, and to protect the state in the cases stated, is explicit and full. But why tender the benefits of this provision only to a state government set up in this particular way? This section of the Constitution contemplates a case wherein the element within a state, favorable to republican government, in the Union, may be too feeble for an opposite and hostile element external to or even within the state; and such are precisely the cases with which we are now dealing. An attempt to guarantee and protect a revived state government, constructed in whole, or in preponderating part, from the very element against whose hostility and violence it is to be protected, is simply absurd. There must be a test by which to separate the opposing elements, so as to build only from the sound, and that test is a sufficiently liberal one which accepts as sound whoever will make a sworn recantation of his former unsoundness.

But if it be proper to require as a test of admission to the political body, an oath of allegiance to the Constitution of the United States, and to the Union under it, why also to the laws and proclamations in regard to slavery? Those laws and proclamations were enacted and put forth for the purpose of aiding

in the suppression of the rebellion. To give them
their fullest effect, there had to be a pledge for their
maintenance. In my judgment they have aided, and
will further aid, the cause for which they were intended. To now abandon them would be not only to
relinquish a lever of power, but would also be a cruel
and astounding breach of faith. I may add at this
point, that while I remain in my present position I
shall not attempt to retract or modify the emancipation proclamation, nor shall I return to slavery any
person who is free by the terms of that proclamation,
or by any of the acts of Congress.

For these and other reasons it is thought best that
support of these measures shall be included in the
oath; and it is believed the executive may lawfully
claim it in return for pardon and restoration of forfeited rights, which he has clear constitutional power to withhold altogether, or grant upon the terms
which he shall deem wisest for the public interest.

It should be observed, also, that this part of the
oath is subject to the modifying and abrogating power
of legislation and supreme judicial decision.

•The proposed acquiescence of the national executive
in any reasonable temporary state arrangement for
the freed people is made with the view of possibly
modifying the confusion and destitution which must
at best attend all classes by a total revolution of labor
throughout whole states.

It is hoped that the already deeply afflicted people
in those states may be somewhat more ready to give
up the cause of their affliction, if, to this extent, this
vital matter be left to themselves; while no power of

the national executive to prevent an abuse is abridged by the proposition.

The suggestion in the proclamation as to maintaining the political frame-work of the states on what is called reconstruction, is made in the hope that it may do good without the danger of harm. It will save labor, and avoid great confusion.

But why any proclamation now upon the subject? This question is beset with the conflicting views that the step might be delayed too long or be taken too soon. In some states the elements for resumption seem ready for action, but remain inactive, apparently for want of a rallying point—a plan of action. Why shall A adopt the plan of B rather than B that of A? And if A and B should agree, how can they know but that the general government here will reject their plan? By the proclamation a plan is presented which may be accepted by them as a rallying point, and which they are assured in advance will not be rejected here. This may bring them to act sooner than they otherwise would.

The objection to a premature presentation of a plan by the national executive consists in the danger of committals on points which could be more safely left to further developments.

Care has been taken to so shape the document as to avoid embarrassments from this source. Saying that in certain terms, certain classes will be pardoned, with rights restored, it is not said that other classes, or other terms will never be included. Saying that reconstruction will be accepted if presented in a specified way, it is not said it will never be accepted in any other way.

The movements, by state action, for emancipation in several of the states, not included in the emancipation proclamation, are matters of profound gratulation. And while I do not repeat in detail what I have heretofore so earnestly urged upon this subject, my general views and feelings remain unchanged; and I trust that Congress will omit no fair opportunity of aiding these important steps to a great consummation.

In the midst of other cares, however important, we must not lose sight of the fact that the war power is still our main reliance. To that power alone we can look yet for a time, to give confidence to the people in the contested regions, that the insurgent power will not again overrun them. Until that confidence shall be established, little can be done anywhere for what is called reconstruction.

Hence our chiefest care must be directed to the army and navy, who have thus far borne their harder part so nobly and well. And it may be esteemed fortunate that in giving the greatest efficiency to these indispensable arms, we do also honorably recognize the gallant men, from commander to sentinel, who compose them, and to whom, more than to others, the world must stand indebted for the home of freedom disenthralled, regenerated, enlarged and perpetuated. A. LINCOLN.

PROCLAMATION OF AMNESTY.

December 8, 1863.

Whereas, in and by the Constitution of the United

States, it is provided that the president " shall have power to grant reprieves and pardons for offenses against the United States, except in cases of impeachment;" and whereas a rebellion now exists whereby the loyal state governments of several states have for a long time been subverted, and many persons have committed and are now guilty of treason, against the United States, and whereas, with reference to such rebellion and treason, laws have been enacted by Congress declaring forfeitures and confiscation of property and liberation of slaves, all upon terms and conditions therein stated, and also declaring that the president was thereby authorized at any time thereafter, by proclamation, to extend to persons who may have participated in the existing rebellion, in any state or part thereof, pardon and amnesty with such exceptions and at such times and on such conditions as he may deem expedient for the public welfare; and whereas, the congressional declaration and limited and conditional pardon accords with well established judicial exposition of the pardoning power; and whereas, with reference to said rebellion, the President of the United States has issued several proclamations, with provisions in regard to the liberation of slaves; and whereas, it is now desired by some persons heretofore engaged in said rebellion to resume their allegiance to the United States, and to reinaugurate loyal state governments within and for their respective states:

Therefore, I, Abraham Lincoln, President of the United States, do proclaim, declare, and make known to all persons who have directly, or by implication, participated in the existing rebellion, except as hereinafter excepted, that a full pardon is hereby granted to them and each of them, with restoration of all rights and property, except as to slaves, and in property cases where rights of third parties shall have intervened, and upon the condition that every such person shall take and subscribe an oath, and thenceforward keep and maintain such oath inviolate : and which oath shall be registered for permanent preservation, and shall be of the tenor and effect following, to wit :

"I, ———— ————, do solemnly swear, in presence of Almighty God, that I will henceforth faithfully support, protect and defend the Constitution of the United States, and the union of the states thereunder: and that I will, in like manner, abide by and faithfully support all acts of Congress passed during the existing rebellion with reference to slaves, so long and so far as not repealed, modified, or held void by Congress, or by decision of the Supreme Court; and that I will, in like manner, abide by and faithfully support, all proclamations of the president made during the existing rebellion having reference to slaves, so long and so far as not modified or declared void by decision of the Supreme Court. So help me God."

The persons excepted from the benefits of the foregoing provisions are all who are, or shall have been, civil or diplomatic officers or agents of the so-called Confederate government; all who have left judicial stations under the United States to aid the rebellion ; all who are, or shall have been, military or **navy** officers of said so-called Confederate government above the rank of colonel in the army, or of lieutenant in the navy; all who left seats in the United States Congress to aid the rebellion; all who resigned commissions in the army or navy of the United States, and afterward aided the rebellion; and all who have engaged in any way in treating colored persons, or white persons in charge of such, otherwise than lawfully as prisoners of war, and which persons may have been found in the United States service as soldiers, seamen, or in any other capacity.

And I do further proclaim, declare, and make known that whenever in any of the states of Arkansas, Texas, Louisiana, Mississippi, Tennessee, Alabama, Georgia, Virginia, Florida, South Carolina, and North Carolina, a number of persons, not less than one-tenth in number of the votes cast in such state at the presidential election of the year of our Lord one thousand eight hundred and sixty, each having taken the oath aforesaid and not having since violated it, and being a qualified voter by the election law of the state existing immediately before the so-called act of secession, and excluding all others, shall re-establish a state government which shall be republican, and in no wise contravening said oath, such shall be recognized as the true government of the state, and the state shall receive thereunder the benefits of the constitutional provision which declares that "the United States shall guarantee to every state in this Union a republican form of government, and shall protect each of them against invasion; and, on application of the legislature, or the executive (when the legislature can not be convened), against domestic violence.

And I do further proclaim, declare, and make known that any provision that may be adopted by such state government, in relation to the freed people of such state, which shall recognize and declare their permanent freedom, provide for their education, and which may yet be consistent, as a temporary arrangement, with their present condition as a laboring, landless, and homeless class, will not be objected to by the national executive. And it is suggested as not improper that, in constructing a loyal state government in any state, the name of the state, the boundary, the subdivisions, the constitution, and the general code of laws, as before the rebellion, be maintained, subject only to the modifications made necessary by the conditions herein before stated, and such others, if any, not contravening said conditions, and which may be deemed expedient by those framing the new state government.

To avoid misunderstanding, it may be proper to say that this proclamation, so far as it relates to state governments, has no reference to states wherein loyal state governments have all the while been maintained. And, for the same reason, it may be proper to further say that whether members sent to Congress from any state shall be admitted to seats constitutionally rests exclusively with the respective houses, and not to any extent with the executive. And, still further, that this proclamation is intended to present the people of the states wherein the national authority has been suspended, and loyal state governments have been subverted, a mode in and by which the national and loyal state governments may be re-established within such states, or in any of them; and, while the mode presented is the best the executive can suggest, with his present impressions, it must not be understood that no other possible mode would be acceptable.

Given under my hand, at the City of Washington, the eighth day of December, A. D. one thousand eight hundred and sixty-three, and of the independence of the United States of America the eighty-eighth.

ABRAHAM LINCOLN.

To Hon. Secretary of War.

Executive Mansion, Washington, Dec. 21, 1863.

[Private.] In regard to the western matter, I believe the programme will have to stand substantially as I first put it.

Henderson, and especially Brown, believe that the social influence of St. Louis would inevitably tell injuriously upon General Pope in the particular difficulty existing there, and I think there is some force in that view.

As to retaining General S. (Schofield), temporarily, if this should be done, I believe I shall scarcely be able to get his nomination through the Senate.

Send me over his nomination, which, however, I am not quite ready to send to the senate.

Yours, as ever, A. LINCOLN.

Letter to O. D. Filley, St. Louis, Mo.

Dec. 22, 1863.

I have just looked over a petition signed by some three dozen citizens of St. Louis, and the accompanying letters, one by yourself, one by a Mr. Nathan Ranney, and one by a Mr. John D. Coalter, the whole relating to the Rev. Dr. McPheeters. The petition prays that in the name of justice and mercy that I will restore Dr. McPheeters to all his ecclesiastical rights. This gives no intimation as to what ecclesiastical rights are withheld. Your letter states that Provost-Marshal Dick, about a year ago, ordered the arrest of Dr. McPheeters, pastor of Pine Street Church, prohibited him from officiating, and placed the management of the affairs of the church out of the control of the chosen trustees; and near the close you state that a certain course "would insure his release." Mr. Ranney's letter says: "Dr. Samuel B. McPheeters is enjoying all the rights of a civilian, but can not preach the gospel!" Mr. Coalter, in his letter, asks: "Is it not a strange illustration of the condition of things, that the question who shall be allowed to preach in a church in St. Louis shall be decided by the *President of the United States?*" Now, all this sounds very strangely; and, withal, a little as if you gentlemen, making the application, do not understand the case alike; one affirming that the doctor is enjoying all the rights of a civilian, and another pointing out to me what will secure his *release*. On the 2d of January last, I wrote to General Curtis in relation to Mr. Dick's order upon Dr. McPheeters; and, as I suppose, the doctor is enjoying all the rights of a civilian, I only quote that part of my letter which relates to the church. It was as follows: "But I must add that the United States Government must not, as by this order, undertake to run the churches. When an individual, in the church or out of it, becomes dangerous to the public interest, he must be checked; but the churches, as such, must take care of themselves. It will not do for the United States to appoint trustees, supervisors, or other agents, for the churches."

This letter going to General Curtis, then in command there, I supposed, of course, it was obeyed, especially as I heard no further complaint from Dr. McPheeters or his friends for nearly an entire year. I have never interfered, or thought of interfering, as to who shall or shall not preach in any church, nor have I knowingly or believingly tolerated any one else to so interfere by my authority. If any one is so interfering, by color of my authority, I would like to have it specifically made known to me.

If, after all, what is now sought is to have me put Dr. M. back over the head of a majority of his own congregation, that, too, will be declined. I will not have control of any church on any side.

Yours respectfully,   A. LINCOLN.

TO MAJOR-GENERAL GILMORE.

Executive Mansion, Washington, Jan. 13, 1864.

I understand an effort is being made by some worthy gentlemen to reconstruct a legal state government in Florida. Florida is in your department, and it is not unlikely you may be there in person. I have given Mr. Hay a commission of major, and sent him to you, with some blank books and other blanks, to aid in the reconstruction. He will explain as to the manner of using the blanks, and also my general views on the subject. It is desirable for all to co-operate, but if irreconcilable differences of opinion shall arise, you are master. I wish the thing done in the most speedy way, so that when done it be within the range of the late proclamation on the subject. The detail labor will, of course, have to be done by others; but I will be greatly obliged if you will give it such general supervision as you can find consistent with your more strictly military duties.

ABRAHAM LINCOLN.

TO MESSRS. CROSBY AND NICHOLS.

Executive Mansion, Washington, Jan. 16, 1864.

Gentlemen:—The number for this month and year of the North American Review was duly received, and for which please accept my thanks.

Of course, I am not the most impartial judge; yet, with due allowance for this, I venture to hope that the article entitled "The President's Policy" will be of value to the country. I fear I am not worthy of all which is therein kindly said of me personally.

The sentence of twelve lines, commencing at the top of page 252, I could wish to be not exactly what it is. In what is there expressed the writer has not correctly understood me. I have never had a theory that secession could absolve states or people from their obligation.

Precisely the contrary is asserted in the inaugural address; and it was because of my belief in the continuation of those *obligations* that I was puzzled, for a time, as to *denying* the legal *rights* of those citizens who remained individually innocent of treason or rebellion. But I mean no more now than to merely call attention to the point.

Yours, very respectfully,   A. Lincoln.

To Major-General Steele.

Executive Mansion, Washington, Jan. 20, 1864.

Sundry citizens of the State of Arkansas petition me that an election may be held in that state, at which to elect a governor; that it be assumed at that election, and thenceforward, that the constitution and laws of that state, as before the rebellion, are in full force, except that the constitution is so modified as to declare that there shall be neither slavery nor involuntary servitude, except in the punishment of crimes whereof the party shall have been duly convicted; that the general assembly may make such provisions for the freed people as shall recognize and declare their permanent freedom, and provide for their education, and which may yet be construed as a temporary arrangement suitable to their condition, as a laboring, landless, and homeless class; that said election shall be held on the 28th of March, 1864, at all the usual places of the state, or all such as voters may attend for that purpose; that the voters attending at eight o'clock in the morning of said day may choose judges and clerks of election for such purpose; that all persons qualified by said constitution and laws, and taking the oath presented in the President's proclamation of December 8, 1863, either before or at the election, and none others, may be voters; that each set of judges or clerks may make returns directly to you on or before the —— day of —— next; that in all other respects said election may be conducted according to said Constitution and laws; that on receipt of said returns, when 5,406 votes shall have been cast, you can receive said votes, and ascertain all who shall thereby appear to have been elected; that, on the —— day of —— next, all persons so appearing to have been elected, who shall appear before you at Little Rock, and take the oath, to be by you severally administered, to support the Constitution of the United States, and said modified Constitution of the State of Arkansas, may be declared by you qualified and empowered to immediately enter upon the duties of the offices to which they shall have been respectively elected.

You will please order an election to take place on the 28th of March, 1864, and returns to be made in fifteen days thereafter. A. LINCOLN.

LETTER TO GOVERNOR HAHN, OF LOUISIANA, MARCH 13, 1864.

Dear Sir:—I congratulate you on having fixed your name in history as the first free state governor of Louisiana. Now you are about to have a convention, which, among other things, will define the elective franchise, I barely suggest, for your private consideration, whether, some of the colored people may not be let in—as, for instance, the very intelligent, and especially those who have fought gallantly in our ranks?

They would probably help, in some trying time to come, to keep the jewel of liberty in the family of freedom.

But this is only a suggestion, not to the public, but to you alone. Yours truly, A. LINCOLN.

ADDRESS AT THE PATENT OFFICE, WASHINGTON, MARCH 16, 1864.

Ladies and Gentlemen:—I appear to say but a word. This extraordinary war in which we are engaged falls heavily upon all classes of people, but the most heavily upon the soldier.

For it has been said, all that a man hath will he give for his life; and while all contribute of their substance, the soldier puts his life at stake, and often yields it up in his country's cause. The highest merit, then, is due to the soldier. In this extraordinary war, extraordinary developments have manifested themselves, such as have not been seen in former wars; and among these manifestations nothing has been more remarkable than these fairs for the relief of suffering soldiers and their families. And the chief agents in these fairs are the women of America. I am not accustomed to the use of the language of eulogy; I have never studied the art of paying compliments to women; but I must say, that if all that has been said by orators and poets since the creation of the world in praise of women were applied to the women of America, it would not do them justice for their conduct during the war. I will close by saying, God bless the women of America.

Lincoln's Description of Grant to a Friend, March, 1864.

Well, I hardly know what to think of him, altogether. He is the quietest little fellow you ever saw. Why, he makes the least fuss of any man you ever knew. I believe two or three times he has been in this room a minute or so before I knew he was here. Its about so all around. The only evidence you have that he's in any place, is that he makes things *git*. Wherever he is things move. Grant is the first general I've had. He's a general; I'll tell you what I mean. You know how its been with all the rest. As soon as I put a man in command of the army, he'd come to me with a plan of a campaign, and about as much as say, "Now, I don't believe I can do it, but if you say so, I'll try it on," and so put the responsibility of success or failure on me. They all wanted me to be the general. Now, it isn't so with Grant. He hasn't told me what his plans are. I don't know, and I don't want to know. I'm glad to find a man that can go ahead without me. You see, when any of the rest set out on a campaign, they'd look over matters and pick out some one thing they were short of, and they knew I couldn't give 'em, and tell me they couldn't hope to win unless they had it; and it was the most generally cavalry. Now, when Grant took hold, I was waiting to see what his pet impossibility would be, and I reckoned it would be cavalry, as a matter of course, for we hadn't horses enough to mount what men we had.

There were fifteen thousand, or thereabouts, up near Harper's Ferry, and no horses to put them on.

Well, the other day Grant sends to me about those very men, just as I expected, but what he wanted to know was whether he should make infantry of 'em or discharge 'em. He doesn't ask impossibilities of me, and he's the first general I've had that didn't.

To Major-General Meade.

Executive Mansion, Washington, March 29, 1864.

My Dear Sir:—Your letter to Colonel Townsend, inclosing a slip from the Herald, and asking a court of inquiry, has been laid before me by the Secretary of War, with the request that I would consider it. It is quite natural that you would feel some sensibility on the subject; yet I am not impressed, nor do I think the country is impressed, with the belief that your honor demands, or the public interest demands, such an inquiry. The country knows that at all events you have done good service, and I believe it agrees with me that it is much better for you to be engaged in trying to do more, than to be diverted as you necessarily would be by a court of inquiry.

Yours, truly, A. Lincoln.

To Mr. A. G. Hodges, of Frankfort, Ky., April 4, 1864.

I did understand, however, that very oath to preserve the Constitution to the best of my ability imposed upon me the duty of preserving, by every indispensable means, that government, that nation of which that Constitution was the organic law. Was it possible to lose the nation and yet preserve the Constitution? By general law, life and limb must be protected, yet often a limb must be amputated to save a life, but a life is never wisely given to save a limb. I felt that measures, otherwise unconstitutional, might become lawful by becoming indispensable to the preservation of the Constitution through the preservation of the nation. Right or wrong, I assumed this ground, and now avow it. I could not feel that, to the best of my ability, I had even tried to preserve the Constitution if to preserve slavery or any minor matter, I should permit the wreck of government, country, and Constitution altogether. When, early in the war, General Fremont attempted military emancipation, I forbade it, because I did not then think it an indispensable necessity. When, a little later, General Cameron, then Secretary of War, suggested the arming of the blacks, I objected, because I did not yet think it an indispensable necessity. When, still later, General Hunter attempted military emancipation, I again forbade it, because I did not yet think the indispensable necessity had come. When, in March, and May, and July, 1862, I made earnest and successive appeals to the border states to favor compensated emancipation, I believed the indispensable necessity for military emancipation and arming the blacks would come, unless averted by that measure.

They declined the proposition, and I was, in my best judgment, driven to the alternative of either surrendering the Union, and with it the Constitution, or of laying strong hand upon the colored element. I chose the latter. In choosing it, I hoped for greater gain than loss, but of this I was not entirely confident. More than a year of trial now shows no loss by it in our foreign relations, none in our home popular sentiment, none in our white military force, no loss by it any how or anywhere. On the contrary, it shows a gain of quite a hundred and thirty thousand soldiers, seamen, and laborers. These are palpable facts, about which, as facts, there can be no caviling. We have the men, and we could not have had them without the measure. And now let any Union man who complains of this measure test himself by writing down in one line that he is for subduing the rebellion by force of arms, and in the next that he is for taking three hundred and thirty thousand men from the Union side, and placing them where they would be best for the measure he condemns. If he can not face his case so stated it is only because he can not face the truth.

I add a word which was not in the verbal conversation. In telling this tale, I attempt no compliment to my own sagacity. I claim not to have controlled events, but confess plainly that events have controlled me. Now, at the end of three years' struggle, the nation's condition is not what either party or any man devised or expected.

God alone can claim it. Whither it is tending seems plain. If God now wills the removal of a great wrong, and wills also that we of the North, as well as you of the South, shall pay fairly for our complicity in that wrong, impartial history will find therein new causes to attest and revere the justice and goodness of God.

Yours, truly,   A. LINCOLN.

WORDS TO GEN. GRANT, ON APRIL 9, 1864.

The Nation's appreciation of what you have done, and its reliance upon you for what remains to be done in the existing great struggle, are now presented with this commission constituting you lieutenant-general in the army of the United States. With this high honor devolves upon you also a corresponding responsibility. As the country herein trusts you, so, under God, it will sustain you. I scarcely need to add that with what I here speak for the Nation goes my own hearty personal concurrence.

SPEECH AT THE BALTIMORE FAIR, APRIL 18, 1864.

Ladies and Gentlemen:—Calling it to mind that we are in Baltimore, we can not fail to note that the world moves. Looking upon the many people I see assembled here to serve as they best may the soldiers of the Union, it occurs to me that three years ago those soldiers could not pass through Baltimore. I would say, blessings upon the men who have wrought these changes, and the ladies who have assisted them. This change which has taken place in Baltimore is part only of a far wider change which has taken place all over the country.

When the war commenced, three years ago, no one expected that it would last this long, and no one supposed that the institution of slavery would be materially affected by it. But here we are. The war is not yet ended, and slavery has been very materially affected or interfered with. So true is it that man proposes and God disposes.

The world is in want of a good definition of the word liberty. We all declare ourselves to be for liberty, but we do not all mean the same thing. Some mean that a man can do as he pleases with himself and his property. With others it means that some men can do as they please with other men and other men's labor. Each of these things are called liberty, although they are entirely different. To give an illustration: A shepherd drives the wolf from the throat of his sheep when attacked by him, and the sheep of course thanks the shepherd for the preservation of his life; but the wolf denounces him as despoiling the sheep of his liberty, especially if it be a black sheep.

This same difference of opinion prevails among some of the people of the north. But the people of Maryland have recently been doing something to properly define the meaning of the word, and I thank them from the bottom of my heart for what they have done and are doing.

It is not very becoming for a president to make a speech of great length, but there is a painful rumor afloat in the country, in reference to which a few words shall be said. It is reported that there has been a wanton massacre of some hundreds of colored soldiers at Fort Pillow, Tennessee, during a recent engagement there, and he thought it fit to explain some facts in relation to the affair. It is said by some persons that the government is not, in this matter, doing its duty. At the commencement of the war, it was doubtful whether black men would be used as soldiers or not. The matter was examined into very carefully, and after mature deliberation, the whole matter resting, as it were, with himself, he, in his judgment, decided that they should. He was responsible for the act to the American people, to a Christian nation, to the future historian, and, above all, to his God, to whom he would have one day to render an account of his stewardship. He would now say that in his opinion the black soldier should have the same protection as the white soldier, and he would have it.

It was an error to say that the government was not acting in the matter. The government has no direct evidence to confirm the reports in existence relative to this massacre, but he himself believed the facts in relation to it to be as stated. When the government does know the facts from official sources, and they prove to substantiate the reports, retribution will be surely given. What is reported, he thought, would make a clear case. If it is not true, then all such stories are to be considered as false. If proved true, when the matter is thoroughly examined, what shape is to be given to the retribution? Can we take the man who was captured at Vicksburg, and shoot him for the victim of this massacre? If it should happen that it was the act of only one man, what course is to be pursued then? It was a matter requiring careful examination and deliberation, and if it should be substantiated by sufficient evidence, all might rest assured that retribution would be had.

Message to Congress.

April 28, 1864.

To the Honorable Senate and House of Representatives:—I have the honor to transmit herewith an address to the President of the United States, and through him to both Houses of Congress, on the condition of the people of East Tennessee, and asking their attention to the necessity for some action on the part of the government for their relief, and which address is presented by the committee or organization called "The East Tennessee Relief Association." Deeply commiserating the condition of those most loyal people, I am unprepared to make any specific recommendation for their relief. The military is doing, and will continue to do, the best for them within its power. Their address represents that the construction of a direct railroad communication between Knoxville and Cincinnati, by way of Central Kentucky, would be of great consequence in the present emergency. It may be remembered that in my annual message of December, 1861, such railroad construction was recommended. I now add that, with the hearty concurrence of Congress, I would yet be pleased to construct the road, both for the relief of those people and for its continuing military importance. ABRAHAM LINCOLN.

To the House of Representatives.

April 28, 1864.

In obedience to the resolution of your honorable body, a copy of which is herewith returned, I have the honor to make the following brief statement, which is believed to contain the information sought:

Prior to and at the meeting of the present Congress, Robert C. Schenck, of Ohio, and Frank P. Blair, Jr., of Missouri, members-elect thereto, by and with the consent of the Senate, held commissions from the executive as major-generals in the volunteer army.

General Schenck tendered the resignation of his said commission and took his seat in the House of Representatives, at the assembling thereof, upon the distinct verbal understanding with the Secretary of War and the Executive that he might at any time during the session, at his own pleasure, withdraw said resignation and return to the field.

General Blair was, by temporary agreement of General Sherman in command of a corps through the battles in front of Chattanooga, and in marching to the relief of Knoxville, which occurred in the latter days of December last, and of course was not present at the assembling of Congress. When he subsequently arrived here he sought and was allowed by the Secretary of War and the Executive the same conditions and promise as was allowed and made to General Schenck.

General Schenck has not applied to withdraw his resignation; but when General Grant was made lieutenant-general, producing some changes of commanders, General Blair sought to be assigned to the command of a corps. This was made known to General Grant and General Sherman, and assented to by them, and the particular corps for him was designated. This was all arranged and understood, as now remembered, so much as a month ago; but the formal withdrawal of General Blair's resignation, and the reissuing of the order assigning him to the command of a corps, were not consummated at the War Department until last week, perhaps on the 23d of April instant.

As a summary of the whole it may be stated that General Blair holds no military commission or appointment other than as herein stated, and that it is believed he is now acting as major-general upon the assumed validity of the commission herein stated and not otherwise.

There are some letters, notes, telegrams, orders, entries, and perhaps other documents, in connection with the subject, which it is believed would throw no additional light upon it, but which will be cheerfully furnished if desired. ABRAHAM LINCOLN.

LETTER TO GENERAL GRANT, APRIL 30, 1864.

Not expecting to see you before the spring campaign opens, I wish to express in this way my entire satisfaction with what you have done up to this time, so far as I understand it. The particulars of your plans I neither know, nor seek to know. You are vigilant and self-reliant; and pleased with this, I wish not to obtrude any restraints or constraints upon you. While I am very anxious that any great disaster, or capture of our men in great numbers, shall be avoided. I know that these points are less likely to escape your attention than they would mine. If there be any thing wanting which is within my power to give, do not fail to let me know it.

And now, with a brave army and a just cause, may God sustain you. Yours, very truly,

A. LINCOLN.

PRESIDENT'S RECOMMEND FOR PRAYER AND THANKSGIVING.

Executive Mansion, Washington, May 9, 1864.

To the Friends of Union and Liberty:—Enough is known of army operations within the last five days to claim our special gratitude to God. While what remains undone demands our most serious prayers to and reliance upon Him (without whom all human effort is vain), I recommend that all patriots, at their homes, at their places of public worship, and wherever they may be, unite in common thanksgiving and prayer to Almighty God. ABRAHAM LINCOLN.

THE PRESIDENT'S IDEA OF DEMOCRATIC POLICY AND STRATEGY.

May, 1864.

The slightest knowledge of arithmetic will prove to any man that the rebel armies can not be destroyed by Democratic strategy. It would sacrifice all the white men of the North to do it. There are now in the service of the United States nearly two hundred thousand able-bodied colored men, most of them under arms, defending and acquiring Union territory.

The Democratic strategy demands that these forces be disbanded, and that the masters be conciliated by restoring them to slavery. The black men who now assist Union prisoners to escape are to be converted into our enemies, in the vain hope of gaining the good will of their masters. We shall have to fight two nations instead of one.

You can not conciliate the South if you guarantee ultimate success, and the experiences of the present war prove their success is inevitable if you fling the compulsory labor of four millions of black men into their side of the scale.

Will you give our enemies such military advantages as insure success, and then depend upon coaxing, flattery, and concession to get them back into the Union.

Abandon all the forts now garrisoned by black men, take two hundred thousand men from our side, and put them in the battle field or corn field against us, and we would be compelled to abandon the war in three weeks. We have to hold territory in inclement and sickly places. Where are the Democrats to do this? It was a free fight, and the field was open to the War Democrats to put down this rebellion by fighting against both the master and slave long before the present policy was inaugurated. There have been men base enough to propose to me to return to slavery our black warriors of Port Hudson and Olustee, and thus win the respect of the masters they fought. Should I do so, I should deserve to be damned in time and eternity.

Come what will. I will keep my faith with friend and foe. My enemies pretend I am now carrying on the war for the sole purpose of abolition. So long as I am president it shall be carried on for the sole purpose of restoring the Union. But no human power can subdue this rebellion without the use of the emancipation policy, and every other policy calculated to weaken the moral and physical forces of the rebellion.

Freedom has given us two hundred thousand men, raised on southern soil. It will give us more yet. Just so much it has abstracted from the enemy, and instead of checking the South, there are evidences of a fraternal feeling growing up between our men and the rank and file of the rebel soldiers. Let my enemies prove to the country that the destruction of slavery is not necessary to the restoration of the Union. I will abide the issue.

RESPONSE TO SERENADE AT WASHINGTON, MAY 13, 1864.

Fellow-Citizens:—I am very much obliged to you for the compliment of this call, though I apprehend it is owing more to the good news received to-day from the army, than to a desire to see me.

I am indeed very grateful to the brave men who have been struggling with the enemy in the field, to their noble commanders who have directed them, and especially to our Maker.

Our commanders are following up their victories resolutely and successfully.

I think, without knowing the particulars of the plans of General Grant, that what has been accomplished is of more importance than at first appears. I believe, I know (and am especially grateful to know), that General Grant has not been jostled in his purposes, that he has made all his points, and to-day he is on his line as he purposed before he moved his armies.

I will volunteer to say that I am very glad at what has happened, but there is a great deal still to be done. While we are grateful to all the brave men and officers for the events of the past few days, we should, above all, be very grateful to Almighty God, who gives us victory.

There is enough yet before us requiring all loyal men and patriots to perform their share of the labor and follow the example of the modest general at the head of our armies, and sink all personal considerations for the sake of the country.

I commend you to keep yourselves in the same tranquil mood that is characteristic of that brave and loyal man. I have said more than I expected when I came before you. Repeating my thanks for this call, I bid you good-bye.

To A New York Meeting, June 3, 1864.

Hon. F. A. Conckling, and others: Gentlemen—Your letter, inviting me to be present at a mass meeting of loyal citizens to be held at New York, on the 4th inst., for the purpose of expressing gratitude to Lieutenant-General Grant for his signal services, was received yesterday. It is impossible for me to attend. I approve, nevertheless, whatever may tend to strengthen and sustain General Grant and the noble armies now under his direction.

My previous high estimate of General Grant has been maintained and heightened by what has occurred in the remarkable campaign he is now conducting. While the magnitude and difficulty of the task before him do not prove less than I expected, he and his brave soldiers are now in the midst of their great trial, and I trust at your meeting you will so shape your good words that they may turn to men and guns moving to his and their support.

Yours truly,   A. LINCOLN.

SPEECH DELIVERED JUNE 9, 1864, TO COMMITTEE INFORMING LINCOLN OF HIS RENOMINATION.

Mr. Chairman and Gentlemen of the Committee:—I will neither conceal my gratification, nor restrain the expression of my gratitude, that the Union people, through their convention, in the continued effort to save and advance the nation, have deemed me not unworthy to remain in my present position.

I know no reason to doubt that I shall accept the nomination tendered, and yet, perhaps I should not declare definitely before reading and considering what is called the platform. I will say now, however, that I approve the declaration in favor of so amending the Constitution as to prohibit slavery throughout the nation. When the people in revolt, with the hundred days explicit notice that they could within those days resume their allegiance without the overthrow of their institutions, and that they could not resume it afterward, elected to stand out, such an amendment of the Constitution as is now proposed became a fitting and necessary condition to the final success of the Union cause. Such alone can meet and cover all cavils. I now perceive its importance and embrace it. In the joint names of Liberty and Union, let us labor to give legal form and practical effort.

Speech to the National Union League, June 9, 1864.

Gentlemen:—I can only say in response to the remarks of your chairman, that I am very grateful for the renewed confidence which has been accorded to me, both by the convention and the National League. I am not insensible at all to the personal compliment there is in this, yet I do not allow myself to believe that any but a small portion of it is to be appropriated as a personal compliment to me. The convention and the nation, I am assured, are alike animated by a higher view of the interests of the country, for the present and the great future, and the part I am entitled to appropriate as a compliment, is only that part which I may lay hold of as being the opinion of the convention and of the league, that I am not entirely unworthy to be intrusted with the place I have occupied for the last three years.

I have not permitted myself, gentlemen, to conclude that I am the best man in the country; but I am reminded in this connection of a story of an old Dutch farmer, who remarked to a companion once that "it was not best to swap horse when crossing a stream."

Speech at a Philadelphia Fair, June 16, 1864.

I suppose that this toast was intended to open the way for me to say something.

War, at the best, is terrible, and this war of ours, in its magnitude and in its duration, is one of the most terrible. It has deranged business, totally in many localities, and partially in all localities. It has destroyed property and ruined homes; it has produced a national debt and taxation unprecedented, at least in this country; it has carried mourning to almost every home, until it can almost be said that the "heavens are hung in black."

Yet the war continues, and several relieving coincidents have accompanied it from the very beginning which have not been known, as I understand or have any knowledge of, in any former wars in the history of the world. The Sanitary Commission, with all its benevolent labors; the Christian Commission, with all its Christian and benevolent labors; and the various places, arrangements, so to speak, and institutions, have contributed to the comfort and relief of the soldiers. You have two of these places in this city—the Cooper Shop and Union Volunteer Refreshment Saloons. And, lastly, these fairs, which I believe began only in last August if I mistake not in Chicago, then at Boston, at Cincinnati, Brooklyn, New York, at Baltimore, and those at present held at St. Louis, Pittsburg and Philadelphia.

The motive and object that lie at the bottom of all these are most worthy; for, say what you will, after all, the most is due to the soldier, who takes his life in his hands and goes to fight the battles of his country. In what is contributed to his comfort when he passes to and fro, and in what is contributed to him when he is sick and wounded, in whatever shape it comes, whether from the fair and tender hand of woman or from any other source, it is much, very much. But I think that there is still that which is of as much value to him in the continual reminders he sees in the newspapers, that while he is absent he is yet remembered by the loved ones at home.

Another view of these various institutions, if I may so call them, is worthy of consideration, I think. They are voluntary contributions, given zealously and earnestly, on top of all the disturbances of business, of all the disorders, of all the taxation, and of all the burdens that the war has imposed upon us, giving proof that the national resources are not at all exhausted, and that the natural spirit of patriotism is even firmer and stronger than at the commencement of the war.

It is a pertinent question, often asked in the mind privately, and from one to the other, When is the war to end? Surely I feel as deep an interest in this question as any other can, but I do not wish to name a day, a month, or a year, when it is to end. I do not wish to run any risk of seeing the time come, without our being ready for the end, for fear of disappointment because the time had come and not the end. We accepted this war for an object, a worthy object, and the war will end when that object is attained. Under God, I hope it never will end until that time. Speaking of the present campaign, General Grant is reported to have said, "I am going through on this line if it takes all summer." This war has taken three years; it was begun or accepted upon the line of restoring the national authority over the whole national domain, and for the American people, as far as any knowledge enables me to speak, I say we are going through on this line if it takes three years more.

My friends, I did not know but I might be called upon to say a few words before I got away from here, but I did not know it was coming just here. I have never been in the habit of making predictions in regard to the war, but I am almost tempted to make one. If I were to hazard it, it is this: that Grant is this evening, with General Meade and General Hancock, and the brave officers and soldiers with him, in a position from whence he will never be dislodged until Richmond is taken, and I have but one single proposition to put now, and perhaps I can best put it in the form of an interrogative. If I shall discover that General Grant and the noble officers and men under him can be greatly facilitated in their work by a sudden pouring forward of men and assistance, will you give them to me? Are you ready to march? [Cries of "Yes!"] Then, I say, stand ready, for I am watching for the chance. I thank you, gentlemen.

To Hon. WILLIAM DENNISON AND OTHERS, A COMMITTEE OF THE UNION NATIONAL CONVENTION.

Executive Mansion, Washington, June 27, 1864.

Gentlemen:—Your letter of the 14th inst., formally

notifying me that I have been nominated by the convention you represent for the Presidency of the United States for four years from the 4th of March next, has been received. The nomination is gratefully accepted, as the resolutions of the convention, called the platform, are heartily approved.

While the resolution in regard to the supplanting of republican government upon the western continent is fully concurred in, there might be misunderstanding were I not to say that the position of the government in relation to the action of France in Mexico, as assumed through the State Department and indorsed by the convention among the measures and acts of the Executive, will be faithfully maintained so long as the state of facts shall leave that position pertinent and applicable. I am especially gratified that the soldiers and seamen were not forgotten by the convention, as they forever must and will be remembered by the grateful country for whose salvation they devote their lives.

Thanking you for the kind and complimentary terms in which you have communicated the nomination, and other proceedings of the convention, I subscribe myself, Your obedient servant,

ABRAHAM LINCOLN.

LINCOLN TO GENERAL GRANT.

July 10, 1864, 2:30 *P. M.*

Your dispatch to General Halleck, referring to what I may think in the present emergency, is shown me. General Halleck says we have no force here fit to go to the field. He thinks that with the hundred-day men and invalids we have here, we can defend Washington, and, scarcely, Baltimore. Besides these, there are about eight thousand, not very reliable, under Howe at Harper's Ferry, with Hunter approaching that point very slowly, with what number I suppose you know better than we. Wallace, with some odds and ends, and part of what came up with Ricketts, was so badly beaten yesterday at Monocacy, that what is left can attempt no more than to defend Baltimore. What we shall get in from Pennsylvania and New York will scarcely be worth counting, I fear. Now what I think is, that you should provide to retain your hold where you are certainly; and *bring the rest with you, personally,* and make a vigorous effort to defeat the enemy's force in this vicinity. I think there is really a fair chance to do this if the movement is prompt. This is what I think—upon your suggestion—and is not an order. A. LINCOLN.

To Whom it may Concern.

Executive Mansion, Washington, D. C., July 18, 1864.

Any proposition which embraces the restoration of peace, the integrity of the whole Union, and the abandonment of slavery, and which comes by and with an authority that can control the armies now at war against the United States, will be received and considered by the Executive Government of the United States, and will be met by liberal terms on other substantial and collateral points, and the bearer or bearers thereof shall have safe conduct both ways.

ABRAHAM LINCOLN.

To LIEUTENANT-GENERAL GRANT, CITY POINT, VA.

Washington, D. C., Aug. 3, 1864, Cypher, 6 P. M.

I have seen your dispatch in which you say—" I want Sheridan put in command of all the troops in the field, with instructions to put himself south of the enemy, and follow him to the death. Wherever the enemy goes, let the troops go also." This, I think, is exactly right, as to how our forces should move. But please look over the dispatches you may have received from here, even since you made that order, and discover, if you can, that there is any idea in the head of any one here, of "putting our army *south* of the enemy" or of "following him to the *death*" in any direction. I repeat to you it will neither be done nor attempted unless you watch it every day, and hour, and force it.
A. LINCOLN.

PRESIDENT LINCOLN'S REPLY TO REV. DR. POHLMAN, OF ALBANY, N. Y., AND OTHERS OF THE GENERAL SYNOD OF THE LUTHERAN CHURCH AT LANCASTER.

August, 1864.

Gentlemen:—I welcome here the representatives of the Evangelical Lutherans of the United States. I accept with gratitude their assurances of the sympathy and support of that enlightened, influential and loyal class of my fellow-citizens in an important crisis, which involves, in my judgment, not only the civil and religious liberties of our own dear land, but in a large degree the civil and religious liberties of mankind in many countries, and through many ages. You well know, gentlemen, and the world knows, how reluctantly I accepted this issue of battle forced upon me, on my advent to this place, by the internal enemies of our country. You all know, the world knows the forces and the resources the public agents have brought into employment to sustain a government against which there has been brought not one complaint of real injury committed against society at home or abroad. You all may recollect that in taking up the sword thus forced into our hands, this government appealed to the prayers of the pious and the good, and declared that it placed its whole dependence upon the favor of God. I now humbly and reverently, in your presence, reiterate the acknowledgment of that dependence, not doubting that if it shall please the Divine Being who determines the destinies of nations, that this shall remain a united people, they will, humbly seeking the Divine guidance, make their prolonged national existence a source of new benefits to themselves and their successors, and to all classes and conditions of mankind.

Hon. Henry J. Raymond.

Executive Mansion, Washington, August 15, 1864.

My Dear Sir:—I have proposed to Mr. Greeley that the Niagara correspondence be published, suppressing only the parts of his letters over which the red pencil is drawn in the copy which I herewith send.

He declines giving his consent to the publication of his letters unless these parts be published with the rest.

I have concluded that it is better for *me* to submit, for the time, to the consequences of the false position in which I consider he has placed me, than to submit the *country* to the consequences of publishing these discouraging and injurious parts.

I send you this, and the accompanying copy, not for publication, but merely to explain to you, and that you may preserve them until their proper time shall come. Yours truly, A. LINCOLN.

TENDER OF NATIONAL THANKS TO FARRAGUT AND CANBY.

Executive Mansion, September 3, 1864.

The national thanks are tendered by the President to Admiral Farragut and Major-General Canby, for the skill and harmony with which the recent operations in Mobile Harbor and against Fort Powell, Fort Gaines, and Fort Morgan were planned and carried into execution. Also to Admiral Farragut and Major-General Granger, under whose immediate command they were conducted, and to the gallant commanders on sea and land, and to the sailors and soldiers engaged in the operations, for their energy and courage, which, under the blessing of Providence, have been crowned with brilliant success, and have won for them the applause and thanks of the nation.

ABRAHAM LINCOLN.

CALL FOR THANKSGIVING.

Executive Mansion, Washington City, Sept. 3, 1864.

The signal success that Divine Providence has recently vouchsafed to the operations of the United States army and navy in the harbor of Mobile, and the reduction of Forts Powell, Gaines, and Morgan, and the glorious achievements of the army under

Major-General Sherman in the State of Georgia, resulting in the capture of the city of Atlanta, call for devout acknowledgments to the Supreme Being, in whose hands are the destinies of nations. It is therefore requested that on next Sunday, in all places of public worship in the United States, thanksgiving be offered to Him for His mercy in preserving our national existence, against the insurgent rebels who so long have been waging a cruel war against the government of the United States for its overthrow, and also that prayers be made for the Divine protection to our brave soldiers and their leaders, in the field, who have so often and so gallantly periled their lives in battling with the enemy, and for blessings and comfort from the Father of Mercies to the sick, and wounded and prisoners, and to the orphans and widows of those who have fallen in the service of their country, and that He will continue to uphold the government of the United States against all the efforts of public enemies and secret foes.

ABRAHAM LINCOLN.

TENDER OF NATIONAL THANKS TO GENERAL SHERMAN.

Executive Mansion, Washington, Sept. 3, 1864.

The national thanks are tendered by the President to Major-General W. T. Sherman and the gallant officers and soldiers of his command before Atlanta, for the distinguished ability and perseverance displayed in the campaign in Georgia, which, under Divine favor, has resulted in the capture of Atlanta. The marches, battles, sieges and other military operations that have signalized the campaign, must render it famous in the annals of war, and have entitled those who have participated therein to the applause and thanks of the nation.   ABRAHAM LINCOLN.

September 5, 1864.

Ordered :—First—That on Monday the 5th day of September, commencing at the hour of twelve o'clock noon, there shall be given a salute of one hundred guns at the arsenal and navy yard at Washington, and on Tuesday, the 6th day of September, or the day after the receipt of this order, at each arsenal and navy yard in the United States, for the recent brilliant achievements of the fleet and the land forces of the United States in the harbor of Mobile in the reduction of Fort Powell, Fort Gaines and Fort Morgan. The Secretary of War and the Secretary of the Navy will issue the necessary directions in their respective departments for the execution of this order.

Second—That on Wednesday, the 7th day of September, commencing at the hour of twelve o'clock noon, there shall be fired a salute of one hundred guns at the arsenal at Washington, and at New York, Boston, Philadelphia, Baltimore, Pittsburg, Newport, Ky., and St. Louis, and at New Orleans, Mobile, Pensacola, Hilton Head, and Newbern, the day after the receipt of this order, for the brilliant achievements of the army under the command of Major-General Sherman in the State of Georgia, and the capture of Atlanta.

The Secretary of War will issue directions for the execution of this order.   ABRAHAM LINCOLN.

Executive Order Returning Thanks to the Ohio Volunteers for One Hundred Days Service.

Executive Mansion, Washington, Sept. 10, 1864.

The term of one hundred days for which the National Guard of Ohio volunteered having expired, the President directs an official acknowledgment of their patriotism and valuable services during the recent campaign. The term of service of their enlistment was short, but distinguished by memorable events in the valley of the Shenandoah, on the Peninsula, in the operations of the James River, around Petersburg and Richmond, in the battle of Monocacy, in the intrenchments of Washington, and in other important service. The National Guard of Ohio performed with alacrity the duty of patriotic volunteers, for which they are entitled, and are hereby tendered, through the Governor of their state, the national thanks.

The Secretary of War is directed to transmit a copy of this order to the Governor of Ohio, and to cause a certificate of their honorable service to be delivered to the officers and soldiers of the Ohio National Guard, who recently served in the military force of the United States as volunteers for one hundred days.

Abraham Lincoln.

Speech at a Serenade, September, 1864.

Soldiers:—You are about to return to your homes and your friends, after having, as I learn, performed in camp a comparatively short term of duty in this great contest. I am greatly obliged to you, and to all who have come forward at the call of their country. I wish it might be more generally and universally understood what the country is now engaged in. We have, as all will agree, a free government, where every man has a right to be equal with every other man. In this great struggle the form of government and every form of human right is endangered if our enemies succeed. There is more involved in this contest than is realized by every one. There is involved in this struggle the question, whether your children and my children shall enjoy the privileges we have enjoyed. I say this in order to impress upon you, if you are not already so impressed, that no small matter should divert us from our great purpose.

There may be some inequalities in the practical application of our system. It is fair that each man shall pay taxes in exact proportion to the value of his property; but if we should wait, before collecting a tax, to adjust the taxes upon each man in exact proportion with every other man, we should never collect any tax at all. There may be mistakes made sometimes; things may be done wrong, while the officers of the government do all they can to prevent mistakes. But I beg of you, as citizens of this great republic, not to let your minds be carried off from the great work we have before us. This struggle is too large for you to be diverted from it by any small matter. When you return to your homes, rise up to the height of a generation of men worthy of a free government, and we will carry out the great work we have commenced. I return to you my sincere thanks, soldiers, for the honor you have done me this afternoon.

To Another Ohio Regiment he Spoke as Follows, September, 1864.

Soldiers:—I suppose you are going home to see your families and friends. For the services you have done in this great struggle in which we are engaged, I present you sincere thanks for myself and the country.

I almost always feel inclined, when I say any thing to soldiers, to impress upon them, in a few brief remarks, the importance of success in this contest. It is not merely for the day, but for all time to come, that we should perpetuate for our children's children that great and free government which we have enjoyed all our lives. I beg you to remember this, not merely for my sake, but for yours. I happen, temporarily, to occupy this big White House. I am a living witness that any one of your children may look to come here as my father's child has. It is in order that each one of you may have, through this free government which we have enjoyed, an open field and a fair chance for your industry, enterprise, and intelligence; that you may all have equal privileges in the race of life, with all its desirable human aspirations—it is for this that the struggle should be maintained, that we may not lose our birthrights, not only for one, but for two or three years, if necessary. The nation is worth fighting for to secure such an inestimable jewel.

To Major-General Sherman.

Washington, D. C., September 19, 1864.

The state election of Indiana occurs on the 11th of October, and the loss of it to the friends of the government would go far toward losing the whole Union cause.

The bad effect upon the November election, and especially the giving the state government to those who will oppose the war in every possible way, are too much to risk if it can be avoided. The draft proceeds, notwithstanding its strong tendency to lose us the state.

Indiana is the only important state voting in October whose soldiers can not vote in the field. Any thing you can safely do to let her soldiers, or any part of them go home to vote at the state election, will be greatly in point.

They need not remain for the presidential election, but may return to you at once.

This is in no sense an order, but is merely intended to impress you with the importance to the army itself of your doing all you safely can, yourself being the judge of what you can safely do.

Yours, truly, A. Lincoln

To Hon. Montgomery Blair.

Executive Mansion, Washington, Sept. 23, 1864.

My Dear Sir:—You have generously said to me, more than once, that whenever your resignation could be a relief to me, it was at my disposal. The time has come.

You very well know that this proceeds from no dissatisfaction of mine with you personally or officially.

Your uniform kindness has been unsurpassed by that of any other friend, and while it is true that the war does not so greatly add to the difficulties of your department as to those of some others, it is yet much to say, as I most truly can, that in the three years and a half during which you have administered the General Post-office, I remember no single complaint against you in connection therewith.

Yours, as ever, A. LINCOLN.

LETTER TO MRS. ELIZA P. GURNEY.

September 30, 1864.

My Esteemed Friend:—I have not forgotten, probably never shall forget, the very impressive occasion when yourself and friends visited me on a Sabbath forenoon two years ago. Nor had your kind letter, written nearly a year later, ever been forgotten. In all it has been your purpose to strengthen my reliance in God. I am much indebted to the good Christian people of the country for their constant prayers and consolations, and to no one of them more than to yourself. The purposes of the Almighty are perfect and must prevail, though we erring mortals may fail to accurately perceive them in advance. We hoped for a happy termination of this terrible war long before this; but God knows best, and has ruled otherwise. We shall yet acknowledge his wisdom and our own errors therein; meanwhile we must work earnestly in the best light He gives us, trusting that so working still conduces to the great end He ordains. Surely He intends some great good to follow this mighty convulsion which no mortal could make, and no mortal could stay. Your people—the Friends—have had, and are having, very great trials on principles and faith opposed to both war and oppression. They can only practically oppose oppression by war. In this hard dilemma some have chosen one horn and some the other.

For those appealing to me on conscientious grounds I have done and shall do the best I could and can in my own conscience under my oath to the law. That you believe this I doubt not, and believing it I shall still receive for my country and myself your earnest prayers to our Father in Heaven.

Your sincere friend, A. LINCOLN.

SPECIAL EXECUTIVE ORDER RETURNING THANKS TO VOLUNTEERS FOR ONE HUNDRED DAYS, FROM THE STATES OF ILLINOIS, INDIANA, IOWA, AND WISCONSIN.

Executive Mansion, Washington, October 1, 1864.

The term of one hundred days for which volunteers from the states of Indiana, Illinois, Iowa, and Wisconsin volunteered, under the call of their respective governors, in the months of May and June, to aid the recent campaign of General Sherman, having expired, the president directs an official acknowledgment to be made of their patriotic service. It was their good fortune to render effective service in the brilliant operations in the south-west, and to contribute to the victories of the national arms over the rebel forces in Georgia, under command of Johnston and Hood. On all occasions, and in every service to which they were assigned, their duty as patriotic volunteers was performed with alacrity and courage, for which they are entitled to and are hereby tendered the national thanks through the governors of their respective states.

The Secretary of War is directed to transmit a copy of this order to the governors of Indiana, Illinois, Iowa, and Wisconsin, and to cause a certificate of their honorable services to be delivered to the officers and soldiers of the states above named, who recently served in the military service of the United States as volunteers for one hundred days.

ABRAHAM LINCOLN.

SPEECH TO THE 148TH OHIO REGIMENT. FALL OF 1864.

Soldiers of the 148*th Ohio:*—I am most happy to meet you on this occasion. I understand that it has been your honorable privilege to stand, for a brief period, in the defense of your country, and that now you are on your way to your homes. I congratulate you, and those who are waiting to bid you welcome home from the war; and permit me in the name of the people to thank you for the part you have taken in this struggle for the life of the nation. You are soldiers of the republic, every-where honored and respected. Whenever I appear before a body of soldiers, I feel tempted to talk to them of the nature of the struggle in which we are engaged. I look upon it as an attempt on the one hand to overwhelm and destroy the national existence, while on our part we are striving to maintain the government and institutions of our fathers, to enjoy them ourselves, and transmit them to our children and our children's children forever.

To do this the constitutional administration of our government must be sustained, and I beg of you not to allow your minds or your hearts to be diverted from the support of all necessary measures for that purpose, by any miserable picayune arguments addressed to your pockets, or inflammatory appeal made to your passions and your prejudices.

It is vain and foolish to arraign this man or that for the part he has taken or has not taken, and to hold the government responsible for his acts. In no administration can there be perfect equality of action and uniform satisfaction rendered by all.

But this government must be preserved, in spite of the acts of any man or set of men. It is worthy your every effort. Nowhere in the world is presented a government of so much liberty and equality. To the humblest and poorest amongst us are held out the highest privileges and positions. The present moment finds me at the White House, yet there is as good a chance for your children as there was for my father's.

Again I admonish you not to be turned from your stern purpose of defending our beloved country and its free institutions by any arguments urged by ambitious and designing men, but stand fast, to the Union and the old flag.

Soldiers, I bid you God-speed to your homes.

The President's Last, Shortest, and Best Speech, in 1864.

On Thursday of last week two ladies from Tennessee came before the president asking the release of their husbands held as prisoners of war at Johnson's Island. They were put off till Friday, when they came again, and were again put off to Saturday. At each of the interviews, one of the ladies urged that her husband was a religious man. On Saturday the president ordered the release of the prisoners, and then said to the lady: "You say your husband is a religious man; tell him when you meet him, that I say I am not much of a judge of religion, but that, in my opinion, the religion that sets men to rebel and fight against this government, because, as they think, that government does not sufficiently help *some* men to eat their bread on the sweat of *other* men's faces, is not the sort of religion upon which people can get to heaven."

To Hon. Henry W. Hoffman.

Executive Mansion, Washington, Oct. 18, 1864.

My Dear Sir: — A convention of Maryland has formed a new constitution for the state; a public meeting is called for this evening at Baltimore, to aid in securing its ratification, and you ask a word from me for the occasion. I presume the only feature of the instrument about which there is serious controversy, is that which provides for the extinction of slavery.

It needs not to be a secret, and I presume it is no

secret, that I wish success to this provision. I desire it on every consideration.

I wish to see all men free. I wish the national prosperity of the already free, which I feel sure the extinction of slavery would bring. I wish to see in progress of disappearing that only thing which could bring this nation to a civil war. I attempt no argument. Argument upon the question is already exhausted by the abler, better informed, and more immediately interested sons of Maryland herself. I only add, that I shall be gratified exceedingly if the good people of the state shall, by their votes, ratify the new constitution.

Yours truly,   A. LINCOLN.

SPEECH AT A SERENADE, OCTOBER 19, 1864.

I am notified that this is a compliment paid me by the loyal Marylanders resident in this district. I infer that the adoption of the new constitution for that state furnishes the occasion, and that, in your view, the extirpation of slavery constitutes the chief merit of the new constitution. Most heartily do I congratulate you and Maryland, and the nation, and the world upon the event. I regret that it did not occur two years sooner, which, I am sure, would have saved to the nation more money than would have met all the private loss incident to the measure.

But it has come at last, and I sincerely hope its friends may fully realize all their anticipations of good from it, and that its opponents may, by its effects, be agreeably and profitably disappointed.

A word upon another subject: Something said by

the Secretary of State, in his recent speech at Auburn, has been construed by some into a threat that, if I shall be beaten at the election, I will, between then and the end of my constitutional term, do what I may be able to ruin the government. Others regard the fact that the Chicago convention adjourned not *sine die*, but to meet again, if called to do so by a particular individual, as the intimation of a purpose that if their nominee shall be elected he will at once seize the control of the government. I hope the good people will permit themselves to suffer no uneasiness on this point.

I am struggling to maintain the government, not to overthrow it. I therefore say that, if I shall live, I shall remain president until the fourth of next March, and that whoever shall be constitutionally elected therefor, in November, shall be duly installed as president on the fourth of March, and that, in the interval, I shall do my utmost that whoever is to hold the helm for the next voyage shall start with the best possible chance to save the ship.

This is due to the people both on principle and under the Constitution. Their will, constitutionally expressed, is the ultimate law for all. If they should deliberately resolve to have immediate peace, even at the loss of their country and their liberties, I have not the power nor the right to resist them. It is their own business, and they must do as they please with their own. I believe, however, they are still resolved to preserve their country and their liberty; and in this office or out I am resolved to stand by them.

I may add, that in this purpose to save the country and its liberties no classes of people seem so nearly unanimous as the soldiers in the field and the seamen afloat. Do they not have the hardest of it? Who should quail while they do not? God bless the soldiers and seamen, with all their brave commanders.

REPLY TO THE PROTEST OF TENNESSEE, OCTOBER 22, 1864.

At the time these papers were presented, as before stated, I had never seen either of them, nor heard of the subject to which they relate, except in a general way, only one day previously. Up to the present moment nothing whatever has passed between Governor Johnson or any one else connected with the proclamation and myself. Since receiving the papers, as stated, I have given the subject such brief consideration as I have been able to do in the midst of so many pressing public duties.

My conclusion is, that I have nothing to do with the matter, either to sustain the plan as the convention and Governor Johnson have initiated it, or to revoke or modify it as you demand. By the Constitution and laws the President is charged with no duty in the conduct of a presidential election in any state; nor do I in this case perceive any military reasons for his interference in the matter.

The movement set on foot by the convention and Governor Johnson does not, as seems to be assumed by you, emanate from the national executive. In no proper sense can it be considered other than as an independent movement of at least a portion of the loyal people of Tennessee.

I do not perceive in the plan any menace of violence or coercion toward any one. Governor Johnson, like any other loyal citizen of Tennessee, has the right to favor any political plan he chooses, and as military governor it is his duty to keep the peace among and for the loyal people of the state.

I can not discern that by this plan he proposes any more. But you object to the plan. Leaving it alone will be your perfect security against it. Do as you please on your own account, peacefully and loyally, and Governor Johnson will not molest you, but will protect you against violence so far as in his power.

I presume that the conducting of a presidential election in Tennessee in strict accordance with the old code of the state is not now a possibility.

It is scarcely necessary to add that if any election shall be held, and any votes shall be cast in the State of Tennessee for President and Vice-President of the United States, it will belong, not to the military agents, nor yet to the executive department, but exclusively to another department of the government, to determine whether they are entitled to be counted, in conformity with the Constitution and laws of the United States.

Except it be to give protection against violence, I decline to interfere in any way with any presidential election. ABRAHAM LINCOLN.

To General Sheridan.

Executive Mansion, Washington, October 22, 1864.

With great pleasure I tender to you and your brave army, the thanks of the nation and my own personal admiration and gratitude for the month's operations in the Shenandoah Valley, and especially for the splendid work of October 19th.

Your obedient servant,   Abraham Lincoln.

Speech at a Seranade by a Club of Pennsylvanians the Night of the Election, November 9, 1864.

Friends and Fellow-Citizens:—Even before I had been informed by you that the compliment was paid me by loyal citizens of Pennsylvania friendly to me, I had inferred that you were that portion of my countrymen who think that the best interests of the nation are to be subserved by the support of the present administration. I do not pretend to say that you who think so embrace all the patriotism and loyalty of the country. But I do believe, and I trust without personal interest, that the welfare of the whole country does require that such support and indorsement be given.

I earnestly believe that the consequences of this day's work, if it be as you assure me, and as now seems probable, will be to the lasting advantage if not to the very salvation of the country.

I can not at this hour say what has been the result of the election, but whatever it may have been, and I have no desire to modify this opinion, that all who have labored to-day in behalf of the Union organization have wrought for the best interests of the country and the world, not only for the present, but for all future ages.

I am thankful to God for the approval of the people. But while deeply grateful for this mark of their confidence in me, if I know my heart, my gratitude is free from any taint of personal triumph.

I do not impugn the motives of any one opposed to me. It is no pleasure to me to triumph over any one, but I give thanks to the Almighty for the evidences of the people's resolution to stand by free government and the right of humanity.

Response to a Serenade by the various Lincoln and Johnson Clubs of the District of Columbia, November 10, 1864.

It has long been a grave question whether any government, not too strong for the liberties of its people, can be strong enough to maintain its existence in great emergencies.

On this point the present rebellion brought our government to a severe test, and a presidential election occurring in a regular course during the rebellion, added not a little to the strain.

If the loyal people united were put to the utmost of their strength by the rebellion, must they not fail when divided and partially paralized by a political war among themselves? But the election was a necessity. We can not have free government without elections; and if the rebellion could force us to forego or postpone a national election, it might fairly claim to have already conquered and ruined us.

The strife of the election is but human nature practically applied to the facts of the case. What has occurred in this case must ever recur in similar cases. Human nature will not change. In the future great national trial compared with the men of this, we will have as weak and as strong, as silly and as wise, as bad and as good. Let us, therefore, study the incidents of this as philosophy to learn wisdom from, and none of them as wrongs to be revenged.

But the election, along with its incidental and undesirable strife, has done good too.

It has demonstrated that a people's government can sustain a national election in the midst of a great civil war. Until now, it has not been known to the world that this was a possibility. It shows, also, how sound and strong we still are. It shows that even among the candidates of the same party, he who is most devoted to the Union and most opposed to treason can receive most of the people's votes.

It shows, also, to the extent yet known, that we have more men now than we had when the war began. Gold is good in its place; but living, brave and patriotic men are better than gold. But the rebellion continues, and, now that the election is over, may not all have a common interest to re-unite in a common effort to save our common country? For my own part, I have striven and shall strive to avoid placing any obstacle in the way.

So long as I have been here, I have not willingly planted a thorn in any man's bosom. While I am duly sensible to the high compliment of a re-election, and duly grateful, as I trust, to Almighty God, for having directed my countrymen to a right conclusion, as I think, for their good, it adds nothing to my satisfaction that any other man may be disappointed by the result.

May I ask those who have not differed with me to join with me in this same spirit toward those who have? And, now, let me close by asking three hearty cheers for our brave soldiers and seamen, and their gallant and skillful commanders.

Letter of Condolence Written to Mrs. Bixby, of Boston, Mass., on the Death of Five Sons on the Field of Battle.

Executive Mansion, Washington, Nov. 21, 1864.

Dear Madam:—I have been shown in the files of the War Department, a statement of the Adjutant-General of Massachusetts, that you are the mother of five sons, who have died gloriously on the field of battle.

I feel how weak and fruitless must be any words of mine which should attempt to beguile you from the grief of a loss so overwhelming. But I can not refrain from tendering to you the consolation that may be found in the thanks of the Republic they died to save. I pray that our Heavenly Father may assuage the anguish of your bereavement, and leave you only the cherished memory of the loved and lost, and the solemn pride that must be yours, to have laid so costly a sacrifice upon the altar of freedom.

Yours very sincerely and respectfully,
Abraham Lincoln.

Fourth Annual Message, December 6, 1864.

Fellow-citizens of the Senate and House of Representatives:—Again the blessings of health and abundant harvests claim our profoundest gratitude to Almighty God. The condition of our foreign affairs is reasonably satisfactory.

Mexico continues to be a theater of civil war. While our political relations with that country have undergone no change, we have, at the same time, strictly maintained neutrality between the belligerents.

. . . .

The proposed overland telegraph between America and Europe, by the way of Behring's Straits and Asiatic Russia, which was sanctioned by Congress at the last session, has been undertaken, under very favorable circumstances, by an association of American citizens, with the cordial good-will and support as well of this government as of those of Great Britain and Russia. Assurances have been received from most of the South American States of their high appreciation of the enterprise, and their readiness to co-operate in constructing lines tributary to that world-encircling communication. I learn with much satisfaction that the noble design of a telegraphic communication between the eastern coast of America and Great Britain has been renewed with full expectation of its early accomplishment.

Thus it is hoped that with the return of domestic peace the country will be able to resume with energy and advantage its former high career of commerce and civilization.

Our very popular and estimable representative in Egypt died in April last. An unpleasant altercation which arose between the temporary incumbent of the office and the government of the Pasha resulted in a suspension of intercourse. The evil was promptly corrected on the arrival of the successor in the consulate, and our relation with Egypt, as well as our relations with the Barbary Powers, are entirely satisfactory.

The rebellion which has so long been flagrant in China, has at last been suppressed, with the co-operating good offices of this government and of the other western commercial states.

The judicial consular establishment there has become very difficult and onerous, and it will need legislative revision to adapt it to the extension of our commerce, and to the more intimate intercourse which has been instituted with the government and people of that vast empire. China seems to be accepting with hearty good will the conventional laws which regulate commercial and social intercourse among the western nations.

Owing to the peculiar situation of Japan, and the anomalous form of its government, the action of that empire in performing treaty stipulations is inconstant, and capricious. Nevertheless, good progress has been effected by the western powers, moving with enlightened concert.

Our own pecuniary claims have been allowed, or put in course of settlement, and the inland sea has been reopened to commerce. There is reason also to believe that these proceedings have increased rather than diminished the friendship of Japan toward the United States.

The ports of Norfolk, Fernandina, and Pensacola have been opened by proclamation. It is hoped that foreign merchants will now consider whether it is not safer and more profitable to themselves, as well as just to the United States, to resort to these and other open ports, than it is to pursue, through many hazards, and at vast cost, a contraband trade with the other ports which are closed, if not by actual military occupation, at least by a lawful and effective blockade.

For myself, I have no doubt of the power and duty of the executive, under the law of nations, to exclude enemies of the human race from an asylum in the United States. If Congress should think that proceedings in such cases lack the authority of law, or ought to be further regulated by it, I recommend that provision be made for effectually preventing foreign slave-traders from acquiring domicile and facilities for their criminal occupation in our country.

It is possible that, if it were a new and open question, the maritime powers, with the lights they now enjoy, would not concede the privileges of a naval belligerent to the insurgents of the United States, destitute, as they are, and always have been, equally of ships of war, and of ports and harbors. Disloyal emissaries have been neither less assiduous nor more successful during the last year than they were before that time in their efforts, under favor of that privilege to embroil our country in foreign wars. The desire and determination of the governments of the maritime states to defeat that design are believed to be as sincere as, and can not be more earnest than our own.

Nevertheless, unforeseen political difficulties have arisen, especially in Brazilian and British ports, and on the northern boundary of the United States, which have required, and are likely to continue to require, the practice of constant vigilance, and a just and conciliatory spirit on the part of the United States, as well as of the nations concerned and their governments. Commissioners have been appointed under the treaty with Great Britain on the adjustment of the claims of the Hudson's Bay and Puget Sound Agricultural Companies in Oregon, and are now proceeding to the execution of the trust assigned to them. In view of the insecurity of life and property in the region adjacent to the Canadian border, by reason of recent assaults and depredations committed by inimical and desperate persons who are harbored there, it has been thought proper to give notice that after the expiration of six months, the period conditionally stipulated in the existing arrangement with Great Britain, the United States must hold themselves at liberty to increase their naval armament upon the lakes if they shall find that proceeding necessary. The condition of the border will necessarily come into consideration in connection with the question of continuing or modifying the rights of transit from Canada through the United States, as well as the regulation of imposts, which were temporarily established by the reciprocity treaty of the 5th June, 1854. I desire however, to be understood, while making this statement, that the colonial authorities of Canada are not deemed to be intentionally unjust or unfriendly toward the United States; but, on the contrary, there is every reason to expect that, with the approval of the imperial government, they will take the necessary measures to prevent new incursions across the borders. . . .

The war continues. Since the last annual message all the important lines and positions then occupied by our forces have been maintained, and our arms have steadily advanced; thus liberating the regions left in the rear, so that Missouri, Kentucky, Tennessee and parts of other states have again produced reasonably fair crops.

The most remarkable feature in the military operations of the year is General Sherman's attempted march of three hundred miles directly through the insurgent region. It tends to show a great increase of our relative strength that our General-in-chief should feel able to confront and hold in check every active force of the enemy, and yet to detach a well appointed large army to move on such an expedition. The result not yet being known, conjecture in regard to it is not here indulged.

Important movements have also occurred during the year to the effect of molding society for durability in the Union. Although short of complete success, it is much in the right direction that twelve thousand citizens in each of the States of Arkansas and Louisiana have organized loyal state governments, with free constitutions, and are earnestly struggling to maintain and administer them. The movements in the same direction, more extensive though less definite, in Missouri, Kentucky and Tennessee, should not be overlooked. But Maryland presents the example of complete success. Maryland is secure to liberty and Union for all the future. The genius of rebellion will no more claim Maryland. Like another foul spirit, being driven out, it may seek to tear her, but it will woo her no more.

At the last session of Congress a proposed amendment of the Constitution abolishing slavery throughout the United States passed the Senate, but failed for lack of the requisite two-thirds vote in the House of Representatives. Although the present is the same Congress, and nearly the same members, and without questioning the wisdom or patriotism of those who stood in opposition, I venture to recommend the reconsideration and passage of the measure at the present session. Of course the abstract question is not changed; but an intervening election shows, almost certainly, that the next Congress will pass the measure if this does not. Hence there is only a question of *time* as to when the proposed amendment will go to the states for their action. And as it is to so go, at all events, may we not agree that the sooner the better? It is not claimed that the election has imposed a duty on members to change their views or their votes, any further than, as an additional element to to be considered, their judgment may be affected by it. It is the voice of the people now for the first time heard upon the question. In a great national crisis like ours, unanimity of action among those seeking a common end is very desirable,—almost indispensable.

And yet no approach to such unanimity is attainable unless some deference shall be paid to the will of the majority, simply because it is the will of the majority. In this case the common end is the maintenance of the Union, and among the means to secure that end, such will through the election is most clearly declared in favor of such constitutional amendment.

The most reliable indication of public purpose in this country is derived through our popular elections. Judging by the recent canvass and its result, the purpose of the people within the loyal states to maintain the integrity of the Union was never more firm nor more nearly unanimous than now.

The extraordinary calmness and good order with which the millions of voters met and mingled at the polls give strong assurance of this. Not only all those who supported the Union ticket, so-called, but a great majority of the opposing party also, may be fairly claimed to entertain and to be actuated by the same purpose. It is an unanswerable argument to this effect, that no candidate for any office whatever, high or low, has ventured to seek votes on the avowal that he was for giving up the Union. There have been much impugning of motives, and much heated controversy as to the proper means and best mode of advancing the Union cause, but on the distinct issue of Union or no Union the politicians have shown their instinctive knowledge that there is no diversity among the people. In affording the people the fair opportunity of showing, one to another and to the world, this firmness and unanimity of purpose, the election has been of vast value to the national cause.

The election has exhibited another fact not less valuable to be known—the fact that we do not approach exhaustion in the most important branch of national resources—that of living men. While it is melancholy to reflect that the war has filled so many graves and carried mourning to so many hearts, it is some relief to know that, compared with the surviving, the fallen have been so few.

While corps and divisions and brigades and regiments have formed and fought and dwindled and gone out of existence, a great majority of the men who composed them are still living. The same is true of the naval service. The election returns prove this. So many voters could not else be found. The states regularly holding elections both now and four years ago, to wit, California, Connecticut, Delaware, Illinois, Indiana, Iowa, Kentucky, Maine, Maryland, Massachusetts, Michigan, Minnesota, Missouri, New Hampshire, New Jersey, New York, Ohio, Oregon, Pennsylvania, Rhode Island, Vermont, West Virginia, and Wisconsin cast 3,982,011 votes now against 3,870,222 cast then.

To this is to be added, 33,762 cast now in the new states of Kansas and Nevada, which states did not vote in 1860, thus swelling the aggregate to 4,015,773 and the net increase during the three years and a half of war to 145,551.

A table is appended showing particulars. To this

again should be added the number of all soldiers in the field from Massachusetts, Rhode Island, New Jersey, Delaware, Indiana, Illinois, and California, who, by the laws of those states, could not vote away from their homes, and which number can not be less than 90,000. Nor yet is this all. The number in organized territories is triple now what it was four years ago, while thousands, white and black, join us as the national arms press back the insurgent lines. So much is shown affirmatively and negatively by the election. It is not material to inquire *how* the increase has been produced or to show that it would have been *greater* but for the war, which is probably true.

The important fact remains demonstrated that we have more men *now* than we had when the war began; that we are not exhausted nor in process of exhaustion; that we are *gaining* strength, and may if need be maintain the contest indefinitely. This as to men. Material resources are now more complete and abundant than ever. The natural resources, then, are unexhausted, and as we believe, inexhaustible. The public purpose to re-establish and maintain the national authority, is unchanged, and, as we believe, unchangeable. The manner of continuing the effort remains to choose. On careful consideration of all the evidence accessible, it seems to me that no attempt at negotiation with the insurgent leader could result in any good. He would accept nothing short of severance of the Union—precisely what we will not and can not give. His declarations to this effect are explicit and oft-repeated. He does not attempt to deceive us. He affords us no excuse to deceive ourselves. He can not voluntarily re-accept the Union, we can not voluntarily yield it. Between him and us the issue is distinct, simple and inflexible. It is an issue which can only be tried by war, and decided by victory. If we yield, we are beaten; if the southern people fail him, he is beaten. Either way, it would be the victory and defeat following war. What is true, however, of him who heads the insurgent cause is not necessarily true of those who follow.

Although he can not re-accept the Union, they can; some of them, we know, already desire peace and re-union. The number of such may increase. They can at any moment have peace simply by laying down their arms and submitting to the national authority under the Constitution.

After so much, the government could not, if it would, maintain war against them. The loyal people would not sustain or allow it. If questions should remain, we would adjust them by the peaceful means of legislation, conference, courts, and votes, operating only in constitutional and lawful channels. Some certain, and other possible, questions are, and, would be, beyond the executive power to adjust, as, for instance, the admission of members into Congress, and whatever might require the appropriation of money.

The executive power itself would be greatly diminished by the cessation of actual war. Pardons and remissions of forfeitures, however, would still be within executive control. In what spirit and temper this control would be exercised can be fairly judged of by the past.

A year ago general pardon and amnesty, upon specified terms, were offered to all, except certain designated classes, and it was, at the same time made known that the excepted classes were still within contemplation of special clemency. During the year, many availed themselves of the general provision, and many more would, only that the signs of bad faith in some, led to such precautionary measures as rendered the practical process less easy and certain. During the same time also special pardons have been granted to individuals of the excepted classes, and no voluntary application has been denied. Thus, practically, the door has been, for a full year, open to all, except such as were not in condition to make free choice—that is, such as were in custody or under constraint. It is still so open to all. But the time may come—probably will come—when public duty shall demand that it be closed; and that, in lieu, more rigorous measures than heretofore shall be adopted.

In presenting the abandonment of armed resistance to the national authority on the part of the insurgents as the only indispensable condition to ending the war, on the part of the government, I retract nothing heretofore said as to slavery. I repeat the declaration made a year ago, that, "while I remain in my present position I shall not attempt to retract or modify the emancipation proclamation, nor shall I return to slavery any person who is free by the terms of that proclamation, or by any of the acts of Congress." If the people should, by whatever mode or means, make it an executive duty to re-enslave such persons, another, and not I, must be their instrument to perform it.

In stating a single condition of peace, I mean simply to say that the war will cease on the part of the government whenever it shall have ceased on the part of those who began it.   A. LINCOLN.

December 6, 1864.

PRESIDENT LINCOLN TO COL. EDMUND D. TAYLOR, OF CHICAGO, ILL., DECEMBER, 1864.

My Dear Colonel Dick:—I have long determined to make public the origin of the greenback, and tell the world that it is one of Dick Taylor's creations. You have always been friendly to me, and when troublous times fell upon us, and my shoulders, though broad and willing, were weak, and myself surrounded by such circumstances and such people that I knew not whom to trust, then I said in my extremity, "I will send for Colonel Taylor; he will know what to do." I think it was in January, 1862, on or about the 16th, that I did so. You came, and I said to you, "What can we do?" Said you, "Why, issue treasury notes bearing no interest, printed on the best banking paper. Issue enough to pay off the army expenses, and declare it legal tender." Chase thought it a hazardous thing, but we finally accomplished it, and gave to the people of this Republic the greatest blessing they ever had—their own paper to pay their own debts.

It is due to you, the father of the present greenback, that the people should know it, and I take great pleasure in making it known. How many times have

I laughed at you telling me plainly that I was too lazy to be any thing but a lawyer.

  Yours truly,   A. LINCOLN, *President.*

TO GENERAL SHERMAN.

Executive Mansion, Washington, D. C., Dec. 26, 1864.

My Dear General Sherman:—Many, many thanks for your Christmas gift, the capture of Savannah. When you were about to leave Atlanta for the Atlantic coast, I was *anxious,* if not fearful; but, feeling that you were the better judge, and remembering that nothing risked nothing gained, I did not interfere. Now, the undertaking being a success, the honor is all yours, for I believe none of us went further than to acquiesce. And, taking the work of General Thomas into the account, as it should be taken, it is indeed a great success. Not only does it afford the obvious and immediate military advantages, but in showing to the world that your army could be divided, putting the stronger part to an important new service, and yet having enough to vanquish the old opposing forces of the whole—Hood's army—it brings those who sat in darkness to see great light.

Please make my grateful acknowledgment to your whole army, officers and men.

  Yours, very truly,   A. LINCOLN.

TO DR. JOHN MACLEAN.

Executive Mansion, Washington, Dec. 27, 1864.

My Dear Sir:—I have the honor to acknowledge the reception of your note of the 20th of December, conveying the announcement that the trustees of the

College of New Jersey had conferred upon me the degree of Doctor of Laws.

The assurance conveyed by this high compliment that the course of the government which I represent has received the approval of a body of gentlemen of such character and intelligence, in this time of public trial, is most grateful to me.

Thoughtful men must feel that the fate of civilization upon the continent is involved in the issue of our contest.

Among the most gratifying proofs of this conviction is the hearty devotion every-where exhibited by our schools and colleges to the national cause.

I am most thankful if my labors have seemed to conduce to the preservation of those institutions under which alone we can expect good government, and in its train sound learning and the progress of the liberal arts. I am, sir, very truly,

Your obedient servant,

A. LINCOLN.

UPON PRESENTING TO THE PRESIDENT A VASE OF SKELETON LEAVES GATHERED ON THE BATTLE FIELD OF GETTYSBURG, JANUARY 24, 1865, THE PRESIDENT SAID:

Reverend Sir, and Ladies and Gentlemen:—I accept with emotions of profoundest gratitude the beautiful gift you have been pleased to present to me.

You will, of course, expect that I acknowledge it. So much has been said about Gettysburg, and so well, that for me to attempt to say more may perhaps only serve to weaken the force of that which has already been said.

A most graceful and elegant tribute was paid to the patriotism and self-denying labors of the American ladies on the occasion of the consecration of the National Cemetery at Gettysburg by our illustrious friend, Edward Everett, now, alas, departed from earth. His life was a truly great one, and I think the greatest part of it was that which crowned its closing years. I wish you to read, if you have not already done so, the eloquent and truthful words which he then spoke of the women of America. Truly, the service they have rendered to the defenders of our country in this perilous time, and are yet rendering, can never be estimated as they ought to be.

For your kind wishes to me personally I beg leave to render you likewise my sincerest thanks. I assure you they are appreciated.

And now, gentlemen and ladies, may God bless you all.

LETTER TO GOVERNOR SMITH, OF VERMONT.

Executive Mansion, Washington, Feb. 8, 1865.

His Excellency, Governor Smith, of Vermont:—Complaint is made to me, by Vermont, that the assignment of her quota for the draft on the pending call is intrinsically unjust, and also in bad faith of the government's promise to fairly allow credits for men previously furnished. To illustrate, a supposed case is stated as follows:

Vermont and New Hampshire must, between them, furnish six thousand men on the pending call, and being equal, each must furnish as many as the other in the long run. But the government finds that on former calls Vermont furnished a surplus of five hundred, and New Hampshire a surplus of fifteen hundred. These two surpluses making two thousand, and added to the six thousand, making eight thousand to be furnished by the two states, or four thousand each, less by fair credits. Then subtract Vermont's surplus of five hundred from her four thousand, leaves three thousand five hundred as her quota on the pending call; and likewise subtract New Hampshire's surplus of fifteen hundred from her four thousand, leaves two thousand five hundred as her quota on the pending call. These three thousand five hundred and two thousand five hundred make precisely six thousand, which the supposed case requires from the two states, and it is just equal for Vermont to furnish one thousand more now than New Hampshire, because New Hampshire has heretofore furnished one thousand more than Vermont, which equalizes the burdens of the two in the long run. And this result, so far from being bad faith to Vermont, is indispensable to keeping good faith with New Hampshire. By no other result can the six thousand men be obtained from the two states, and at the same time deal justly and keep faith with both, and we do but confuse ourselves in questioning the process by which the right result is reached. The supposed case is perfect as an illustration.

The pending call is not for three hundred thousand men, subject to fair credits, but is for three hundred thousand remaining after all fair credits have been deducted, and it is impossible to concede what Vermont asks without coming out short of three hundred thousand men, or making other localities pay for the partiality shown her.

This upon the case stated: If there be different reasons for making an allowance to Vermont, let them be presented and considered.

Yours truly, ABRAHAM LINCOLN.

PRESIDENT LINCOLN DICTATED THE FOLLOWING TO SECRETARY STANTON, TO BE SENT TO GENERAL GRANT.

March 3, 1865.

The president directs me to say to you that he wishes you to have no conference with General Lee, unless it be for the capitulation of Lee's army, or on some minor or purely military matter. He instructs me to say that you are not to decide, discuss, or confer upon any political question. Such questions the President holds in his own hands, and will submit them to no military conferences or conventions. In the meantime you are to press to the utmost your military advantages.

SECOND INAUGURAL ADDRESS, MARCH 4, 1865.

Fellow-Countrymen:—At this second appearing to take the oath of the presidential office, there is less occasion for an extended address than there was at the first. Then a statement somewhat in detail of a course to be pursued seemed very fitting and proper. Now, at the expiration of four years, during which public declarations have been constantly called forth on every point and phase of the great contest which still absorbs the attention and engrosses the energies of the nation, little that is new could be presented.

The progress of our arms, upon which all else chiefly depends, is as well known to the public as to myself, and it is, I trust, reasonably satisfactory and encouraging to all. With high hope for the future, no prediction in regard to it is ventured. On the occasion corresponding to this four years ago, all thoughts were anxiously directed to an impending civil war. All dreaded it; all sought to avert it. While the inaugural address was being delivered from this place, devoted altogether to *saving* the Union without war, insurgent agents were in the city seeking to *destroy* it without war—seeking to dissolve the Union and divide effects by negotiation. Both parties deprecated war; but one of them would *make* war rather than let the nation survive, and the other would *accept* war rather than let it perish. And the war came. One-eighth of the whole population were colored slaves, not distributed generally over the Union, but localized in the southern part of it.

These slaves constituted a peculiar and powerful interest. All knew that this interest was somehow the cause of the war. To strengthen, perpetuate and extend this interest was the object for which the insurgents would rend the Union, even by war, while the government claimed no right to do more than to restrict the territorial enlargement of it.

Neither party expected for the war the magnitude or the duration which it has already attained. Neither anticipated that the *cause* of the conflict might cease with, or even before, the conflict itself should cease. Each looked for an easier triumph, and a result less fundamental and astounding.

Both read the same Bible, and pray to the same God; and each invokes His aid against the other.

It may seem strange that any man should dare to ask a just God's assistance in wringing their bread from the sweat of other men's faces; but let us judge not, that we be not judged.

The prayers of both could not be answered. That of neither has been answered fully. The Almighty has His own purposes.

"Woe unto the world because of offenses, for it must needs be that offenses come: but woe to that man by whom the offense cometh." If we shall suppose that American slavery is one of these offenses, which in the providence of God must needs come, but which, having continued through His appointed time, He now wills to remove, and that He gives to both North and South this terrible war as the woe due to those by whom the offense came, shall we discern therein any departure from those divine attributes which the believers in a living God always ascribe to Him? Fondly do we hope, fervently do we pray, that this mighty scourge of war may speedily pass away. Yet, if God wills that it continue until all the wealth piled by the bondman's two hundred and fifty years of unrequited toil shall be sunk, and until every drop of blood drawn with the lash shall be paid with another drawn with the sword; as was said three thousand years ago, so still it must be said, "The judgments of the Lord are true and righteous altogether."

With malice toward none, with charity for all, with firmness in the right, as God gives us to see the right, let us strive on to finish the work we are in; to bind up the nation's wounds; to care for him who shall have borne the battle, and for his widow and orphans; to do all which may achieve and cherish a just and a lasting peace among ourselves and with all nations.

PRESIDENT LINCOLN TO THURLOW WEED.

Executive Mansion, Washington, March 15, 1865.

Dear Mr. Weed:—Every one likes a compliment. Thank you for yours on my little notification speech and on the recent inaugural address. I expect the latter to wear as well as, perhaps better than, any thing I have produced; but I believe it is not immediately popular.

Men are not flattered by being shown that there has been a difference of purpose between the Almighty and them.

To deny it, however, in this case, is to deny that there is a God governing the world.

It is a truth which I thought needed to be told, and, as whatever of humiliation there is in it falls most directly on myself, I thought others might afford for me to tell it. Truly, yours, A. LINCOLN.

INTRODUCED BY GOVERNOR MORTON, FROM NATIONAL HOTEL, WASHINGTON, D. C., MARCH 17, 1865, AND THE PRESIDENT'S RESPONSE.

Fellow-citizens:—It will be but a very few words that I shall undertake to say. I was born in Kentucky, raised in Indiana, and lived in Illinois; and now I am here, where it is my business to care equally for the good people of all the states.

I am glad to see an Indiana regiment on this day able to present the captured flag to the governor of Indiana.

I am not disposed, in saying this, to make a distinction between the states, for all have done equally well.

There are but few views or aspects of this great war upon which I have not said or written something, whereby my own opinion might be known. But there is one—the recent attempt of our erring brethren, as they are sometimes called, to employ the negro to fight for them. I have neither written nor made a speech on that subject, because that was their business, not mine; and if I had a wish upon the subject, I had not the power to introduce it, or make it effective. The great question with them was whether the negro, being put into the army, will fight for them. I do not know, and therefore can not decide. They ought to know better than we. I have in my lifetime heard many arguments why the negroes ought to be slaves; but if they fight for those who would keep them in slavery, it will be a better argument than all I have yet heard. He who will fight for that ought to be a slave. They have concluded at last to take one out of four of the slaves and put them in the army; and that one out of four who will fight to keep the others in slavery ought to be a slave himself, unless he is killed in a fight.

While I have often said that all men ought to be

free, yet would I allow those colored persons to be slaves who want to be, and next to them those white people who argue in favor of making other people slaves. I am in favor of giving an appointment to such white men to try it on for these slaves. I will say one thing in regard to the negroes being employed to fight for them. I do know he can not fight and stay at home and make bread too. And as one is about as important as the other to them, I don't care which they do. I am rather in favor of having them try them as soldiers. They lack one vote of doing that, and I wish I could send my vote over the river so that I might cast it in favor of allowing the negro to fight. But they can not fight and work both. We must now see the bottom of the enemy's resources. They will stand out as long as they can, and if the negro will fight for them, they must allow him to fight. They have drawn upon their last branch of resources, and we can now see the bottom. I am glad to see the end so near at hand. I have said now more than I intended, and will therefore bid you goodbye.

CITY POINT, VIRGINIA, APRIL 2, 8:30 P. M.

At 4:30 P. M. to-day General Grant telegraphs as follows:

We are now up, and have a continuous line of troops, and in a few hours will be intrenched from the Appomattox below Petersburg to the river above. The whole captures since the army started out will not amount to less than twelve thousand men, and probably fifty pieces of artillery. I do not know the number of men and guns accurately, however. A portion of Foster's Division, Twenty-fourth Corps, made a most gallant charge this afternoon, and captured a a very important fort from the enemy, with its entire garrison.

All seems well with us, and every thing is quiet just now. A. LINCOLN.

CITY POINT, VIRGINIA, APRIL 2, 2 P. M.

At 10:45 A. M. General Grant telegraphs as follows:

Every thing has been carried from the left of the Ninth Corps. The Sixth Corps alone captured more than six thousand prisoners. The Second and Twenty-fourth Corps captured forts, guns and prisoners from the enemy, but I can not tell the numbers. We are now closing around the works of the line immediately enveloping Petersburg. All looks remarkably well. I have not yet heard from Sheridan. His headquarters have been moved up to Bank's House, near the Boydton road, about three miles south-west of Petersburg. A. LINCOLN.

TELEGRAM TO THE SECRETARY OF WAR.

At 12:30 P. M. to-day General Grant telegraphed me as follows:

There has been much hard fighting this morning. The enemy drove our left from near Dabney's house back well toward the Boydton pland-road. We are now about to take the offensive at that point, and I hope will more than recover the lost ground.

Later he telegraphed again as follows:

Our troops, after being driven back to the Boydton plank-road, turned and drove the enemy in turn, and took the White Oak road, which we now have. This gives us the ground occupied by the enemy this morning. I will send you a rebel flag captured by our troops in driving the enemy back. There have been four flags captured to-day.

Judging by the two points from which General Grant telegraphs, I infer that he moved his headquarters about one mile since he sent the first of the two dispatches. A. LINCOLN.

To E. M. STANTON, SECRETARY OF WAR.

City Point, Virginia, April 2. 1865, 8:30 A. M.

Last night General Grant telegraphed that General Sheridan, with his cavalry and the Fifth Corps, had captured three brigades of infantry, a train of wagons, and several batteries; the prisoners amounting to several thousand.

This morning General Grant, having ordered an attack along the whole line, telegraphs as follows:

Both Wright and Parke got through the enemy's lines. The battle now rages furiously. General Sheridan, with his cavalry, the Fifth Corps, and Miles' Division of the Second Corps, which was sent to him this morning, is now sweeping down from the west.

All now looks highly favorable. General Ord is engaged, but I have not yet heard the result in his front. A. LINCOLN.

DISPATCH TO SECRETARY STANTON, APRIL 3, 1865.

This morning Lieutenant-General Grant reports Petersburg evacuated, and he is confident that Richmond also is.

He is pushing forward to cut off, if possible, the retreating rebel army.   A. LINCOLN.

PRESIDENT'S ORDER.

Headquarters Armies of the United States,
City Point, April 6, 1865.

It has been intimated to me, that the gentlemen who have acted as the legislature of Virginia, in support of the rebellion, may now desire to assemble at Richmond, and take measures to withdraw the Virginia troops, and other support from resistance to the general government. If they attempt it, give them permission and protection, until, if at all, they attempt some action hostile to the United States, in which case you will notify them, give them reasonable time to leave, and at the end of which time arrest any who remain. Allow judge Campbell to see this, but do not make it public. Yours, etc.,

A. LINCOLN.

LAST PUBLIC SPEECH EVER DELIVERED BY PRESIDENT LINCOLN, APRIL 11, 1865.

After the fall of Richmond and the surrender of the Army of Northern Virginia, President Lincoln was called upon in Washington, and made these remarks:

[We meet this evening, not in sorrow, but in gladness of heart. The evacuation of Petersburg and Richmond, and the surrender of the principal insurgent army, give hope of a righteous and speedy peace, whose joyous expression can not be restrained. In the midst of this, however, He from whom all blessings flow must not be forgotten. A call for a national thanksgiving is being prepared and will be duly promulgated. Nor must those whose harder part give us the cause of rejoicing be overlooked. Their honors must not be parceled out with others. I myself was near the front, and had the high pleasure of transmitting much of the good news to you, but no part of the honor, for plan or execution, is mine. To General Grant, his skillful officers, and brave men all belongs. The gallant navy stood ready, but did not in reach to take active part.

By these recent successes, the reinauguration of the national authority, reconstruction, which has had a large share of thought from the first, is pressed much more closely upon our attention. It is fraught with great difficulty. Unlike the case of a war between independent nations, there is no authorized organ for us to treat with. No one man has authority to give up the rebellion for any other man. We simply must begin with and mold from disorganized and discordant elements. Nor is it a small additional embarrassment that we, the loyal people, differ among ourselves as to the mode, manner, and means of reconstruction.

As a general rule, I abstain from reading the reports of attacks upon myself, wishing not to be provoked by that to which I can not properly offer an answer. In spite of this precaution, however, it comes to my knowledge that I am censured from some supposed agency in setting up and seeking to sustain the new state government of Louisiana. In this I have done just so much as and no more than the public knows. In the annual message of December, 1863, and accompanying proclamation, I presented a plan of reconstruction (as the phrase goes), which I promised, if adopted by any state, should be acceptable to and sustained by the executive government of the nation. I distinctly stated that this was not the only plan which might possibly be acceptable, and I also distinctly protested that the executive claimed no right to say when or whether members should be admitted to seats in Congress from such states. This plan was in advance submitted to the then cabinet, and distinctly approved by every member of it. One of them suggested that I should then and in that connection apply the Emancipation Proclamation to the theretofore excepted parts of Virginia and Louisiana; that I should drop the suggestion about apprenticeship for freed people, and that I should omit the protest against my own power, in regard to the admission of members of Congress, but even he approved every part and parcel of the plan which has since been employed or touched by the action of Louisiana.

The new constitution of Louisiana, declaring emancipation for the whole state, practically applies the proclamation to the part previously excepted. It does not adopt apprenticeship for freed people, and it is silent, as it could not well be otherwise, about the admission of members to Congress. So that, as it applies to Louisiana, every member of the cabinet fully approved the plan.

The message went to Congress, and I received many commendations of the plan, written and verbal, and not a single objection to it from any professed emancipationist came to my knowledge until after the news reached Washington that the people of Louisiana had begun to move in accordance with it. From about July, 1862, I had corresponded with different persons supposed to be interested, seeking a reconstruction of a state government for Louisiana. When the message of 1863, with the plan before mentioned reached New Orleans, General Banks wrote me he was confident that the people, with his military co-operation, would reconstruct substantially on that plan. I wrote him and some of them to try it. They tried it, and the result is known.

Such only has been my agency in getting up the Louisiana government. As to sustaining it, my promise is out, as before stated. But as bad promises are better broken than kept, I shall treat this as a bad promise and break it whenever I shall be convinced that keeping it is adverse to the public interest. But I have not yet been so convinced.

I have been shown a letter on this subject, supposed to be an able one, in which the writer expresses regret that my mind has not seemed to be definitely fixed on the question whether the seceded states, so called, are in the Union or out of it.

It would, perhaps, add astonishment to his regret, were he to learn that, since I have found professed Union men endeavoring to make that question, I have *purposely* forborne any public expression upon it. As appears to me, that question has not been, nor yet is, a practically material one, and that any discussion of it, while it thus remains practically immaterial, could have no effect other than the mischievous one of dividing our friends. As yet, whatever it may hereafter become, that question is bad as a basis of a controversy, and good for nothing at all as merely a pernicious abstraction. We all agree that the seceded states, so called, are out of their proper practical relation with the Union, and that the sole object of the government, civil and military, in regard to those states, is to again get them into that proper practical relation. I believe it is not only possible, but in fact easier, to do this without deciding, or even considering, whether these states have ever been out of the Union, than with it. Finding themselves safely at home, it would be utterly immaterial whether they had ever been abroad. Let us all join in doing the acts necessary to restoring the proper practical relations between these states and the Union, and each forever after innocently indulge his own opinion whether, in doing the acts, he brought the state from without into the Union, or only gave them proper assistance, they never having been out of it.

The amount of constituency, so to speak, on which the new Louisiana government rests, would be more satisfactory to all if it contained fifty, thirty, or even twenty thousand, instead of only about twelve thousand, as it really does. It is also unsatisfactory to some that the elective franchise is not given to the colored men. I would myself prefer that it were now conferred on the very intelligent, and on those who serve our cause as soldiers. Still, the question is not whether the Louisiana government, as it stands, is quite all that is desirable. The question is, "Will it be wise, take it as it is, and help to improve it, or to reject and disperse it?" "Can Louisiana be brought into proper practical relation with the Union *sooner* by *sustaining* or by *discarding* her new state government?"

Some twelve thousand voters in the heretofore slave state of Louisiana have sworn allegiance to the Union, assumed to be the rightful political power of the state, held elections, organized a state government, adopted a free state constitution, giving the benefit of public schools equally to black and white, and empowering the legislature to confer the elective franchise upon the colored man. Their legislature has already voted to ratify the constitutional amendment recently passed by Congress abolishing slavery throughout the nation. These twelve thousand persons are thus fully committed to the Union, and to perpetual freedom in the states—committed to the very things and nearly all the things the nation wants—and they ask the nation's recognition, and its assistance to make good that committal.

Now, if we reject and spurn them, we do our utmost to disorganize and disperse them. We, in effect, say to the white men, "You are worthless, or worse; we will neither help you nor be helped by you." To the blacks we say, "This cup of liberty which these, your old masters, hold to your lips, we will dash from you, and leave you to the chances of gathering the spilled and scattered contents in some vague and undefined when, where, and how." If this course, discouraging and paralyzing both black and white, has any tendency to bring Louisiana into proper practical relations with the Union, I have, so far, been unable to perceive it. If, on the contrary, we recognize and sustain the new government of Louisiana, the converse of all this is made true.

We encourage the hearts and nerve the arms of the twelve thousand to adhere to their work and argue for it, and proselyte for it, and fight for it, and feed it, and grow it, and ripen it to a complete success. The colored man, too, seeing all united for him, is inspired with vigilance, and energy, and daring, to the same end. Grant that he desires the elective franchise, will he not attain it sooner by saving the already advanced steps toward it than by running backward over them? Concede that the new government of Louisiana is only to what it should be as the egg is to the fowl; we shall sooner have the fowl by hatching the egg than by smashing it.

Again, if we reject Louisiana, we also reject one vote in favor of the proposed amendment to the National Constitution.

To meet this proposition, it has been argued that no more than three-fourths of those states which have not attempted secession are necessary to validly ratify the amendment

I do not commit myself against this further than to say that such a ratification would be questionable, and sure to be persistently questioned, whilst a ratification by three-fourths of all the states would be unquestioned and unquestionable.

I repeat the question, " can Louisiana be brought into proper practical relation with the Union *sooner* by *sustaining* or by *discarding* her new state government?" What has been said of Louisiana will apply generally to other states. And yet so great peculiarities pertain to each state, and such important and sudden changes occur in the same state, and, with all, so new and unprecedented is the whole case, that no exclusive and inflexible plan can safely be prescribed as to details and collaterals. Such exclusive and inflexible plan would surely become a new entanglement. Important principles may, and must, be inflexible.

In the present situation, as the phrase goes, it may be my duty to make some new announcement to the people of the south. I am considering, and shall not fail to act when satisfied that action will be proper.

LAST PUBLIC UTTERANCES OF PRESIDENT LINCOLN,
APRIL 14, 1865.

Mr. Colfax—I want you to take a message from me to the miners whom you visit. I have very large ideas of the mineral wealth of our nation. I believe it practically inexhaustible. It abounds all over the western country, from the Rocky Mountains to the Pacific, and its development has scarcely commenced. During the war, when we were adding a couple millions of dollars every day to our national debt, I did not care about encouraging the increase in the volume of our precious metals. We had the country to save first. But now that the rebellion is overthrown, and we know pretty nearly the amount of our national debt, the more gold and silver we mine, we make the payment of that debt so much the easier. Now, I am going to encourage that in every possible way. We shall have hundred of thousands of disbanded soldiers, and many have feared that their return home in such great numbers might paralyze industry, by furnishing, suddenly, a greater supply of labor than there will be a demand for. I am going to try to attract them to the hidden wealth of our mountain ranges, where there is room enough for all. Immigration, which even the war has not stopped, will land upon our shores hundreds of thousands more per year from overcrowded Europe. I intend to point them to the gold and silver that wait for them in the west. Tell the miners for me, that I shall promote their interests to the utmost of my ability, because their prosperity is the prosperity of the nation; and we shall prove, in a very few years, that we are indeed the treasury of the world.

IN CARRIAGE GOING TO THEATER. LAST WRITTEN WORDS.

Allow Mr. Ashmun and friend to come to me at 9 o'clock A. M. to-morrow, April 15, 1865.

A. LINCOLN.

FUNERAL HYMN.

> Rest, noble martyr; rest in peace;
> Rest with the true and brave,
> Who, like thee, fell in freedom's cause,
> The nation's life to save.

Thy name shall live while time endures,
    And men shall say of thee,
"He saved his country from its foes,
    And bade the slave be free."

These deeds shall be thy monument,
    Better than brass or stone;
They leave thy fame in Glory's light,
    Unrivaled and alone.

This consecrated spot shall be,
    To Freedom ever dear;
And Freedom's sons of every race,
    Shall weep and worship here.

O God! before whom we, in tears,
    Our fallen Chief deplore;
Grant that the cause for which he died,
    May live forever more.

THE END.

THE NATIONAL LINCOLN MONUMENT, SPRINGFIELD, ILL.
FACING SOUTH.
(From Power's History of the Attempt to Steal the Body of Lincoln.)

THE NATIONAL LINCOLN MONUMENT.
FACING NORTH.

INDEX.

	PAGE.
Address to Committee notifying him of his First Nomination to the Presidency, May 18, 1860	13
Address at Springfield, Ill., February 11, 1861	18
Address at Indianapolis, Ind., February 11, 1861	19
Address at Indianapolis, Ind. (evening), February 11, 1861	20
Address at Cincinnati, O., February 12, 1861	22
Address at Columbus, O., February 13, 1861	25
Address at Pittsburg, Pa., February 15, 1861	27
Address at Albany, N. Y., February 18, 1861	31
Address at Albany, N. Y. (evening), February 18, 1861	32
Address at Troy, N. Y., February 18, 1861	34
Address at Hudson, N. Y., February 19, 1861	34
Address at Poughkeepsie, N. Y., February 19, 1861	35
Address at Fishkill Landing, N. Y., February 19, 1861	36
Address at Peekskill, N. Y., February 19, 1861	36
Address at New York City, N. Y., February 20, 1861	37
Address at Trenton, N. J., February 21, 1861	39
Address at Philadelphia, Pa., February 22, 1861	41
Address at Harrisburg, Pa., February 22, 1861	42
Address at Serenade, Washington, D. C., February 28, 1861	47
Address to Delegates from Virginia, April 13, 1861	64
Address to Frontier Guards, April 28, 1861	69
Address to Baltimore Committee, April 28, 1861	69
Address on Retirement of General Scott, November 1, 1861	105
Address to the Senators and Representatives of the Border States, July, 1862	171
Address at a Union Meeting in Washington, August 6, 1862	184
Address on Colonization, August 14, 1862	186
Address Respecting the Issue of Emancipation Proclamation, September 13, 1862	196

(427)

Address at Serenade in Honor of Emancipation Proclamation, September 24, 1862.. 204
Address to Major John J. Key, September 26, 1862. 205
Address to Army of the Potomac, December 22, 1862......... 281
Address at a Serenade, July, 1863.. 281
Address at the Dedication of Gettysburg Cemetery, November 19, 1863.. 329
Quotation from Speech of Daniel Webster............................ 330
Address at Patent Office, Washington, March 16, 1864......... 349
Address at the Baltimore Fair, April 18, 1864...................... 354
Address at Serenade at Washington, D. C., May 13, 1864...... 362
Address to Committee on Re-nomination, June 9, 1864........ 364
Address to National Union League, June 9, 1864................. 365
Address at Philadelphia Fair, June 16, 1864....................... 366
Address at Serenade, September, 1864................................ 376
Address to 148th Ohio Regiment, September, 1864.............. 382
Address to another Ohio Regiment, September, 1864........... 378
Address, called his last, shortest, and best, September, 1864.. 384
Address at a Serenade, October 19, 1864............................ 385
Address at a Serenade by Club of Pennsylvanians, November 9, 1864.. 389
Address at a Serenade to Lincoln and Johnson Clubs, November 10, 1864.. 390
Address upon Receipt of Vase of Skeleton Leaves, January 24, 1865... 406
Address from National Hotel, Washington, March 17, 1865.. 412
Address, last delivered by Lincoln, April 11, 1865 417

INAUGURAL ADDRESSES.

Address, First Inaugural, March 4, 1861............................. 48
Address, Second Inaugural, March 4, 1865.......................... 409

LETTERS TO HIS GENERALS.

Letter to Major-General Fremont, August 15, 1861.............. 96
Letter to Major-General Fremont, September 2, 1861........... 98
Letter to Major-General Fremont, September 22, 1861......... 100
Letter to Major-General Fremont, May 24, 1862................... 142
Letter to Major-General Fremont, May 24, 1862................... 143

INDEX. 429

Letter to Major-General Fremont, May 29, 1862.................. 149
Letter to Major-General Fremont, June 9, 1862 155
Letter to Major-General Fremont, June 12, 1862................ 155
Letter to Major-General Fremont, June 13, 1862................ 155
Letter to Major-General Fremont, June 15, 1862................ 156
Letter to Major-General Fremont, June 16, 1862................ 158
Letter to Major-General Fremont, September 11, 1862.......... 193
Letter to Major-General Halleck, December 2, 1861 121
Letter to Major-General Halleck, January 1, 1862.............. 124
Letter to Major-General Halleck, January 15, 1862............. 124
Letter to Major-General Halleck, February 16, 1862............ 127
Letter to Major-General Halleck, May 24, 1862................. 144
Letter to Major-General Halleck, July 2, 1862................. 168
Letter to Major-General Halleck, July 6, 1862................. 284
Letter to Major-General Halleck, July 6, 1863................. 170
Letter to Major-General Halleck, July 29, 1863................ 293
Letter to Major-General McClellan, February 3, 1862........... 125
Letter to Major-General McClellan, April 9, 1862.............. 133
Letter to Major-General McClellan, May 9, 1862................ 138
Letter to Major-General McClellan, May 21, 1862 141
Letter to Major-General McClellan, May 25, 1862............... 141
Letter to Major-General McClellan, May 25, 1862............... 145
Letter to Major-General McClellan, May 28, 1862............... 148
Letter to Major-General McClellan, May 31, 1862............... 154
Letter to Major-General McClellan, June 1, 1862............... 154
Letter to Major-General McClellan, June 20, 1862.............. 160
Letter to Major-General McClellan, June 21, 1862.............. 161
Letter to Major-General McClellan, June 26, 1862.............. 162
Letter to Major-General McClellan, June 28, 1862.............. 163
Letter to Major-General McClellan, July 1, 1862............... 166
Letter to Major-General McClellan, July 2, 1862............... 167
Letter to Major-General McClellan, July 3, 1862............... 168
Letter to Major-General McClellan, July 4, 1862............... 169
Letter to Major-General McClellan, July 13, 1862.............. 171
Letter to Major-General McClellan, October 13, 1862........... 207
Letter to Major-General McClellan, October 25, 1862........... 213
Letter to Major-General McClellan, October 26, 1862........... 213
Letter to General Buell, January 6, 1862...................... 124

INDEX.

Letter to General Buell, January 7, 1862... 122
Letter to General Buell, January 13, 1862....................................... 123
Letter to General Buell March 10, 1862 131
Letter to General Saxton, May 24, 1862.. 142
Letter to General Saxton, May 25, 1862... 144
Letter to General Saxton, May 25, 1862... 146
Letter to General Saxton, May 25, 1862... 147
Letter to General McDowell, May 24, 1862...................................... 143
Letter to General McDowell, May 28, 1862...................................... 148
Letter to Major-General Hooker, January 26, 1863............................ 247
Letter to Major-General Hooker, April 15, 1863................................ 255
Letter to Major-General Hooker, May 6, 1863................................... 256
Letter to Major-General Hooker, May 6, 1863................................... 257
Letter to Major-General Hooker, May 7, 1863................................... 257
Letter to Major-General Hooker, May 8, 1863................................... 258
Letter to Major-General Hooker, May 14, 1863................................. 259
Letter to Major-General Hooker, June 5, 1863.................................. 261
Letter to Major-General Hooker, June 10, 1863................................ 262
Letter to Major-General Hooker, June 14, 1863................................ 276
Letter to Major-General Hooker, June 14, 1863................................ 276
Letter to Major-General Hooker, June 16, 1863................................ 278
Letter to Major-General Schofield, May 27, 1863.............................. 260
Letter to Major-General Schofield, June 22, 1863.............................. 279
Letter to Major-General Schofield, October 1, 1863........................... 311
Letter to Major-General Schofield, October 28, 1863......................... 325
Letter to Major-General Grant, July 13, 1863.................................... 286
Letter to Major-General Grant, August 9, 1863.................................. 305
Letter to Major-General Grant, April 30, 1864................................... 359
Letter to Major-General Grant, July 10, 1864.................................... 369
Letter to Major-General Grant, August 3, 1864.................................. 371
Letter to Major-General Grant, March 3, 1865................................... 409
Letter to Major-General Meade, March 29, 1864................................ 351
Letter to Major-General Dix, June 30, 1862...................................... 166
Letter to Major-General Dix, May 9, 1863. 258
Letter to Major-General Hunter, June 30, 1862................................. 165
Letter to Major-Generals Hunter and Lane, Feb. 10, 1862.................. 127
Letter to Major-General Sherman, September 19, 1864....................... 389
Letter to Major-General Sherman, December 26, 1864........................ 405

Letter to Major-General Burnside, January 8, 1863............ 244
Letter to Major-General Burnside, July 27, 1863 293
Letter to Major-General Curtis, January 2, 1863................ 242
Letter to Major-General Curtis, July 5, 1863...................... 282
Letter to General Schurz, June 16, 1862........................... 160
Letter to General Schurz, November 24, 1862 217
Letter to Major-General Hurlburt, May 22, 1863............... 260
Letter to Major-General Banks, August 5, 1863.................. 302
Letter to Major-General Rosecrans, October 4, 1863............ 315
Letter to Major-General Gilmore, January 13, 1864............ 345
Letter to Major-General Steele, January 20, 1864................ 347
Letter to Major-General Sheridan, October 22, 1864........... 389
Letter to General Hunter and Admiral Du Pont, April 14, 1863... 254
Letter to Commander of Department of the West, October 24, 1861... 103
Letter to Flag Officer Goldsborough, May 7, 1862.............. 137
Letter to Flag Officer Goldsborough, May 10, 1862............ 139
Letter to Lieutenant-General Scott, November 1, 1861........ 105
Letter to General Lorenzo Thomas, July 8, 1863................. 285

LETTERS TO GOVERNORS.

Letter to Governor Hicks and Mayor Brown, April 20, 1861.. 68
Letter to Governor B. Magoffin, August 24, 1861................ 97
Letter to Governor Andrew Johnson, April 27, 1862........... 137
Letter to Governor Morton, July 3, 1862........................... 169
Letter to Governor Andrew Johnson, July 11, 1862 171
Letter to Governor Andrew G. Curtin, September 11, 1862... 194
Letter to Governor Andrew G. Curtin, September 12, 1862... 195
Letter to Governor Andrew G. Curtin, May 1, 1863............ 255
Letter to Governor Andrew G. Curtin, May 2, 1863............ 256
Letter to Governor Seymour, July, 1863............................ 289
Letter to Governor Seymour, August 7, 1863..................... 303
Letter to Governor Bradford, November 2, 1862................. 214
Letter to Governor Hahn, March 13, 1864........................ 348
Letter to Governor Smith, February 8, 1865...................... 407
Letter to Governor Joel Parker, July 20, 1863.................... 290
Letter to Governor Joel Parker, July 25, 1863.................... 291

LETTERS TO MEMBERS OF CABINET.

Letter to Secretary of State Seward, June 29, 1862............ 164
Letter to Secretary of State Seward, June 30, 1862............ 165
Letter to Secretary of Navy Wells, May 11, 1861.............. 72
Letter to Secretary of Treasury Chase, May 25, 1862.......... 147
Letter to Secretary of War Stanton, August 17, 1861.......... 97
Letter to Secretary of War Stanton, September 18, 1861....... 100
Letter to Secretary of War Stanton, January 31, 1862......... 125
Letter to Secretary of War Stanton, December 21, 1863........ 343
Letter to Secretary of War Stanton, April 2, 1865............ 414
Letter to Secretary of War Stanton, April 2, 1865............ 415
Letter to Secretary of War Stanton, April 2, 1865............ 415
Letter to Secretary of War Stanton, April 2, 1865............ 416
Letter to Secretary of War Stanton, April 3, 1865............ 417
Letter to Postmaster-General Blair, July 24, 1863............ 291
Letter to Postmaster-General Blair, September 23, 1864....... 379

LETTERS TO CIVILIANS.

Letter to Committee notifying him of his First Nomination to the Presidency, May 23, 1860............................ 14
Letter to John B. Fry, August 15, 1860....................... 14
Letter to Thurlow Weed, August 17, 1860...................... 15
Letter to Thurlow Weed, December 17, 1860.................... 16
Letter to Thurlow Weed, February 4, 1861..................... 17
Letter to Senor Molina, March 17, 1861....................... 63
Letter to Mrs. General Fremont, September 12, 1861........... 99
Letter to Hon. O. H. Browning, September 22, 1861............ 100
Letter to Cuthbert Bullitt, July 28, 1862.................... 187
Letter to Horace Greeley, August 22, 1862.................... 192
Letter to Hon. Alexander Henry, September 12, 1862........... 196
Letter to Major John J. Key, September 26, 1862.............. 206
Letter to Thomas H. Clay, October 8, 1862.................... 207
Letter to Thomas R. Smith, October 21, 1862.................. 212
Letter to Hon. Fernando Wood, December 12, 1862.............. 238
Letter to Workingmen of Manchester, England, February 9, 1863.. 248
Letter to Rev. Alexander Reed, February 22, 1863............. 250

INDEX. 433

Letter to New York Democrats, June 12, 1863.................... 263
Letter to Ohio Democrats, July 29, 1863........................... 294
Letter to Illinois Convention, August 26, 1863 305
Letter to Hon. Charles Drake and Others, October 5, 1863... 316
Letter to Thurlow Weed, October 14, 1864...................... 323
Letter to E. E. Motriol and Others, October 28, 1863.......... 327
Letter to O. D. Filley, December 22, 1863....................... 344
Letter to Crosby and Nichols, January 16, 1864................ 346
Letter to A. G. Hodges, April 4, 1864............................ 351
Letter to F. A. Conckling, June 3, 1864.......................... 363
Letter to Hon. William Dennison and Others, June 27, 1864.. 368
Letter to Rev. Dr. Pohlman, August 15, 1864.................... 371
Letter to Hon. Henry J. Raymond, August 15, 1864............. 372
Letter to Mrs. Eliza P. Gurney, September 30, 1864............ 380
Letter to Hon. Henry W. Hoffman, October 18, 1864........... 384
Letter of Reply to Protest of Tennessee, October 22, 1864.... 387
Letter to Mrs. Bixby, November 21, 1864........................ 392
Letter to Colonel E. D. Taylor, December 27, 1864 401
Letter to Dr. John Maclean, December 27, 1864................ 405
Letter to Thurlow Weed, March 15, 1865........................ 412
Letter to Mr. Ashmun and Friend, April 14, 1865............... 425
Letter to Hon. J. K. Dubois, July 11, 1863 286
Letter to Hon. J. K. Moorehead, June 18, 1863.................. 279

MESSAGES TO CONGRESS.

First Message to Congress, July 4, 1861........................... 72
First Annual Message to Congress, December 3, 1861............ 110
Message of Recommendation to Congress, March 6, 1862..... 128
Message to Congress, April 16, 1862............................. 136
Message to Congress, May 29, 1862.............................. 149
Message to Congress, July 17, 1862 176
Second Annual Message, December 1, 1862..................... 219
Message to Congress, January 19, 1863.......................... 244
Third Annual Message, December 8, 1863 330
Message to Congress, April 28, 1864............................. 357
Fourth Annual Message, December 6, 1864...................... 393

PROCLAMATIONS

Proclamation, April 15, 1861	66
Proclamation, May 3, 1861	70
Proclamation, April 10, 1862	135
Proclamation, May 19, 1862	139
Proclamation, September 22, 1862	200
Proclamation, November 16, 1862	216
Proclamation, January 1, 1863	240
Proclamation, March 31, 1863	252
Proclamation, June 15, 1863	277
Proclamation, July 15, 1863	287
Proclamation, October 3, 1863	313
Proclamation, December 8, 1863	338

ORDERS.

Memorandum of Military Programme, July 23, 1861	95
General War Order No. 3, March 8, 1862	130
General War Order, March 13, 1862	131
Presidential Orders, June 22, 1862	161
Order Establishing Provisional Court, October 20, 1862	211
President's Order Relieving General McClellan, November 5, 1862	215
Approval of Court-Martial Proceedings, January 21, 1863	246
War Bulletin—Official, July 31, 1863	301
Orders for National Salutes, September 5, 1864	375
Thanks to Ohio Volunteers, September 10, 1864	376
Thanks to Volunteers of Illinois, Indiana, Iowa, and Wisconsin, October 1, 1864	381
Presidential Order, April 6, 1865	417

CALLS FOR NATIONAL THANKS.

Call for Thanksgiving and Prayer, July, 1863	287
Call for Thanksgiving and Prayer, May 9, 1864	360
National Thanks to Farragut and Canby, September 3, 1864	373
National Thanks to General Sherman, September 3, 1864	374
Call for National Thanksgiving, September 3, 1864	375

MISCELLANEOUS.

Lincoln's Statement of how he Entered Washington, February 23, 1861	45
Letter on Missouri Matters, November 5, 1861	106
Nomination of John Pope as Major-General, March 22, 1862	132
Nomination of Fitz John Porter as Major-General, July 16, 1862	175
Letter Regarding Thomas W. Knox, March 20, 1863	251
Announcement of the Success of the Army of the Potomac, July 4, 1863	280
Communication to the House of Representatives, November, 1863	327
Lincoln's Description of Grant to a Friend, March, 1864	350
Communication to House of Representatives, April 28, 1864	358
Interview Published in New York Tribune, January 30, 1861	16
Words to General Grant, April 9, 1864	354
The President's Idea of Democratic Policy and Strategy, May, 1864	360
Last Public Utterances of President Lincoln, April 14, 1865	424
To Whom it May Concern, July 18, 1864	370
Last Written Words, April 14, 1865	425
To Whom it May Concern, November 1, 1862	213
To Whom it May Concern, October 27, 1863	324

POEMS AND HYMNS.

Oh! Why Should the Spirit of Mortal be Proud?	61
Closing Hymn at Lincoln's Burial	425